T0339658

"Since Victorian times, Western medicine has endorsed a model which has prioritized curing over healing. It has had spectacular scientific and technical success but, in recent decades, its shortcomings have become increasingly clear. A number of pioneers have already pointed to the direction which is required, an integration of arts and sciences as well as the spiritual and material. In his varied and illustrious medical career, Paul Dieppe exemplifies just what is needed if this new model is to take hold. His book should be required reading for all health care professionals and complementary therapists and will also appeal to a wider audience who want to see medicine fulfill its potential for healing".

David Greaves, formerly Senior Lecturer in
Medical Humanities at Swansea University, UK,
and author of *The Healing Tradition* (Routledge, 2004)

"Medicine and healing have been the twin themes of my career for 60 years, my journey as well as Paul Dieppe's. I am profoundly glad that our paths converged and profoundly grateful for the vision he brings to the shared vocation of all who tread the same path. The courage and honesty with which he combines personal experience and insight with diligent enquiry and academic authority are moving and powerful, and richly evoke the healing that medicine needs".

Jeremy Swayne, doctor and priest; one-time general
practitioner, Dean of the Faculty of Homeopathy UK, and
Chair of the Bath and Wells Diocesan Healing Advisory Group,
UK, and author of *Remodelling Medicine* (Saltire Books, 2012)

"Healing often draws meaning from suffering. It encompasses trustworthy relationships that include kindness, a sense of being known and unconditional love.

The author of this book shares his deep knowledge of the healing process. From hard-won personal experience and research that involves deep listening to others' journeys, he recounts authentic experiences that can serve as lenses, or sometimes even as mirrors, for us to understand and grow in our own healing journeys. Whether we are experiencing our roles as healers or as people in need of healing, this book offers us practical wisdom for the individual, collective and systemic changes needed to foster healing".

"Professor Dieppe brings to this book a lifetime of outstanding clinical and research experience as an internationally acclaimed academic physician, combined with his personal insights and experiences of healing. It is the most rigorously researched and insightful book on human healing to date.

This book should be read by everyone involved in the delivery of health care, whether as doctors, nurses, allied healthcare professionals or therapists. It is a powerful rallying call to move beyond the blinkered confines of reductionism to elevate medicine to a new plane – as a healing art and science. And it serves as an illuminating guide for anyone interested in self-care – and that should be all of us – to embark on a healing journey whatever their stage of life".

"As we navigate through challenging times, this book offers a refreshing perspective on the role of healing in medicine. This book is a must-read for professional health care trainees and anyone seeking a deeper understanding of healing and its role in our lives".

"*Healing and Medicine: A Doctor's Journey Toward Their Integration* adds a unique voice to the twenty-first-century entreaty that health must be viewed as more than the absence of disease. The remarkable message of this book is that a more complete level of health is achievable not solely through improved techniques, technology and pharmaceuticals, but through a deeper understanding of the many facets of healing itself.

Dr. Dieppe shares with readers how his several life-threatening personal challenges as much as his keen observations of physician–patient clinical encounters set him on the journey to explore the nature of healing. We travel with him to interview those who heal and those who have been healed, to visit hospitals, community health fairs and Lourdes, and to explore healing through clinical trials and public art. What emerges are insights and hypotheses that will pique the interest of all who rely on, all who practice and all who are committed to improving contemporary health care".

Richard Hammerschlag, Co-Director of Research and Innovation, Consciousness, and Healing Initiative, La Jolla, CA, USA. Emeritus Research Director, Oregon College of Oriental Medicine, Portland, OR, USA

"How should healing, that mysterious process we all know, be studied? Dr Dieppe is one of those rare researchers who seeks out and listens carefully to people whose accounts of healing are typically dismissed. He examines closely experiences of his own that most choose to ignore. Building on this attentiveness, he gives us the story of his journey from a biomedical approach to healing to one that takes the powers of the body to be at the heart of healing's mystery.

Dieppe's style is that of a gifted raconteur. His story of discovery becomes ours in the course of his telling. His vision of the body as fundamentally spiritual offers a picture of healing as the activity of living with love into our connections with all that is".

David Schenck, Co-author of *Healers: Extraordinary Clinicians at Work* and *What Patients Teach: Everyday Ethics of Healthcare*, and the author of *Into the Field of Suffering: Finding the Other Side of Burnout*

"In medicine, we learn to discount what doesn't fit our biomedical version of reality. Lately, though, it seems ever clearer that biomedicine is but a small part of the long art. Our profession should be thankful, then, that this distinguished clinician and researcher has stayed faithful to his own experience and been so rigorously curious about inexplicable recovery and reconciliation".

David Peters, Professor Emeritus,
University of Westminster, UK. Editor-in-Chief,
Journal of Holistic Healthcare & Integrative Medicine

"Paul Dieppe is an internationally renowned rheumatologist with an esteemed career in academia and evidence-based medicine. In this book, he has courageously and creatively charted different waters, mostly unexplored and sadly neglected by the medical profession. His professional and personal journey plumbs the depths of healing, and what that actually means to each of us as people. This resonates deeply with physicians like me and will with those grappling with illness or trauma. We increasingly have to question the limitations of our scientific biomedical approach, with its focus on curing alone. This book brings messages of hope that are, themselves, healing".

Brian M. Berman, Professor Emeritus, Family and
Community Medicine, University of Maryland School of Medicine;
Founder and President, Nova Institute for Health; Founder and
Director, Cochrane Complementary Medicine Field; Bravewell
Leadership Award in Integrative Medicine

Healing and Medicine

Healing is on many people's minds today. In the wake of the COVID-19 pandemic and a host of other disruptions and disasters, many of us feel that we need healing – in our personal lives, for the environment and for our planet. But healing is rarely defined and is not an accepted part of medicine in the West. This book examines the relationship between healing and medicine through the eyes of an academic physician who changed his interests from biomedical research to healing late in his career in medicine. It is based on his experiences and stories of his encounters with patients, practitioners and others for whom healing has had a particular significance, as well as his rigorous research into the subject. A central theme of the book is that modern medicine needs to be more pluralistic in its approach to health and accept that spirituality and healing techniques have roles to play alongside scientific medicine, which currently has its base in materialism alone.

Healing and Medicine

A Doctor's Journey Toward
Their Integration

PAUL DIEPPE

with Cinder Hypki

Foreword by Dr. Michael Dixon OBE

Routledge
Taylor & Francis Group

A PRODUCTIVITY PRESS BOOK

First published 2024
by Routledge
605 Third Avenue, New York, NY 10158

and by Routledge
4 Park Square, Milton Park, Abingdon, Oxon, OX14 4RN

Routledge is an imprint of the Taylor & Francis Group, an informa business

ISBN: 978-1-032-61063-4 (hbk)
ISBN: 978-1-032-61059-7 (pbk)
ISBN: 978-1-003-46181-4 (ebk)

DOI: 10.4324/9781003461814

Typeset in Minion
by Deanta Global Publishing Services, Chennai, India

To Liz, Clare and Torie – thank you

"The most beautiful experience we can have is the mysterious.
It is the fundamental emotion that stands at the cradle
of true art and true science" (Albert Einstein)

Contents

SECTION Three: Integration

Foreword

Professor Paul Dieppe is a remarkable man and this is a remarkable book. I first met him when he was one of the nation's most respected hospital doctors with an impressive research record behind him and at the very top of his game.

Many years later, he was to have his "Road to Damascus" moment, recognizing that modern biomedicine was failing to answer too many of the health issues facing us as individuals and communities. In his words, "The success of modern medicine has led to the erroneous belief in Western society that doctors can cure anything". He goes on to say that modern medicine can treat many diseases but "It does not do well with chronic illness and suffering; they often need healing". That is the message of this extraordinary book – namely that we need to "integrate the art of healing with the science of curing".

This book should be compulsory reading for all health professionals, whether they be doubters of anything that stands outside standard evidence-based medicine or whether they are among the increasing number who feel unarmed to cope with the complexity of symptoms and suffering that they face. This is also a book for anyone who has an interest in how we heal, particularly if they or those around them are failing to find sufficient answers from conventional medicine.

As someone who has stood at the pinnacle of biomedicine, Professor Dieppe is best qualified to help us understand how medicine can regain its ability to heal as well as alleviate symptoms. He is also best qualified to guide us, in his own words, toward "A more inclusive approach to modern medicine, and the acceptance of some alternative "unscientific" views of the world". That world, and medicine itself, is changing fast. Today, our doctors are taught to use population-based evidence to decide what is best for the average patient. Yet, like most doctors, I have yet to meet an average or normal patient, and medicine must regain its roots in treating each of us as individuals – respecting our hopes, aspirations, beliefs and pasts. The move to a much more personal interpretation of medicine is being led by science, with the discovery of the genome and the microbiome. It thus points the way toward a new medicine that better respects our individuality, our personal needs and our need to heal as well as to cure or treat the symptoms.

Like Professor Dieppe, I have been fascinated watching the success of various healers with my patients for whom there can be no conventional scientific explanation. I have also witnessed the long-term beneficial effects of patients going to Lourdes. These healing effects can be achieved without medicines but should not be ignored because our conventional mindset rejects them.

In the twenty-first century, most disease is what is considered long-term and therefore, by its very nature, incurable. We can arrest progression and improve symptoms but, as health professionals, we must not only regain our ability to heal but also enable our patients to heal themselves. That means respecting the relationship between mind, body and spirit and not assuming that the job is done when the symptom has been sorted or the physical pain relieved.

As you turn the pages of this book, it will become clear that you are on a journey with a great doctor and a great healer. Professor Dieppe provides us with a unique insight into the power of healing and our potential both as patients and doctors to achieve it.

Dr. Michael Dixon, OBE.
General Practitioner, Chairman of the College of Medicine,
Health Advisor to King Charles, and
author of *Time to Heal: Tales of a Country Doctor*
(Unicorn Press, Lewes UK, 2020)

Preface

I am a retired academic physician who practiced medicine in English university hospitals for most of my working life. The work was a pleasure as well as a great privilege. I think I was able to help many of the patients who consulted me, by giving them access to the wonders of modern biomedicine. These included drugs and surgery, as well as the therapy provided by the wonderful nurses, physiotherapists and occupational therapists that I worked alongside.

However, due to a number of unusual life experiences outlined in this book, I became increasingly disillusioned by the exclusivity of biomedical science, and its rejection of all other approaches to health. So, toward the end of my career, I switched my research interests away from medicine to the phenomenology of healing.

Initially, my exploration of healing was largely driven by curiosity. I wanted to understand my own spiritual and healing experiences. I wanted to know what happened when I was told I had been healed, aged 16. I needed to know more about the strange, spiritual things that occurred during and after I was held hostage in Kuwait and Iraq. And I needed to heal.

But, as I began my work on healing, I became confused and a little bit angry. Colleagues in medicine in whom I confided seemed to think I was crazy to take an interest in healing, several of them warning me against doing anything so "unscientific". Some of them told me that it would mean the end of my career. But, reading around the subject, I discovered that the evidence to support the value of healing was extensive. In addition, the existence of paranormal events (such as premonitions, near-death experiences, telepathy and telekinesis) was irrefutable. But mainstream medicine was having none of it. I had also learnt that quantum theory was offering an alternative way of understanding our world that might account for phenomena such as healing transformations, and that many quantum physicists thought that consciousness was not produced by the brain but was a fundamental property of the Universe. But biomedicine, I discovered, was having none of that either; medicine "knew" that consciousness was produced within our individual, isolated heads. The implication of this belief is, of course, that we are separate "pieces of meat" with no free will. I don't believe that.

These discoveries made me determined to find out more about healing and to try to help open the eyes of my profession to other possibilities. This book is based on 15 years of research into healing. It is written as an attempt to help bridge the gap between the materialistic world of medicine and the spiritual and metaphysical world of healing.

Western academics who do research on healing are more likely to be anthropologists than doctors. And they tend to go to far-flung places to study the healing rituals and practices of Indigenous peoples. Although such work is interesting and provides us with many insights, there is often a hint of the "clever folk from developed countries studying the strange practices of unsophisticated people in the developing world" to this approach. I have not done that. There are many practicing healers and several different healing approaches going on in my country in a culture that I understand and of which I am a part. That is what I have been studying.

Healing is indeed a cultural issue; different types of healing have arisen in different places throughout space and time. For example, Shamanic healing is common in parts of Africa, South America and elsewhere, and healers who use rituals and local plants remain common in many parts of the world. Specific healing techniques have also developed within whole systems of medicine. Ayurvedic medicine in India has many of its own approaches, including meditation and yoga, whereas Traditional Chinese Medicine uses other practices such as acupuncture. Many of these approaches have now been introduced to modern Western societies and altered to suit their culture. Cultural appropriation of ancient healing methods is hugely prevalent in the West, although largely to develop ways of promoting improved wellbeing and happiness, rather than for treating disease and illness.

In many societies, the people sanctioned as health care professionals are the local healers, but, in the West, we have now given that job exclusively to those of us trained in biomedicine. The science that underpins our approach claims that most healing interventions, both ancient and modern, are ineffective and nonsensical. I believe that this is a terrible mistake. Modern medicine is very effective at dealing with many forms of disease and illness ("curing" some things), but I fear that this has led to an erroneous belief in Western society that doctors can cure anything, and an arrogance and hubris within my profession that allows it to dismiss other approaches, however steeped in history, as "hocus pocus". Furthermore, whereas modern biomedicine is good at understanding and treating many diseases, it does not do well with chronic illness and suffering; they often need healing.

Throughout the first half of my career in medicine, I believed that scientific biomedicine was the only way forward. But life experiences led me to think this might be wrong. Subsequently, my glimpse into the world of healers and healing has forced me to take a more pluralistic view of the world. I now "know" – experientially as much as scientifically – that we are spiritual beings with souls, and that there is more to our world than materialism alone. My long-held belief, that caring, compassion and love should be central to all health care provision, has been strongly reinforced by my work on healing. So, I am now appealing for a more inclusive approach to modern medicine, and the acceptance of some alternative "unscientific" views of the world.

We all live in our stories; they define us. This book is based on my stories of things I have experienced and patients I have seen. Although exclusively my story, the telling of it has only been made possible and enhanced by my collaboration with colleague and friend Cinder Hypki, a writer and artist interested in the healing of communities. Scientists need to work with artists like Cinder and other humanities scholars to forward the understanding of healing. I passionately believe that we need to integrate the art of healing with the science of curing.

I think that health care professionals need to learn more about healing and be more accepting of "unscientific" approaches to health care. So, this book is written primarily for them. But I hope it will be of interest to others as well. All of us experience health problems and trauma during our lives. Many of these cannot be cured but need healing. This is not a self-help book about how to heal, but I hope that many general readers might be able to find the right way forward for them within these pages. And at the end of the book, I do offer some conclusions about how we might contribute to healing ourselves, others and our planet.

Paul Dieppe, May 2023, Bristol, UK

Acknowledgements

This book could not have been written without the help of a huge number of people, including many of the wonderful patients and colleagues I have been lucky enough to work with throughout my medical career.

My amazing, selfless wife Liz has been my rock and support for the majority of the journey described in this book, and I could not have done it without her. My wonderful daughters Clare and Torie have also been very supportive. Several old friends and colleagues encouraged me to write the book and have been key to its genesis. In that respect, I am particularly grateful to Fiona and Howard Croft and to Jeremy Swayne.

Over the past few years, I have been fortunate enough to be part of a small research team of academics who share my interest in healing. The group has included – in alphabetical order – Dr Sarah Goldingay, Dr Natalie Harriman, Dr Ayesha Nathoo, Dr Emmylou Rahtz, and Professor Sara Warber. I am profoundly indebted to each of them, particularly for the many hours of stimulating discussion about healing.

The Baltimore based Nova Institute for Health of People, Places, and Planet (Novainstituteforhealth.org) has provided me with both financial and intellectual support for many years now, and I am particularly grateful to the leaders of the Institute – Brian and Sue Berman – for their support and generosity.

Several other friends and colleagues were kind enough to read early drafts of this book, and/or advise me about it. Those whose comments were particularly helpful included Dr Richard Hammerschlag, Professor Rachel Gooberman-Hill, Dr Steven Oliver and Rev Dr Jeremy Swayne. Thank you.

The book contains information gathered from interviews with many health care professionals and healers, as well as members of the public. I cannot thank each of them individually, but I do want to acknowledge their help and generosity in giving me the time and opportunity. I was profoundly humbled by what I learnt about healing from many of these people, as I hope is apparent within the book.

Finally, a massive thank you to Cinder Hypki, whom I first met many years ago through the Nova Institute for Health. When I started out on this project, during the days of the COVID-19 "lockdown", I did not really know what I was doing. I contacted Cinder for some advice, and she patiently and gently moved me in the right direction. She then put in an enormous amount of work editing the words I wrote and helping to shape the book. Cinder and I have had hours of discussion about the manuscript, and those discussions helped me sort out what really mattered to me and allowed me to express those ideas in these pages.

About the Author and Contributor

 *Professor Paul Dieppe* BSc, MD, FRCP, FFPH is an emeritus professor at the Universities of both Exeter and Bristol in the UK. He qualified as a doctor in 1970 and his past jobs have included Professor of Rheumatology and subsequently Director of Research and Dean of the Faculty of Medicine at the University of Bristol; Director of the MRC Health Services Research Collaboration, and then Professor of Health and Wellbeing in University of Exeter, UK. He has published more than 500 peer-reviewed articles in journals and authored or co-authored several medical books. He is based in Bristol, UK.

Contributor

Ms. Cinder Hypki, M.S., is an artist, educator, writer and editor. Her work as a community-based artist facilitates creative expression for community building, celebration and healing through creative workshop design and public projects. She aids non-profit organizations, neighborhoods, groups and individuals in their efforts to create thriving communities and to build a sense of place, purpose and joy. Based in Baltimore USA, she has taught at Maryland Institute College of Art for nearly a decade. Recent book projects include editing *Drawing in the Dark: The Art of Michael Iampieri*, by John C. Wilson and authoring *Far Field Farm: Stories of A Sturdy Dream*.

Section One

Preparation

1

Early Influences

A CLINIC WITH DR BALME

It was a very long time ago (early 1970), but I can still picture the setting: a large, light and airy corner room, situated on the second floor of the main hospital building, with a big window looking out over the famous Barts (St Bartholomew's Hospital, London) square and its central fountain. I was a final-year medical student and had decided to observe an outpatient clinic held by one of the consultants, Dr Harold Wykeham Balme, a general physician with an interest in arthritis. Wykeham Balme was a somewhat larger-than-life character in the medical school; a big jovial Yorkshire man who was President of the rugby club, and who was often to be found drinking with the "rugger buggers", where his loud laugh and risqué stories could be heard by everyone nearby. But he did very little teaching and was known to become somewhat grumpy if asked to go out of his way to teach.

I found him sitting at his consulting desk in that big room and asked him if I could sit in on the clinic.

"No, bugger off lad, I don't like students in my clinic", he said, without looking up.

"But Dr Balme, sir, I am a medical student here, this is a teaching hospital and, as I understand it, I have a right to sit in and observe clinics when I want to".

"Oh hell, alright then, well, sit in that chair back there behind me, and, for goodness' sake, don't say anything when patients are in the room".

DOI: 10.4324/9781003461814-2

He pointed toward one of the hard metal chairs at the back of the room, regularly used by student observers when more teaching-friendly consultants were in these rooms. He was sitting in a large chair with a leather seat and imposing wooden arms. In front of him was a huge desk, with several thick sets of patient notes on it. He was dressed in the expected smart suit and tie, with a crisp white coat on over it. He was a large figure, aged in his mid-50s, with thinning hair on top and the largest, bushiest eyebrows you could imagine. He was reading medical notes, looking serious, so that the usual jovial smile was not apparent.

After a while, he called out "Send the first patient in, Sister".

An elderly lady appeared, staggering awkwardly with the aid of sticks. It was clear, from the appearance of her deformed hands and her gait, that she had severe arthritis. Dr Balme indicated that she should sit in the chair on the other side of the desk from him, which she did, gingerly.

He looked up at her and said "What have you done to your hair, Doris, it looks awful".

She smiled: "Oh, thank you for noticing Dr Balme, I had it done especially for you".

"And how are those no-good sons of yours, Doris – still in prison?"

"No, Dr Balme, Barney is out now and helping in the garage. Thank you for asking".

"Mmm, and your lay-about husband?"

She paused and looked worried. "Well, not so good actually, Dr Balme, he had a heart attack a few weeks ago, and has been flat on his back at home ever since. We have been praying for him, of course, and I think that has helped …".

Dr Balme visibly changed when he heard this. He sat forward in his chair, laid one of his hands gently on Doris', and looked at her in a concerned way. For a while, he said nothing, and then "Oh, I am sorry, Doris, this must be very hard, with the arthritis and everything; how have you been managing?"

She was crying now. "Yes, very difficult, doctor. Thank you for asking".

He gave her some time, and, after she had collected herself, continued with the conversation in the same vein for a time, while I sat at the back of the room, fascinated by what was going on. Then he switched mode.

He got up from his chair and walked around to stand next to the one Doris was sitting in. "So, I suppose I had better have a look at those joints of yours, Doris, see how the arthritis is doing. Hold out your hands for me".

She held her hands out, turned them over when requested to do so, and smiled as Dr Balme gently felt the skin and joints.

He beamed down at her, back to his usual jovial persona. "Doris, that's marvelous, the arthritis is not very active at all, you have done brilliantly; in spite of all this stress, you have things under control. Well done, you".

It was her turn to beam. "Oh, thank you, Dr Balme; thank you so much".

He went back to his chair, scribbled something in the notes, and then sat back and smiled at the patient.

"So, you can bugger off now, Doris, you have had your time".

"When can I come back to see you again, Dr Balme?"

"Not much point is there, Doris? I don't do anything; I don't prescribe any medicine".

"*But you are my medicine, Dr Balme*".

He grinned at her. "OK then, come back in three months' time; tell Sister I said that on your way out".

And out she went, moving more easily than on her arrival, I thought, while Dr Wykeham Balme went back to the notes on his desk.

I was struggling to understand what I had just witnessed. It was completely different from any other clinical encounter I had seen in my time in medical school. This was not the usual formal, scripted, inhumane interview and examination of a nervous, powerless patient by an all-powerful doctor – the *modus operandi* I was used to seeing. Here was someone who treated the patient as another human of equal status to himself, and he knew all about her and her family. I did not know what to ask, but I was bursting to get him to talk about it.

"What was going on during that consultation, Dr Balme?" I ventured from behind him.

He glanced around and met my eye. "Ah lad, sorry, forgot you were there, good question ... well, I suppose you could call that the art of medicine – not the science of medicine, you see". He then looked at me in a strange way and added "You can stay and learn more about it if you want but stay quiet".

I realized this was a special favor. I stayed. I was quiet. I learnt a lot.

Why was that event so important to me, and so extraordinary? Perhaps something about my background and reasons for going into medicine might help explain that.

BECOMING INTERESTED IN MEDICINE

I was born in 1946, into a sheltered, conservative, middle-class English family. My father was an accountant, my mother a teacher. I was the third of their three post-war children, all boys. Our parents looked after us well and went to great trouble to give us a good education, but there was little love or affection within our suburban home near London. Our parents did not make friends or go out much; we played tennis in the back garden, we went to church and were occasionally taken to see rugby matches, but there was very little excitement, culture or exposure to the outside world for us boys.

For many years, I was unaware of the fact that I was always my parent's favorite son. Early on, this may have been because I had more humor, charm and charisma than my brothers, and, as a little boy, my blond curls, smiling face and bright blue eyes made a pretty picture. Then, as I got older, it became clear that I was also good at most things, including games, which was particularly important to my father. I was intensely curious about the world, particularly the natural world of plants and animals, from a young age. But, while growing up, I had little or no idea where life was taking me, until one day, when I was about ten years old, I went on a bike ride with my brothers.

Being out with them was a new, exciting experience and it was probably the first time they had let me join them when they went out together. We cycled up to Kenley airport, one of the bases for Second World War Spitfires. I had been pedaling like mad to keep up – they were three and six years older than me – but now we slowed down, and they started talking. They began to discuss what they were going to do when they left school. One wanted to be an engineer; I forget what the other one was hoping to do. Then one turned to me: "So, what are you going to do, squirt, when you grow up?" Without pause, I said "I am going to be a doctor". I don't know where that came from; I had not considered the question before, but, as soon as I said it, I knew that this was indeed what I would do. I "knew" in some ineffable way that I would indeed become a doctor. My brothers were scornful – there was no one medical in our family, and none of us knew anything about the subject – they told me I was being silly. But I stuck to that unbidden and unconsidered idea and consolidated my decision to become a doctor.

So, life went on, and I became obsessed with just two things: sports, and my future attempt to become a doctor. And my curiosity became centered on the human body and its disorders, as this was going to be my future.

Then, when I was 16, I had my first major life event.

AN INJURY AT SCHOOL

It was an autumn day in 1962 and, as I awoke, I gradually became aware that I was not in my own bed. It smelt strange and there were unfamiliar railings around it. As I looked around, I saw that I was in a huge white room filled with a lot of other beds. The smell was that sickly sweet and highly distinctive smell of the antiseptic fluids used to clean hospitals years ago. I could feel severe pain on the right side of my back, just below the rib cage – a sickening sort of pain, quite unlike that of a cut or a bruise – and I was sweating: the bedclothes were damp. Gradually, I realized I was in a hospital bed, and slowly it all began to come back to me.

I remembered that, on the previous day, I had been injured playing rugby at school. I had received a heavy blow in the back, which winded me. I played out the match (my proud first appearance for the school's first fifteen), but soon understood that things were not right, and I took myself to the school sanatorium. Matron took one look at me and panicked. She rang my parents; she also telephoned for an ambulance. Soon, I was in the local hospital's casualty department, where I was told that I had ruptured a kidney and lost a lot of blood. Tubes were inserted; blood was given intravenously. Later, the doctors said that I might need an operation to remove the damaged kidney.

So, I lay there in pain in that strange bed, while decisions were being made by the medical team to take me to theatre and remove my right kidney. But, apparently, other things were going on as well; some weeks later, I learnt that my parents had organized a prayer meeting for me with their local vicar, at our home not far away.

It was then that something very strange happened.

A group of white-coated men appeared at my bedside, accompanied by a very smart-looking nurse in a blue uniform and a white cap; they were all looking grave. "How are you feeling, Paul?" one of them asked me. He seemed to be the one in charge. I looked up at him, and suddenly I felt OK; in fact, I felt terrific.

I sat up in bed, looked at the group of worried medical people and cheerfully said "I feel fine, thanks". I did! The pain was no longer there, and I was seeing them and everything else around me with amazing clarity. I knew that they had no need to be so worried and that everything was right with the world. It was a wonderful, joyous moment for me. The medical consultation continued for a while; I was prodded a bit, charts were examined and whispered conversations were going on around me. I felt strangely removed from all that, but I knew that everything was OK with me and with all creation, and I continued to smile cheerfully, while sitting up in my bed.

Then, the man in charge said something along the lines of "OK, he does seem to be doing well just now, so let's not rush in; we won't do it today". And they all went away.

Almost as soon as they left, I slumped back down in my bed, feeling awful.

I never had that operation. I went through a rocky few days and spent the best part of a month in the hospital. I underwent a lot of investigations, including several cystoscopies and intra-venous pyelograms, but no major surgery. Slowly, I recovered. About two months after the injury, I was back at school. I still have one-and-a-half functioning kidneys.

It was only afterwards that my parents told me how sick I had been on those first few days, and about their prayer meeting. "The doctors thought you might die, but you were saved and healed as a result of our prayer meeting", my mother confidently told me one afternoon, as I went for a cautious, convalescent walk with her.

The Aftermath

What was a shy, naïve 16-year-old schoolboy to make of that? – the idea that my kidney, and maybe my life, had been saved as a result of a miracle facilitated by a Christian prayer meeting? And what on earth was that extraordinary experience, that amazing "moment" of joy and understanding?

Back then, those things were very difficult for me to grasp. God seemed to be the only possible answer. I had been brought up in a Church of England home. My parents took us boys to church every Sunday, and our school was faith-based. But religion seemed to be something for Sundays alone; it did not impinge much on everyday life. After my recovery, I tried hard to become more fully immersed in the Christian church and lifestyle. But I failed, I could never make sense of the possibility of a loving God sending people to eternal punishment in hell, or of the idea that, if you did not have the opportunity to believe in this particular god, well – bad luck you! I struggled to make sense of it all.

I was told that I could not play rugby again, or indeed any "contact sport". That was harsh; sport, particularly rugby, had been my savior at school. It was something I was quite good at, and it compensated for my small stature and shyness. People did not mess with me or bully me because they could see how I tackled others on the rugby field. Rugby was also one of the few things of interest to my father, who was very proud of my sporting achievements; but that all had to go. My father was amazing while I was sick; although he hated hospitals, he came in most days and sat at my bedside for long periods of time. But, after my recovery, his depression worsened, and his interest in rugby and other sports seemed to dwindle. I felt this was my fault, and that I needed to atone for that in some way.

So, I was experiencing a strange mixture of loss, anger and frustration at a future that had little or no sport left in it, and I was burdened with guilt about my father. I probably hid my confusion and turmoil from my family and friends, particularly my two older brothers, who now seemed resentful of me in some way. Yet, my life had been "saved", as my mother put it, and I felt a sense of awe, wonder and gratitude at my survival with one-and-a-half kidneys. I had a feeling that maybe I was special in some way, and destined for greatness – after all, what else would I have been "saved" for?

Obviously, this injury was a hugely important moment in my life, but I have rarely talked about it to other people, and I don't think many of my medical student friends ever knew about it. Amazingly, it was never discussed at home. My parents never spoke about it, nor did my brothers, and, to this day, we have never shared our understanding of my apparent healing event.

For me, two wonderful things remain at the forefront of this story. The first is that moment of joy and of knowing that all was well – that transformational, spiritual "noetic" moment*. That was special and it was not to be my last. The second was that my injury led indirectly to my getting into medical school.

*Noetic moments: The word "noetic" is derived from "gnosis" or knowing. A noetic moment is one of those special spiritual moments of knowing that we are part of something bigger than ourselves and that we are all connected. They are usually joyous. They can be linked to healing, as discussed later.

MEDICAL SCHOOL

How could my injury lead indirectly to my getting into medical school? The "old doctor" who led the team treating me (who was not very old!) helped me get a place in his alma mater in London – St Bartholomew's Hospital Medical College, known as Barts. I was academically able enough, but my shyness, lack of interests outside of sports and the fact that no one in my family had ever been involved in medicine became apparent problems at interviews in various other medical schools prior to my acceptance at Barts. At the interview there, I saw a letter written by my doctor being read by the interview panel. That was how things worked in the 1960s.

I spent six tumultuous years of training at Barts, initially as a very unworldly young man, lacking in self-confidence. I nearly got thrown out after the first two years of medical science teaching because I could not do anatomy (I have very poor spatial intelligence and cannot read maps – or understand human anatomy) but I scraped through the retake exam with the somewhat illicit help of our anatomy professor.

Having done well in the other subjects, I was allowed to take a year out to do an intercalated BSc in Physiology. That year made a huge difference to me. Being free of the worry of regular exams and of anatomy, I was able to grow up. I read widely and voraciously, with a particular emphasis on psychology and the history of medicine. I got a first-class honors degree, which helped rid me of my feelings of inadequacy and increased my confidence.

So I progressed to the clinical phase of the training as a more mature person, and I soon discovered that I seemed to understand clinical medicine better than many of my peers. But I also found much of the medicine we were being taught strange and sometimes inhumane. Compassion and kindness were not high on the agendas of most of our teachers, and our patients were often viewed as an organ system ("the heart failure in bed six") rather than people. I felt we were being taught to be "body mechanics" rather than caring physicians, and that the disease focus allowed the whole person to be ignored. That frustrated me. The only subject that really attracted me was psychiatry; I won the psychiatry prize in our year and thought that I was heading toward a career as a psychiatrist. At the same time, I continued to pursue my interests in psychology and parapsychology. There, I found evidence of the human understanding of people that seemed to me to be lacking at Barts.

So, there it was: psychology and psychiatry for me. Until, that is, I met Dr Harold Wykeham Balme and Doris. Being a witness to that consultation between them changed my life. "Wykeham", as I came to know him, showed me that you could practice humane, caring medicine without having to be a psychiatrist. He knew his patients as people, living their individual lives, in a particular context; he was able to swear at them, insult them, and tease them because he really *knew* them, and they loved it. And I now understand that the consultation I had first witnessed was also about healing. This is something that I will return to toward the end of this book.

Wykeham became my key mentor when I was a young doctor, someone who helped me understand myself. And subsequently, I became a trusted colleague and friend, with my family visiting him in his beloved Yorkshire on several occasions.

Once he told me that when I got older, I would stop dishing out drugs to people as if there was no tomorrow, like everyone else does, and learn to just "be there" for my patients. I think he was right.

I ended up becoming a rheumatologist rather than a psychiatrist. This was not an overnight thing. I was ambitious and driven, and rheumatology was thought of as a "second-class specialty" at the time, and not something worthy of a high-flyer. Arthritis was just too boring, I was told. But as I went through the years of junior hospital jobs, I became increasingly disillusioned with psychiatry, which seemed to lack any firm basis for its practices. Arthritis, in contrast, seemed increasingly interesting, and rheumatology was gradually being seen as important. So, I managed to get myself back to Barts to work with Wykeham again. During that spell, in the 1970s, I also did some laboratory-based research work and gradually became intoxicated by the beauty and power of medical science. After a while, I got lucky with some research and my career as a rheumatologist took off. I even became thought of as the natural successor to Wykeham at Barts. But there were aspects of the work and role that London medical consultants were expected to play – such as private practice in Harley Street – that I did not want to be a part of, so I looked for jobs elsewhere.

A CAREER IN MEDICINE

My early-career breakthrough came from the discovery of apatite (bone) crystals in the joints of people with arthritis, something that the research group I was working with at Barts found and published a few months before two American groups made the same discovery. Our paper, published in the prestigious journal *The Lancet* in 1976 (1), had my name as first author, so I became the person identified with this finding, which the world of rheumatology thought to be important at the time.

The publication of our paper led to invitations to give talks around the world. I relished this and found that academic medicine was something I could succeed at, that it rewarded me and that such success could fulfill my ambitions and need for recognition (in place of sport). I also knew it would make my parents proud. I was probably trying to assuage my guilt about my father by becoming a successful academic doctor. This success resulted in my appointment as a consultant senior lecturer in rheumatology in Bristol at the very young age of 32. So, my wife and I and our two small daughters (ten months and three years old) made a rapid move to Bristol and I began my new job.

It was a difficult start for me in Bristol, due to my inexperience. But, after a few years, I became very successful there, establishing a well-known osteoarthritis research unit that attracted many trainees from abroad. I was also running a clinical service and doing a lot of teaching – all with the help of those overseas trainees and a wonderful team of young people. In 1987, aged just 41, I was promoted to the position of professor of rheumatology in Bristol.

During those first hectic ten years in Bristol, I became fully "enculturated" into the world of Western biomedicine and biomedical sciences. It is a very seductive and successful profession that has led to greatly improved health and longer lives for millions of us, even though it is only some 100 years since the invention of antibiotics and other wonder drugs, and safe surgery. It was a privilege and an honor to be able to practice as a doctor, teacher and medical scientist then, even though, in the 1970s and 1980s, we had relatively little to offer those of our patients with severe arthritis (except our caring selves).

If you have no good drugs or other treatments, you are left with the all-important need to care for the other person. You are the central component of the treatment, as Doris said to Wykeham – *"Dr Balme, you are my medicine"*. My interest in psychology and psychiatry, as well as Wykeham, had introduced me to such ideas, and I had read the works of Michael Balint (2) and others, who also championed the idea of "the doctor as the treatment". Michael Balint was a hugely influential Hungarian psychoanalyst who spent much of his career working in London. He introduced "Balint Groups" to primary care in the UK, which are still active today. They are discussion groups in which the importance of the relationship between the doctor and the patient is the main focus. His central hypothesis was that "the most frequently used drugs in general practice is the doctor himself".

I was unashamedly reveling in and using the wonders of scientific biomedicine to help treat patients, while advancing my academic career. But I was also becoming increasingly aware of the importance of humane, caring, compassionate interactions in health care.

In addition, I was seeing some patients whose disease and illness did not follow the expected trajectory, or in whom things happened that made no sense within our scientific understanding of how the body and diseases worked. Here, I will share a few personal early-career clinical experiences of this sort.

Holding a Dying Man's Hand

I was doing my first medical job at Barts, a few months after qualifying in 1970. The boss I was working for was a famous Harley Street cardiologist, of whom I was in awe. He did his rounds at Barts just once a week; they were very serious, highly choreographed "events". I had to go down to the square to meet his chauffeur-driven Rolls Royce on its arrival, precisely at 2 pm, open the door for him, and escort him up to his wards, where the rest of his retinue of doctors and nurses was waiting. He remembered absolutely everything that had been said or done the previous week, and God help you if you had not done something which had been requested last time. This particular week, we had a patient in with a dissecting aortic aneurysm* that had been deemed inoperable, and, at his last ward round, the boss had said it was going to burst out the front of his chest, probably in about a week's time, and there was nothing we could do about it. He was never wrong. So, when he came for his ward round the following week, the aneurysm was indeed about to burst, and we (the medical and nursing team) had agreed that he should be the first patient that we presented to the boss.

A "dissecting aortic aneurysm" is a rare condition in which the walls of the main artery leaving the heart weaken and tear; occasionally (back in the 1970s, when surgical options were more limited), this could lead to the aorta coming through the front of the chest and bursting.

We took him to the bed, which we had surrounded with curtains to mask the impending disaster from other patients. He went in, looked at the pulsing mass at the front of the man's chest and carefully felt around it, but said nothing to the patient. He came out and said to me "Go in there and put a bucket over his chest and stay with him until it is over". Sister found me a bucket and I did as I was told. There I was, putting an old metal bucket over the chest of a fully conscious man, while we waited for his aneurysm to burst and for him to die; the remainder of the ward round went on, in hushed tones, around us. I had no idea how to behave, or what to do.

I asked the patient if he understood what was happening. "Yes, I think I am about to die", he said, and I told him that we agreed on that, and explained (again), as carefully as I could, that the big blood vessel coming from his heart was about to burst through his chest wall. Then I held his hand. "Thank you", he said, "please stay with me".

We stayed like that for a while, me gently holding his hand. I asked him about his family and his life, and he told me a lot about himself. He was calm and collected and did not seem to have any regrets. He asked me about my life, and I enjoyed telling him about my fiancée and my upcoming marriage. We bonded; we connected; we were as one together. It was rather beautiful for me, in a very strange way, and, as it went on, I sensed that he became more relaxed and "ready". And then it happened: the aneurysm burst and he exsanguinated into the bucket I was holding over his chest, and died. I felt the gradual, ethereal disappearance of the "person" whose hand I was holding, as the blood went on pumping out of him, into my bucket.

By this time, the boss and his team had moved on to our other ward, on the opposite side of the hospital. I took a little while to compose myself and then left the scene to tell the nurses what had happened. One of them gave me a hug and told me to go back to the rounds; they would take over now and clean up the mess, she said.

I went across to the other ward and caught up with the ward round. The boss caught my eye and nodded at me, almost imperceptibly. Nothing was said. Nobody on the team ever asked me what had happened or talked about that event with me, and I never shared it with anyone else either. That's how things were done in those days.

Comment

This case brings tears to my eyes as I recall it. But strangely I had "forgotten" all about it until relatively recently. Perhaps I had forgotten because it was so traumatic, and the way of dealing with such things in those days was to shut it away and move on. Today, the young doctor would probably be offered counseling, be expected to suffer PTSD and be told to take time off. But, because of the changes in the culture of medicine that have occurred over recent years, such an incident could not happen now – a young doctor would not be left alone in that situation. I remembered the case again at a meeting in Canada about 15 years ago; I attended a workshop where we were asked to write a short story about a traumatic medical encounter in our lives. It was this incident that immediately popped into my head. I wrote it and read it to the rest of the people at the workshop and cried inside.

A key point for me was experiencing the importance of just being with someone, really being there for them and connecting with them, at any point in life, or indeed in death. The sense of a deep "connection" with another living person is something that has become increasingly important to me later in my life, as I discuss in this book. In addition, it was the first time that I felt that moment of departure of another human being, their soul leaving their body. It brought a strange sense of loss, mixed with relief, an experience which I cannot describe, but one that gave me belief in things beyond our physical world, as I will explore later on. "Soul separation" was something that I was soon going to learn more about, as discussed in Chapter 2.

In retrospect, I now believe that this man "died healed", another concept I will return to later.

A Case of Back Pain

In the 1980s, the NHS had long waiting lists; I inherited long waits for arthritis patients when I started work in Bristol. My attempt to manage this appropriately was to develop a system of scanning referral letters to try and assess urgency. If, for example, a referral letter said that the GP thought the patient had early rheumatoid arthritis, we would give that person high priority, as the earlier that gets diagnosed and treated, the better the outcome. But if the GP said it was chronic lower back pain, we would give it a low priority and the patient would have to wait longer; our reasoning was that chronic back pain rarely has a sinister cause, often undergoes spontaneous remission and is something we were not much good at treating.

"Clive" had waited nearly six months to get to see me, as the GP referral letter simply said "chronic low back pain". He was a well-dressed man in his mid-60s, who greeted me warmly and thanked me for seeing him before he had even sat down. Almost as soon as I saw him, I thought something was seriously wrong. He told me that he had been having increasing pain in his lower back for the last nine months or so, and that he had not been feeling well; "and I have lost a bit of weight", he told me. I examined him and detected severe tenderness when I tapped on the lumbar vertebrae. I knew that that was a bad sign, a "red flag" in the world of back pain. I sent him to the radiology department, asking for urgent X-rays of the spine to be returned with the patient to the clinic as soon as possible. After I had seen one or two other patients, he came back with his X-rays. One glance confirmed my fears – there was clear evidence of prostate cancer metastases in his spine, which have a very characteristic appearance that is hard to miss. I sat him down and told him, as gently as I could, what I thought the problem was, apologizing for the fact that he had waited a long time to see me. He did not seem fazed. He thanked me for seeing him and getting to the bottom of it so quickly, then asked me what could be done. I told him that I wanted to consult with a colleague, but that I thought the sooner we began treatment, the better. He said that was fine, and thanked me yet again.

I rang my urology colleague and told him about the case. "OK, Paul", he said, "let's get him into hospital today and do an orchidectomy* and take it from there. I will fix the surgery if you could tell him what we are going to do and find a bed somewhere". I found a bed for "Clive" and told him the plan. I thought he would be furious; after all, he had waited for months, only to be told he was going to have his testicles cut off on the day he gets seen, because it is urgent that we do that! I was anxious and apologetic. But Clive was fine about it and thanked me for sorting things out for him.

Orchidectomy is removal of the testicles; this is done to reduce testosterone levels that drive prostate tumor growth. These days, we do that with tablets, rather than surgical removal; at the time, in the early 1980s, that sort of medication was not available.

So, Clive had his testicles removed that night and was started on chemotherapy for his prostate cancer the following day. I went to see him on the ward before he was discharged, still half-expecting him to be angry with us. But he remained grateful and asked me what else he could do about the cancer. He said that the surgeon had explained about the orchidectomy and the medicines, but that he wondered if there were other things that he could do for himself, to get some control over it. I told him about an American doctor whom I had heard presenting at a medical conference around that time. This specialist seemed to have quite good evidence that diet and lifestyle changes could improve the outcomes of cancer, so I gave Clive some literature about this approach.

He did well. His cancer came under control, and, after a second course of chemotherapy, the urology department gave him the all-clear. When I found out about that, I was relieved, as I had been feeling guilty about him having to wait so long to see us and get the diagnosis, as his cancer was spreading. If we had seen him earlier, I was thinking, he might still have his testicles, poor man.

I saw Clive one more time in our clinic. He came in beaming at me. "So, doctor, thanks to you, Reiki healing has cured my cancer", he said. I was stunned. "Reiki healing, Clive?" He explained that he had read all the literature I had given him about the American doctor's approach and had done some of his own research on it and found a Reiki practitioner locally who could advise him about the lifestyle and dietary changes recommended, and who could also give him some healing treatments for his cancer. "She started doing this weird stuff with me", he said, "waving her arms around over me whilst in deep concentration; but it worked. Soon after the first session with her, they told me my PSA* was coming down. And now, after some more treatments from her, it is right down, back in the normal range" he explained.

"That's great, Clive", I said, "but maybe the chemotherapy and orchidectomy had some influence on the cancer regressing, don't you think?" "No doctor, I am sure it was the Reiki and lifestyle changes that did it, and I am so grateful to you for steering me in that direction". "And the back pain, Clive – has that gone away?" "Yes, thanks, doctor, I am fine now, all thanks to you".

*PSA = Prostate-specific antigen; its measurement in the blood is used to assess prostate cancer activity.

Comment

At the time, I was convinced that the medical treatment was the reason for Clive's recovery from his prostate cancer, and I remain of that view. He had waited for a while to get the diagnosis, which might have made the prognosis worse, but, when we saw him, we got onto it straight away and gave him what was "state-of-the-art" treatment at the time.

Clive's case taught me about the concept of *attribution*. What we doctors think is the reason for someone getting a disease, or being cured of it, might be very different from the views of the patients themselves. And who is to say who is right? Maybe the Reiki healing and lifestyle changes did cure Clive's cancer. He certainly made me consider that possibility, and he was one of a number of people who made me think that what we call "complementary and alternative" treatments might actually do something useful. I even wondered whether strange practices like Reiki healing might be of value, but I most likely dismissed those thoughts as "New Age, woo-woo nonsense" at the time. Doctors often talk about practices like Reiki in this derogatory way. The "New Age" reference comes from the idea that many of these practices have been imported from other, predominantly Eastern, countries and are incorporated into rituals and remedies used by believers in things like witchcraft. The "woo-woo" label was more about indicating that you thought people who believed in any of these things were quite mad, and "away with the fairies". Although attitudes have now changed for the better and many doctors are increasingly inclusive and pluralistic in their thinking about complementary and alternative practices, some of these negative attitudes persist amongst medical professionals.

The Army Curate

This man remains very vivid in my memory. He is someone that I have talked and written about previously – my interactions with him had a big effect on me, on the way I see things and how I subsequently practiced medicine.

I was doing a routine rheumatology clinic in Bristol in the early 1980s, with three or four junior doctors working alongside me. Although each of us had our own list of patients to see, my "juniors" would often be popping in to ask me to see someone, or to help them with a difficult case. That morning, just before we got started, "James", the rheumatology registrar, came into my room to ask if I would be able to see the Reverend White. "Sure", I said, "but why don't you want to see him again?" "Well, I saw him for the first time several months ago, and then again a couple of weeks ago, and I just couldn't figure him out, so I asked him back to see you. He has ankylosing spondylitis*, which does not seem too severe either clinically or radiologically, but he is sort of a wreck, and I didn't know why. I thought maybe you could get to the bottom of it?" "OK, let me see what I can do, and I will tell you what I make of him".

Ankylosing spondylitis – now known as axial spondyloarthritis – is an inflammatory form of arthritis, mainly affecting the joints of the spine. It is more common in men than women. The inflammation causes pain and stiffness of the spine and can lead to fusion of the joints, resulting in a fixed spine, often in a characteristic curve. It usually starts in early adulthood and the inflammation tends to decrease or go away as you get older (called "burn-out").

So, in due course, in came the Reverend White. He was a thin man of medium height, dressed neatly, but exclusively in black, and he had his dog collar on. I had seen from the notes that he was in his late 60s and had been diagnosed with ankylosing spondylitis since the early 1950s. He was walking badly, somewhat bent over, and sighing and grimacing with pain (presumably) as he made the three- or four-meter walk from the door to my desk, where I was inviting him to sit. He did indeed, as James had said, look a wreck. I introduced myself, going through the usual formalities, and asked him our routine questions about the arthritis – what his pain was like, how much morning stiffness he had and for how long? – that sort of thing. I was trying to ascertain how much discomfort he was in and how restricted his physical functioning was. I also wanted to know if the arthritis was still active or not. He responded with profound sadness in voice and manner and, although he gave clear, concise answers, like James, I was finding him a bit of a puzzle – his pain and disability seemed disproportionate to the disease severity.

While the Reverend White was getting ready for my examination, I went over the notes more thoroughly and looked at his X-rays. The records did not help much: he seemed in good general health, and his recent blood tests and X-rays suggested that the arthritis had indeed "burnt-out". So why was he so miserable and disabled? Was this depression, I wondered? I examined him and, while doing that, asked some routine questions about possible depression, such as what did he feel like when he woke up first thing in the morning and was his appetite OK? I drew a blank with all my questions and, when I examined him, I could find very little wrong with him, apart from a stiff spine, as expected.

When he limped back into the main consulting space, sighing and cautiously taking a seat, still behaving as if in terrible pain, I decided to take a different approach. "So how did this all start?" I asked. He looked at his shoes. I waited. Finally, he blurted out "It was in the war". "Go on", I prompted. He looked very embarrassed, and there was another long pause, before finally – "I have never really told the story before". "But you can tell it now", I said softly, giving him time, and, after a while and with a little help, he did tell me his story.

The Reverend White had been a young trainee curate serving overseas toward the end of the Second World War. He developed a discharge from his penis which alarmed him, so he went to see the Army medical officer. The medic examined him and said "Oh dear, you must have gone to the brothel with the lads, Father". "No sir", he responded, "I have never been with a woman". The medic did not believe him and told him that he must have "sinned"; he would give him an antibiotic, and, if that cleared up the discharge, it would be proof that it was indeed a venereal disease that he had contracted. He took the antibiotics, and the discharge quickly cleared up. So he assumed he must have "been to the brothel with the lads" as the medic had said, and then erased it from his memory. What other explanation could there be?

Soon after that, he developed red eyes, "and then, a bit later, my back pain and stiffness started", he explained. After he got back from the war, medical consultations indicated that he had a condition called "Reiter's disease", a form of inflammatory reaction often triggered by a venereal infection, and one that can lead to ankylosing spondylitis. "So, I must have been to that brothel, even though I remember nothing", he told me through tears. "I am so ashamed, and I have never dared to even talk to a woman in any friendly sort of a way since, in case I lose control again. And I just live with this terrible guilt".

I listened and was waiting to hear if there was more. And then suddenly I "knew" what had happened to him. I had a clear, intuitive moment of complete understanding of how this unfortunate, sad man had developed his disease. It was a certainty for me, although I didn't know how or why. And how was I to explain this to him?

Finally, I asked him "Do you remember if there was any diarrhea going around in the camp at that time?"

He paused, thought for a while, and then told me that yes, he thought there had probably been many bad attacks of the "squits" going around the camp in the weeks before he got his venereal infection, and that he might have been one of those to get it.

I wondered again how I was going to tell him, and whether this was the right time and place. "I don't think you went to the brothel, Father", I said eventually. "Certain types of diarrhea can trigger Reiter's disease. I reckon that was what happened, as you can get the penile discharge, as well as the red eyes, from a reaction to the gut infection, without there being any sexual contact".

His reaction was profound. Suddenly, he was muttering to himself, and his body language and facial expressions were changing. As I tried to listen to him, and studied his face and demeanor, I picked up a torrent of conflicting emotions: confusion, shock and disbelief, and then perhaps a dawning of a new understanding, and of what I can only describe as hope.

It took us both a while to sort ourselves out emotionally.

He then questioned me a bit, clearly wanting to believe me, and I gave him one of our patient's booklets about Reiter's disease. As I gave it to him, I said "I think you should read this, and look up what else you can about dysentery as a cause of your disease. Have a think about it, and about what we have said today, and come back and see me again in a few weeks". He agreed, thanking me profusely. As he walked out, his gait already seemed a bit different: quicker and freer.

I had spent a long time with him, and some of my colleagues, as well as many other patients, were queuing up outside to see me and ask me a torrent of questions. I had no time to dwell on what had happened. I cannot even remember if I ever got around to talking to James about it (I hope so), but that consultation has stayed with me.

When I saw the Reverend White again a few weeks later, he was a different man. He was walking better, he had lost that haunted look and there was no grimacing with pain. He was even dressed differently, with a colored shirt on, and some rather jaunty socks; I wondered if he might have put some weight on. He told me that, as soon as he got home after the previous consultation, he "knew" that I had been right, and that this realization had changed his life. "The burden of guilt has been lifted from my shoulders", he told me, "and I no longer feel frightened of women".

To the best of my knowledge, he never came back to see us in the rheumatology clinic after that. I presume he did not need us anymore. I think he was healed.

Comment

What I think I did for this man was to provide him with a safe and compassionate space in which he could tell his story and thus facilitate a re-interpretation of the narrative.

I think he healed himself when he realized he had been in the "wrong story" for the last 40 years of his life. He then found the "right story" and was able to move on, leaving behind the terrible, negative and damaging feelings of guilt. Psychiatrists and psychologists sometimes talk about this phenomenon as "reframing". I think much healing can come through people changing their stories from a negative narrative to a more positive one.

This case was also one of those relatively uncommon, but amazing, occasions in which a sudden medical "intuition" helped me in my clinical work: a sudden sense of "knowing" what the answer was, or that there was something seriously wrong that I needed to find out about, or, conversely, that it was safe not to investigate or treat a particular patient's symptoms. I will never know if most of these moments of intuition were correct, although, in the case of this man, I feel sure it was. Nor do I know what intuition in medical practice is about; some people say it is just about experience, but I think that's unlikely, and the moments feel profound, almost as if something has come to you from outside. I met an American lady at a conference a couple of years ago who told me that she was Professor of Medical Intuition at a medical school in the USA ("How good is that", I thought!). She believed it was important to teach medics how to "listen" – not only to the patient, but also to their intuitive thoughts and feelings, and to learn to trust them. I agree.

A Healer Cures Arthritis

"Joan" was feeling very tired, and she was stiff all over in the mornings. She had also developed aches and pains in her hands and feet. This had all started a few weeks after the birth of her second child, so she put it down to the stress of looking after two small children at first. But it got so bad that she had difficulty getting out of bed in the mornings, and the pains in her hands and feet made it difficult to do things. She found she had real trouble changing the babies' nappies. Her husband persuaded her to go to the doctor, who said that it was probably nothing to worry about, but she might be anemic, so she was going to run a few blood tests. A couple of days later, the doctor contacted Joan to say that there were problems with her blood, and could she come back to the surgery to discuss it?

On her second visit to the GP, the doctor took more time, and looked carefully at the aching hands and feet. Joan told me the doctor had squeezed her hand across the knuckles which made her yelp with pain. The doctor then told Joan that it might be a touch of arthritis and said that she was going to get an urgent appointment with a rheumatologist.

That was where I came in. I saw Joan a couple of weeks later at our rheumatology clinic. By then, there was obvious swelling in some of her joints, and the distribution of the affected joints in her hands and feet, along with the story, indicated that she had probably developed rheumatoid arthritis* – one of the most severe forms of joint disease. Joan cut a sorry sight; she looked pale and tired and was close to tears as she talked to me.

The baby in the pram with her was sniveling and crying a lot. Joan looked to be at the end of her tether. I always find it difficult to tell people that they have rheumatoid arthritis; for many, it felt like a life sentence, and back then, in the late 1970s when I first saw Joan, it often was. I told her that I suspected that she might have arthritis, but that I needed to get some more tests done to be sure, that I would get those done as quickly as possible and see her again very soon to discuss what we should do about it. In the meantime, I told her we could give her something that would make the pain and stiffness easier. I prescribed an anti-inflammatory drug for her and gave her some advice about pacing herself and protecting her hands and feet as much as possible. I asked her if she might be able to bring her husband along next time so that we could all talk about the results of the tests together.

> *Rheumatoid arthritis. Rheumatoid disease/rheumatoid arthritis is a severe form of inflammatory arthritis that can affect almost any joint in the body, but commonly starts in the hands and feet. It is more common in women than in men, and often starts in the reproductive years. Relentless inflammation of the joint lining causes severe pain and stiffness, and also leads to the destruction of the joint tissues and erosion of the underlying bone. These erosions can be seen on X-rays, and that, along with the characteristic immunological abnormalities in the blood, are diagnostic features. In the past, it often led to severe disability, but the development of new biological treatments in the last 20 years have improved the prognosis.*

When I next saw Joan, she seemed a bit happier. Her husband could not get time off work today, she told me, but she hoped he might be able to come to some of her appointments in the future – which he did. The tablets had helped, she said, although they had given her a bit of indigestion. But I was certainly no happier about her situation. The blood tests, as I had feared, showed very high levels of the antibody, or "rheumatoid factor", that appears in most people with rheumatoid arthritis as well as evidence of quite severe anemia and a lot of inflammation in the body. The tests, along with the clinical picture, were telling me "severe rheumatoid arthritis with a poor prognosis". We talked about it, I changed the anti-inflammatory drug in the hope of getting a good effect without indigestion and we discussed "joint protection" strategies (how to use the inflamed joints with the least risk of damaging them) and going straight onto gold injection therapy – our preferred way of treating rheumatoid arthritis at that time. She agreed.

The next few months were very difficult for Joan and her family. She could not tolerate gold or penicillamine, the other suppressive drug we were using then, and the anti-inflammatory drugs only gave modest relief to her symptoms. Her joints were getting worse, and the disease was affecting her whole family. Her husband was having to take time off work to help Joan manage with the house and children, and they were all feeling depressed. X-rays of her hands and feet showed that she had developed the erosive changes in her bones that are characteristic of joint damage in rheumatoid arthritis – changes that we consider irreversible.

I had been seeing Joan very regularly in those first few months, in part because of the need to carefully monitor her drug therapy. But then there was a gap of a couple of months or so when I did not see her. Given all the patients we were dealing with, I did not give her that much thought. But when I did next see her, she was transformed. She looked well, and she and her husband were smiling. They came in together, sat down and beamed at me, telling me that the arthritis had gone away. I was skeptical; that does not happen. So, I examined her, and could find no evidence of arthritis. I told them I was both delighted and amazed, as I had to agree that the arthritis seemed to have gone away; I asked them why they thought that might be. It was Joan's husband who told the story, a little apologetically, clearly anxious about my reaction. He said something like this: "Well, you have been very good to us, doctor, and were clearly doing your best, but we could see that the arthritis was getting worse and that you did not have much else you could do. And we heard about this energy healer in the village, so we thought why not, and went to see her. She has seen Joan three times now, and done energy healing with Joan, and it has worked".

This all happened long before I had become familiar with healers and the concept of "energy healing" and I remained skeptical. But I had learnt not to contradict the beliefs of my patients unless I thought those beliefs were doing them harm, and, in this case, I had to admit that Joan was much better, so I went along with them on the healing. I said I would like to redo the blood tests and X-rays, to see if they showed remission of the arthritis, to which they readily agreed, and we fixed up to meet again a few weeks later. The blood tests were entirely normal, and there was now no evidence of erosions on the X-rays. Joan had indeed been "cured" of her rheumatoid arthritis. A remission of the inflammation, I could just about accept, but the complete disappearance of X-ray changes in such a short time – that was impossible! I asked Joan and her husband if they would mind me seeing them again, doing some more tests and examinations, and then discussing her case with my colleagues. They happily agreed.

Joan was indeed an amazing case from a medical point of view. I took care to be sure that we had not made mistakes of identity with respect to X-rays or blood tests. I talked to her and her husband again, searching for clues as to why the arthritis might have gone away. And then I took her to one of our "Grand Rounds" and presented her case to my medical colleagues. (Grand Rounds were held weekly in our hospital at the time; all senior doctors were expected to attend, and we took turns to present a case that we thought particularly educational or difficult.) My colleagues were shocked by Joan's story. As I expected, they were skeptical (as I had been) and asked if I was sure that those first X-rays, showing erosions, were really hers, as erosions do not go away quickly like that. They asked her about dietary changes or other things that might have happened in her life to explain it. She and her husband patiently explained that, as far as they were concerned, it was all thanks to the healer. No other explanation was forthcoming as we discussed it with Joan and her husband.

After they had left the room, the discussions continued. The general comments were along the lines of "There must be some rational explanation for this, but what is it?" My medical colleagues were not willing to accept the concept of the disappearance of rheumatoid arthritis thanks to a healer. Alternative ideas were put forward. Finally, a consensus emerged. She "*must*" have got some viral infection which altered her immune status, leading to the inflammation, which is thought to be immunologically driven, to disappear. And the X-rays getting better must be due to an unusual ability to heal bone, perhaps a genetic variant.

We had to have a biomedical explanation, which I was reasonably happy to go along with, even though there was no evidence to support it.

I vividly remember one of the young doctors on my team taking me aside after our "Grand Round" and asking me "Paul, could it have been the healer do you think?" And I replied "Well, maybe yes, but that is not an acceptable view for us doctors to take in public; let's both keep an open mind about it".

Comment

This case shook me up. It was the first time I had heard of "energy healing", and the idea that a healer might be able to cure arthritis – something that we specialists could not do – was literally "unbelievable". So, I sort of went along with the story that my colleagues wanted to believe in: there *must* be a biomedical explanation. But must there be? There are regular reports of "spontaneous remissions" of diseases like cancer in the medical literature – people being cured of diseases for no apparent reason – and we doctors like to try to explain these away. And I had my doubts about our explanation of Joan's "remission". But perhaps Joan helped me on my path toward the study of healing. Perhaps her case allowed me to become a bit more open-minded than many of my colleagues about "unscientific" healing practices. But, at the time, I had no idea that this was where my career would take me in the future.

What These and Other Patients Were Teaching Me

My medical training had been of its time. We were taught to take the history of the patient's problems and then examine them in order to diagnose a disease (I discuss the "tyranny of diagnosis" toward the end of this book). We were then taught how to treat the disease we had diagnosed. It was all done by organ system; we did sessions of cardiology, gastroenterology or neurology, etc. So, the patient's illnesses became reduced to pathology in a certain system of the body, which should be treated by a specialist in that condition, using drugs and surgery.

But some of my patients were telling me a different story. I was hearing several messages from them. First, that illness and disease occur in the wider context of someone's life and affect the whole person, not just a single organ. Second, that strange things can happen during the course of illness and disease, such as so-called "natural regression", or healing, that are not explicable by medical science. Third, that the doctor–patient relationship is a critical and powerful weapon in our armory. As Doris had said, and Balint's writings had taught me, the doctor could be the treatment. Active, non-judgmental listening was clearly important, and I was also learning to listen to my intuition. Compassion and honesty were also clearly critical to the successful outcomes for these patients. Sometimes you just have to "be there" for people. Wykeham had taught me that. But how did that fit in with the scientific understanding of disease that I had been taught? And why was the interaction with patients so important? I did not know.

And then there was Joan's energy healer, and Clive's Reiki healer. "What on earth is going on?", a part of me wondered.

Furthermore, there were clear parallels between some of these patients' stories and my own experience of being healed. And I had also had strange, spiritual experiences, such as that "noetic moment" in hospital or my suddenly "knowing" I was going to be a doctor. So, there was some difficult "cognitive dissonance" within me – in other words, a conflict between my scientific work and beliefs and many of my ineffable experiences. I simply could not resolve that conflict. Science was wonderful and seemed to be the only way to explore my curiosity – but my spiritual experiences suggested that there was something else as well, that was not within the reach of science.

Where I Was at This Stage of My Career

I think I was in the sort of quandary that I have seen in other doctors. On the one hand, I was totally seduced by scientific biomedicine, doing lots of research in it, believing in it and seeing some wonderful results when using it for many of my patients. On the other hand, I was occasionally seeing patients who were presenting me with a different paradigm of disease, illness and their outcomes.

On balance, however, biomedical science was winning. My wife and children remind me that, at this stage of my career, I was dismissive of so-called "complementary and alternative medicine", and totally wedded to medical science. My scientific research into osteoarthritis was going well, and I was enjoying the rewards that came with that: international travel, recognition and awards. I was frantically busy with a mixture of clinical work, teaching and research, following the expected course of an academic physician. I was doing well in those conventional terms. I also had a lovely home in Bristol, a wonderfully supportive wife and two wonderful, clever daughters. Apart from working too hard, to my family's detriment, life was good.

I was suppressing any anxiety induced by my spiritual experiences and the anomalies I was witnessing because my success as an academic doctor was fulfilling most of my needs. In retrospect, I think one of the reasons for my pushing myself so hard to be successful was my relationship with my father. He had high hopes for me, initially as a sportsman. But that had been taken away from us. I was probably trying to replace that by becoming a successful academic doctor. And I think that worked. When I was made a professor in Bristol in 1988, my father came to my inaugural lecture and clearly was proud of my achievements.

I could not have known at the time how radically my life was to change just two years later. Nor could I have foreseen how those changes would eventually prevent me from ignoring the spiritual aspects of my life and work. Instead, it was full steam ahead with my career until, in 1990, when I was 44, everything changed.

REFERENCES

1. Dieppe PA, Crocker P, Huskisson EC, Willoughby DA. Apatite deposition disease. A new arthropathy. *Lancet*, 1976; 1: 266–269.
2. Balint M. *The Doctor, His Patient and the Illness*. Churchill Livingstone, 1957.

2

Kuwait and Iraq

By 1990, my career in British medicine seemed to be "riding high". My research team's work on osteoarthritis and crystal-related arthritis had an international profile, and young doctors from all over the world were coming to Bristol to train in rheumatology with us. I was serving on committees of the Royal College of Physicians, the British Society for Rheumatology and the Arthritis Research Council. I was, I think, being "groomed" as a probable future President of some of these Institutions. My future seemed clear and I was happy with that.

A SEA CHANGE

But then everything fell apart, simply because I changed a planned flight to Kuala Lumpur. I was going there to do some teaching and had been sent a ticket for a Malaysian Airways flight departing in the morning of 1 August, 1990. But, at the last minute, I changed it to the evening British Airways flight so that I could finish off some work in the hospital that morning. Therefore, I was a passenger on the ill-fated BA flight 149, which was refueled in Kuwait as Iraq invaded that country, and I did not get back home again until the middle of December.

What happened has been well documented by several journalists and writers. If you want to know more, the best source is probably the recent book by investigative journalist Stephen Davis (1).

I am writing about some aspects of the event here because it led indirectly to changes in my career path, and ultimately to my research on healing.

DOI: 10.4324/9781003461814-3

Briefly, the facts for me were as follows. I got on the plane unaware of the situation in Kuwait, and not realizing that we were going to refuel there. The flight was delayed to allow some Special Forces men, and some of the Kuwaiti royal family to board. The plane was allowed to land in Kuwait after Iraq had started its invasion of that country. The SAS boys and royals disappeared. All of the remaining crew and passengers were taken hostage by the Iraqi army, and the plane (with our luggage in it) was blown up on the tarmac.

For the first few weeks, we were put up in hotels in Kuwait City. We were then split into small groups, our passports were taken from us and we were driven to a variety of different sites. I was in a small bungalow near Kuwait City docks, initially with seven other men and three women. After about a week, the women were released, and then some nationalities, including the one Frenchman in our group, were also allowed home.

After more than three months in Kuwait, our group was bussed to a hotel in Baghdad, where we met many other British and American hostages. We were then split into new groups and taken to military installations around Iraq, to be used as "human shields", supposedly to prevent the bombing of those sites. I was in a poison gas factory near Fallujah. Then, in early December, we heard we might be released. A few days later, we were bussed back to the Mansour Melia Hotel in Baghdad, and met by UK Foreign Office men, who gave us back our passports. On 10 December, we were flown back to London on an Iraqi Airways plane.

What Was It Like?

So what was it like being a hostage, a "human shield" or "a guest of Saddam Hussein" (as our guards called us) for 19 long, hot weeks?

Many people have asked me that question, and I have mostly given evasive answers, told them a simple, palatable (often amusing) story about a single event or just made a joke of it all. It is hard to talk honestly about such experiences.

I was very lonely, I was often terrified and it was incredibly unsettling. Kuwait was the place where I confronted my own death for the very first time. Before taking that flight on 1 August, 1990, I was living a stable, predictable life: I had a comfortable bed of my own to sleep in, I could eat what I liked when I wanted to, I was able to plan visits to almost anywhere in the world and I was blessed with solid, loving relationships with my wife and two teenage daughters. I did not want for toothpaste or a haircut, and I felt in control of things. When I awoke each morning, I felt fairly certain about what was going to happen that day.

But all of that was taken away from me in a single moment; taken away forever, perhaps. Every day during those endless weeks felt as if it could be my last. Early on I had a panic attack, which was truly awful, and I remained anxious for much of the time I was there.

At first, when we were being held in hotels in Kuwait, some sense of normality was maintained; good meals were served three times a day, and we were able to socialize with the many other hostages who were there, including some women and children. I remember sharing my belief (hope) that Margaret Thatcher and the Special Forces would get us out of this mess. But then, after a couple of weeks, when the Iraqis took my passport away, bundled me into a mini bus with ten strangers, and took me to a small, filthy bungalow near the Kuwait docks, any sense of such hope evaporated. I knew none of the people I was with and had very little in common with any of them. I had no way of contacting my wife and children and did not know if they were alive or dead (and they did not know where I was, or if I was alive).

I was in that bungalow for 99 days, mostly with just six other men. In the first few weeks, it was stiflingly hot, we were given very little food, never knew if or when another delivery might turn up and had little or nothing in the way of clothes or toiletries. We could not see or hear much outside the bungalow and we were not allowed to leave it (being guarded by Kalashnikov-carrying young boys who spoke no English other than "no mister, no"). We had no idea what was going on. We heard regular bursts of gunfire and explosions nearby. It was the first time I had heard gunfire used in anger – I never want to hear it again. Sometimes, our guards threatened to shoot us, and we saw evidence of their atrocities. No wonder I was anxious.

"What did you do all day?", people asked me afterwards. Not a lot. Unlike most of my fellow hostages, I slept reasonably well, particularly after they started letting us out of the house to get some exercise each day. I did quite a lot of writing, some longhand, some on an abandoned home computer that we got working in the bungalow. There were a few books in the house that we could read, including the wonderful Encyclopedia Britannica (I think the owner had been an academic working at the nearby Kuwait

University). We found a pack of cards and four of the seven of us played bridge every evening.

When I was relocated to the poison gas factory near Fallujah in northern Iraq, I felt as if I had to "start again". I was with a new group of men with whom I had nothing in common. I had to "muck in" and get to know them; it was a quite different environment and routine to try to settle into. Life was also a little easier in some ways – food was served regularly and was not too bad, and we could exercise freely. But there were no books and no computers. One of the lads had somehow acquired a short-wave radio, so we had some idea what was happening in the outside world. That fuelled a constant fear that the allies would target our poison gas factory early on in their Iraq offensive, which we were hearing was planned to start soon. I did not think I would ever get out of there.

And I lost faith in humanity. I saw terrible things being done to people and to places, for no apparent reason. I witnessed callous disrespect for human life. Would I be behaving like these people if I was in their situation, I wondered? I feared the answer might be "yes" – if I had been brought up in Saddam Hussein's Iraq. Perhaps I would be "toeing the line" and carrying out some of the atrocities I was seeing from his troops.

After just three weeks near Fallujah, we were bussed back to Baghdad and told that we were on the way home. We had no idea why or how this had happened, but some real hope and elation surfaced again, particularly as we were given back our passports. But for me, that sense of happiness was dashed by learning, in a rather cruel way from a British Foreign Office man, that my father had died some weeks previously.

I was not in good shape when I got off the plane at Gatwick Airport in London, in the middle of December, to be met by my family, including my grieving mother.

After my release and return home, I am not sure I ever regained any certainty about the future. To this day, I no longer feel I have complete control over my life, and the experiences have made me much more empathic toward people with anxiety disorders.

But It Was Not All Awful

My months as a hostage was a terrible, life-changing experience.

But it was not all awful. Amid the chaos, the uncertainty, the loss of freedom, the near starvation, the unbearable heat, the awful gunfire and the rest, there were people and things that shone through the darkness. Here are a few examples:

Nature: I loved the large, pink bougainvillea that grew at the front of "our" bungalow in Kuwait. I spent time just "being with it", admiring this magnificent bush that grew and flowered so beautifully in spite of the chaos around it, the blistering heat and the lack of water.

The night sky: For a while, we were able to climb onto the roof of that bungalow in Kuwait (before our guards caught us at it and blocked up the entrance). I used to sit up there at night with one of the other men whom I became friendly with. We would marvel at the night sky, the stars, the constellations and the continuing movement of the moon. The vast, wonderful expanse around us that was untroubled by what was happening in our tiny, insignificant corner of the Universe.

People: Many of my fellow hostages were wonderful people. For example – Peter ("Pete the poof" as he was called) was a source of joy throughout our time in Kuwait docks. Sadly, he died not long after our release (like several other men I met out there). He was very camp, very funny, and took control of the appearance of "his boys" and the space they were living in. He cleaned, he washed, he fussed a lot and he kept me amused (although sadly he did not play cards). Thank you, Peter.

Wide-open spaces: I found being driven through the bleak, wide-open spaces of Northeastern Iraq, around Fallujah, near our poison gas factory "home", rather wonderful. During my time there, groups of us were taken out in a truck, about once a week, to a strange little shop where we could try to make brief telephone calls home (things had improved for us by then). This involved an elderly, wizened Iraqi man twisting wires together, then trying to dial international numbers that we gave him, before he decided he needed the wires twisted together in a different sequence – you could not make this up! I found those bizarre rides a source of great comfort, not only because of the chance to snatch a few treasured seconds of talk with my wife but also because of the opportunity to be in the wide-open spaces around the town, with the wolf packs howling, the dust swirling and the never-ending space around us.

Togetherness: In England, grown men seldom cry in public, except at football matches. But there were times when we were able to cry together, to comfort each other, to hug, to share, to connect over some particular horror or news. So, I suppose my faith in humanity was not completely lost.

Having fun: In spite of everything, we could joke and play together. Toward the end of our time in Kuwait, we met up with three other British men, who were being held in another bungalow nearby, with whom we exchanged things like books, paper and pencils. And in the evenings, we had some fun together. One of our new friends liked to spend his time drawing; he did cartoons of each of us. His drawing of me is shown in Figure 2.1.

FIGURE 2.1
A cartoon of me, drawn by a fellow hostage in Kuwait. It illustrates my obsession with trying to exercise, my new beard and long hair, and the huge amount of weight loss that had occurred.

TRANSFORMATIONAL EVENTS IN KUWAIT AND IRAQ

Many strange things happened during my time as a hostage. Some high drama, some shocking, some ridiculous or hilarious (such as the time a young Iraqi army recruit shot himself in the foot in front of me – he made a poor job of it and I was able to patch his foot up easily enough!). In addition, there were, for me, three particularly important moments that have stayed with me and have contributed to my subsequent change.

Confronting My Own Death for the First Time

This event took place during my first few hours in Kuwait, on 2 August, 1990. A group of us were loaded onto a bus to take us from the airport terminal building to the nearby airport hotel. As the bus trundled off, we saw soldiers with automatic weapons on the tarmac and a tank in the distance. Suddenly our bus stopped, and a young soldier rushed up to the opening doors and shouted "Passports, passports".

I was next to the door; I didn't know where my passport was, so I gave him my boarding pass, the one that I was given when entering the transit lounge to allow me to get back on the plane. He spat on it, threw it on the tarmac and dragged me out of the bus. I picked up my boarding pass: I still have it. He then got onto the bus and dragged a few others off because they could not immediately locate a passport. It was hot outside, and there was that airport smell of ozone and jet engine fuel. He and one other young soldier marched us out, about 40 yards away from the bus, and told us to stand in a line. "My God, they are going to shoot us" said one of our small, strange party; and indeed, it looked that way. The two young men raised their automatic weapons and pointed them at us. Suddenly I knew it was true; they were indeed going to shoot us right there and then. But rather than fear, a great feeling of calm descended upon me. I thought "What a strange and futile way for my life to end", but I was not worried about it; quite the opposite, I got a sense that all was well with the world and that things would be just great for me and everyone else. It was a feeling of joy and love, rather than fear. Total tranquility. But they did not shoot us. Another older soldier rushed up and shouted at the two younger men, they put down their weapons and looked a bit sheepish; they ushered us back onto the bus, which trundled on to the airport hotel.

What I Took Away from That Moment

There were other times at which I thought I might be shot, but this is the one that stands out in my memory, not for its horror, but for its beauty. But there was so much more to it than that. Once I had processed it, I realized that this was a form of "near-death experience" (NDE) – I had been allowed a brief glimpse into the world beyond our bodily existence – and it is full of love, joy and light. WOW! I knew nothing about NDEs at the time, but have since read several books about the subject and the "science" behind them (2, 3). Also, the experience had similarities to that "noetic moment" I described in Chapter 1, when I was ill in hospital, aged 16.

(This event was also featured in a film about flight BA149, made a year or two after our return. But they got it all wrong – the actor playing my part was tall (I am very short!) and he was a redhead (I am not!)).

A Premonition

This event took place toward the end of September 1990, when I was in the bungalow in Kuwait. Conditions there were not good at the time.

We had established a routine, which included keeping our diaries. On this day, in the middle of the morning, when scribbling in my diary, I had a sudden sense of loss that overwhelmed me. I felt awful. I "knew" that something terrible had happened. I thought it might be my parents, but I was not sure. Then, there was some sort of a sense of my father trying to communicate with me. I didn't know what was going on, and it is hard to remember exactly what happened. I know I felt listless and depressed for the rest of that day, and I never wrote in that diary again.

I had no communication with the outside world while in Kuwait (there was no internet nor were there mobile phones in 1990), but, toward the end of November, when we got bussed up to Baghdad, we were able to receive a telephone call from home. I was very nervous, because of the premonition of some disaster. My wife came on the phone and told me everyone was fine, and I burst out crying. I don't think she knew why. The children were fine, and she was doing well, she told me. "What about my parents?" I asked. "Yes, they are also OK" she replied. She told me later that this was the one and only time she has ever lied to me about anything important.

I presumed that the day of my premonition was the day of my father's death.

What I Took from This Experience

This was another death-related experience, as I subsequently learnt that this occurrence was indeed at the time of my father's death. This was what is sometimes called a "shared-death experience" (SDE rather than NDE)*. I was being contacted by my dying father, who was some 3,500 miles away. More evidence of a world beyond the physical one we live in. Again, WOW!

* Shared-death experiences have been extensively studied by William J Peters (among others) For further information on SDEs, follow his "Shared Crossing Project" https://www.sharedcrossing.com

What do I make of that now? I remain awed by what happened. In addition, it helped me understand the rather strange relationship I had with my father. He was bipolar and also suffered from severe eczema (which I have inherited). Although I knew he loved and liked me, as a child I often felt that he was slightly disappointed in me. Much of what I was doing as a young adult was an effort to make him proud of me and to atone for my guilt that my rugby accident had worsened both his depression and his eczema. It bothers me that I was not there when he was dying, that I could not attend the funeral and that I don't know why he died. A part of me still feels responsible for his relatively young death. I think of him often, to this day, with a mixture of both love and guilt. But I have not felt any further contact or sense of connection.

A Healing Conversation

This conversation took place in the camp near Fallujah at the end of November, just after I had been moved there, and billeted with an American man I had never met before.

We were sitting on our bunks in the small wooden hut that was our current "home". It was fairly tidy, as we had cleaned it the day before when the two of us were first put into this little room. That was when we first met, him an American engineer, me an English medic; both of us trapped in Iraq as part of Saddam Hussein's "human shield". The only furnishing in the hut, apart from the two bunks, was one table and a chair; there was nothing on the wooden slatted walls. There was a small bathroom in one corner of the hut, with a flushing loo and a small shower, and we had been provided with some soap and a towel each (luxury!). Otherwise, we had very little, apart from the clothes we stood up in and a few paltry possessions that we had acquired over the last few months of captivity.

"Frank" and I had just eaten with the other hostages in the camp; he was a tall man, with a scraggly beard, and he was very thin. He looked immensely weary and sad. After our meal, we walked back to our hut together and then sat on our bunks, looking at each other. We had already introduced ourselves, but not shared our stories. Now seemed to be the time; I think we both sensed that. I started by asking Frank what he was doing in Kuwait/Iraq. He told me that he was an engineer who worked for one of the oil companies based in Kuwait. "What about you?", he asked. I explained that I had been on the BA plane that had refuelled in Kuwait as Iraq invaded and had been "taken" there – I did not need to elaborate, the story was well known among the hostages. I told him briefly about being in a flat in Kuwait for a long time, some of it without much food or any chance to exercise, and then being moved through Baghdad, and then to this place. I told him how much I missed my family, and how worried I was that there would be no good end to this. "The coalition will be bound to target this place early on in any offensive against Iraq", I said. He agreed. "Yes, we are sitting ducks here, stuck in one of Saddam Hussein's poison gas factories".

"So, what is your story, Frank?" I prompted. He said nothing for a while, but tears started running down his cheeks. I went over to his bunk and held him, allowing him to cry properly. "You do not have to tell me", I said. "No, I want to, I want to tell the story, I need to tell the story", he responded. And, slowly, he told me.

He had been living in a small apartment block in central Kuwait for some months when Iraq invaded. He was unprepared for the invasion and did not know what was going on for the first few days, but he knew a lot of local Kuwaiti people, and they kept him informed. One day, soon after the invasion, one of his Kuwaiti friends told him that the Iraqis were rounding up all the Americans they could find and taking them off to camps. He offered to help Frank hide and to keep him supplied with food, and they both agreed to this plan. He was shown a disused lift shaft in the building, and it was suggested that he hide there if the soldiers came looking for people in the building. Sure enough, a day or two later, the building was stormed by Iraqi soldiers who went from room to room looking for people and for evidence of any foreigners. Frank hid in the lift shaft, and they did not find him. His Kuwaiti friends brought him some food the next day and told him that it was dangerous outside. They suggested that he stay in the building, hiding in the shaft if anyone came in. He did just that, and they went on finding ways to bring some food into the building for him for some weeks. He ventured out of his lift shaft relatively rarely, as he was frightened, and whenever he looked out of a window, he saw Iraqi soldiers everywhere. Then there was silence and no food for a couple of days. Cautiously, he ventured out of the lift shaft and looked out of the window. What he saw was one of his Kuwaiti friends lying dead on the pavement outside, his throat slit. That was it for Frank; soon afterwards, he walked out of the building, hands above his head, and handed himself over to the soldiers. "I thought they might shoot me there and then", he said, "but they didn't, they took me off to some camp where there were other hostages, some of them American. I got some food there, but I could not talk at all. Then I got moved here, and now I am talking. Thank you".

We both wept.

We never spoke of these things again during the three weeks we were together in "Chlorine B" (our nickname for the camp). We passed pleasantries, we joked a little together, but we had nothing much in common, and he spent a lot of his time with the other Americans in the camp, while I gravitated to the British men. But, after that evening, he seemed a lot better, and, on several occasions, he thanked me for listening.

Why That Conversation Had Such a Big Impact on Me

This event, like the previous two, is something that I did not dwell on then, nor did it concern me for some time afterwards but I am now immensely grateful for it. At the time, the experience was valuable and important, as we were both mentally better afterwards. But I did not think much more about it until I was working on placebo effects and healing (as described in the next chapters). Then, I realized that this had been one of those rare moments of meaningful connection between two different souls that had a healing effect on both of us. It was my first experience of "reciprocal healing". When with Frank that day, I somehow knew what to do – just to be with him and listen compassionately. I think I was in the role of the healer that day.

THE AFTERMATH

I came home in December 1990. I was a mess of mixed emotions that included large amounts of grief and guilt. I was grieving for my lost father and my lost life. I felt guilty about my father's death – I thought my absence had caused it, or at least that, had I been around, I might have been able to prevent it. I felt guilty about the negative impact my absence had had on my wife and daughters. Why had I changed that flight? I was also extremely frail, both physically and emotionally.

The simple thing to write now would be along the lines of "But I slowly got stronger and, once I was able to return to work, I decided I needed to change my focus, and start working on placebos and healing". It would be simple to write, and maybe it is not so far from the truth in some ways, but it is absolutely NOT what it was like or what happened.

You might think that when one comes back to normal life after trauma of this sort, that you get some help with Post-Traumatic Stress Disorder (PTSD) and the like, and then re-appraise your situation and move on, perhaps in a different direction. But, for me, it did not work like that at all. I was stuck with an irrational mess of thoughts and feelings about all aspects of both home and work life which were very uncomfortable and went on for years. I suffered from flashbacks and nightmares. Somehow, I muddled through in the end, but it took a long time. I made no clear decisions about what to do; I just sort of found out what I was most comfortable doing as the months and years went by.

First, I needed to understand what had happened to me, why I was in such a sorry mental state, and how to get better. In other words, I had to heal.

Several key experiences set me on that path.

Connecting With Nature

The first few days after I came back home were hard for me and my family. I did not know what to do with myself. On the second or third day, my wife suggested something wonderful. "Let's go for a walk together, and you can tell me the whole story", she said. "OK, let's go to the lake we used to sail on, and walk around that", I agreed. We drove to the reservoir, and did the 50-minute walk around it, me talking for the whole time, recounting what had happened. Telling the story was helpful, but so were the water, the trees, the birdsong and the space: being at one with familiar natural surroundings.

After Christmas, my wife and I decided we needed to go away for a few days; to escape from the gaze of local friends, neighbors and colleagues, who were treating us strangely, and to be on our own, talk more and try to re-establish our relationship. "I want to be at the seaside, preferably in Cornwall", I said. So we borrowed a flat from a colleague in a seaside town in Cornwall and went there to "hide" on our own for a week.

It was a wonderful week. The sea, the headland, and the coastal walks were refreshing. And the good seafood and noisy pubs in the evening did me no harm either.

Why Was This So Important?

In those early days, I realized how important nature, particularly the seaside and the woodland, were to me, how much I had missed them, and how they helped me reconnect.

I walked and I talked, I looked at the trees and listened to the birds. I saw beauty everywhere and was enveloped in the wonderful sight and sound of waves crashing on shorelines. But why was that so wonderful and important? Was it simply that I was seeing and doing things that had always been important to me, but which I had been removed from for nearly five months? I think it was more than that. I felt real joy and at times enchantment at these simple activities. Nature seemed to be telling me something, trying to calm and reassure me in some unfathomable way. It did that in Iraq, through the pink bougainvillea and the night sky. And it still does now. (I will discuss nature and healing in some detail in a later chapter)

The Diagnosis: "Soul Separation"

In 1991, very little was known about Post-Traumatic Stress Disorder (PTSD) and it was not something that most people were aware of. Today, it seems to be something that is an expected aftermath if you have experienced trauma, and it is the diagnostic label that I would have been given. I am not sure that PTSD is a clearly defined entity, and I am certain it is not the same for everyone. I think it includes a complicated spectrum of many different responses. I certainly had many of the features of classic PTSD, such as flashbacks, but I did not identify myself as having PTSD. I briefly discussed my issues with a psychiatrist and a counselor after my return, but neither of them mentioned PTSD, nor were they much help. I concluded that my medical profession had little to offer me.

A year or so after my return, I was still not well, (although I was doing my best to hide my problems from those around me). It was then that I became aware of the problem of PTSD among troops returning from service in Iraq and Afghanistan. A colleague was working with these men; she believed that water immersion therapies, including spas, could work wonders for them. She encouraged me to help her popularize this idea and wanted me to help her research the area and learn more about it. I felt for these men and wanted to help. My friend asked me to visit her at her home for a discussion about it and to look at videos she had of servicemen who had tried the form of water/spa therapy she was interested in.

So there I was, sitting in her front room, surrounded by beautiful antique furniture. My delightful friend set up her laptop on the coffee table in front of the settee that I was on. She said she would set the video going and then disappear to the kitchen while I watched it.

On came the video, initially showing a group of some six servicemen who had been traumatized while serving in Iraq, telling their stories. They had suffered horribly; for example, being in trucks that were blown up by IEDs, and being the only survivor, looking at their mates spread around them, dead. These were troubled men with grim stories that they only seemed to be touching on rather gingerly when asked to speak to camera.

Then we saw them at a spa center in Germany; there was footage of them helping each other in and out of the spa pools, hugging each other and having a laugh. At this point, I was not really giving the video my full attention, I was worrying about what I was going to say to my friend, as I was beginning to realize that I found it difficult to deal with these stories of trauma in Iraq, and that helping these men might not be for me.

Then, the video showed them being interviewed about their experience of being in the spa center. A few said it had helped them but in a somewhat downbeat way. Then, on came another man, a chap who looked about 21, and who spoke more fluently than some of his colleagues. He said he had found the water therapy hugely helpful, as it had allowed him to connect with his colleagues in a new way, and to reconnect with nature and with life. He was filmed looking right into the camera, his voice was arresting, and I was now paying full attention to the film.

And then came the "moment". I do not remember his exact words, but they were something like this:

> "Before I came here, I was in a bit of a mess, I was not connected. Being here has helped me reconnect. What I came to realize while I was here was that my trauma had resulted in soul separation, my body and mind had been separated from my soul, and now I have reconnected all parts of me, so I am whole again".

As I heard that, I thought to myself: "*Soul separation: Oh my God, that is my problem!*" I was shaking as what he had said hit me. Suddenly, I understood what had happened to me and what had been "missing" over the past couple of years. I had been "dead" in the sense that my soul, my essence, had been separated from me through the inhumane things I had witnessed and experienced in Kuwait/Iraq. And I think that moment of realization allowed me to start to "reconnect".

I did not watch the rest of the video, but I think it finished soon after my "moment". My friend came back and asked how I had found it. I had no idea what to say, but, that afternoon, I agreed to visit the spa with her to see for myself.

The Impact of This Event

This was a big moment for me. I had a diagnosis. Not a medical one, but one that made sense to me. The notion of soul separation is one that is difficult for many of us within our modern worldview, so dependent on materialistic science for its "truth". I do not remember the concept of the soul being mentioned at medical school, or in most of my medical career. But all religions recognize this concept. Christianity and some other belief systems equate soul separation with death. Other ancient belief systems and animistic/panpsychic thinking say that all things have a soul. They maintain that there is a world of spirits and souls that we can interact with, perhaps with the help of a shaman, who can use rituals to allow the soul to return home to the host body. Later, I realized that this concept had been one that I had experienced before when I held the hand of the dying man described in Chapter 1, and "felt" his soul depart from his body. What with this and the death-related experiences in Kuwait, it was hard for me to go on ignoring the strange, indescribable experiences that were running through my life.

Revisiting Kuwait

I think one of the most important things I did to aid my recovery was to go back to Kuwait a few years after my return to England.

I was invited to lecture on a post-graduate course on rheumatology to be held in Kuwait City and, after careful discussions with the family, I agreed to go on the condition that my wife could accompany me and that we could have some time to ourselves. My hosts, who knew the backstory, agreed. So, off we went, a little nervously.

The two of us walked around the hotel where I had spent the first three weeks, now derelict but still bearing the marks of the gunfire that we had heard when we were first billeted there. Then we found the bungalow where I had spent 99 uncomfortable nights, and saw it in its present circumstances, with university students bustling about. The bougainvillea was still there, looking wonderful. And we visited the park in which, when hostages, we had been allowed to exercise. Now, as my wife and I walked slowly around, there was no one pointing a Kalashnikov at me. Being back there felt unreal. This was not the awful place that I had been in, it was normal. Had it all been a dream? No. The bougainvillea and bullet marks told me that, but it felt very strange to be back there among normal life.

Why This Helped

There is plenty of evidence that revisiting the site of a traumatic event, once normality has been restored, can be helpful for those with PTSD. Some therapists use "site visits" with their patients as part of their therapy (4), but I think it might be better to let folks do it for themselves, especially if they can be accompanied by a loved one, as I was. That visit to Kuwait and seeing the sites of my captivity again certainly helped me. The frequency of flashbacks and nightmares decreased very soon after my return. I think this visit, particularly seeing the areas of Kuwait, in which I had been held, looking "normal", with happy, contented people wandering about freely, allowed me to reprocess and reframe the experience in some unfathomable way.

"The Lights Are Back On"

It was an afternoon early in 1993, I think, and I was sitting at my desk in the outpatient suite in one of the smaller hospitals near Bristol, looking at the list of patients I was due to see. I had not been able to get back to a full clinical workload since my return but had wanted to go on doing some work with patients. As my salary was being paid by the University, not the NHS, I could dictate terms for my clinical work. I arranged to do clinics in some of the smaller hospitals in our group and give plenty of time to each patient I saw. I now understood, in a new way, that giving people enough time to tell their stories was a hugely important component of my clinical practice. So, that afternoon, I had only two new patients to see, each of whom had been allotted a 45-minute slot, and three follow-ups, each allotted 20 minutes. I saw a familiar name among the follow-up group. "Oh no! How has 'Peggy' got herself onto this list?" I wondered. She was a lovely but rather demanding lady with severe arthritis whom I had been seeing every four months or so since around 1980, but who always went to the main Bristol hospital for her appointments. I had seen her there once since getting back from Iraq and had explained to her that I was unable to give her further appointments, as I would not be doing clinics in that hospital anymore. I transferred her care to one of my colleagues. Part of my strategy of working in the smaller hospitals was to avoid seeing a number of patients, like Peggy, whom I thought had got used to seeing me (addicted to me?) prior to my enforced "holiday", and for whom I thought I could no longer provide the same support as I had done previously.

Sure enough, later that afternoon, Peggy limped into the clinic. She sat herself down, looked up at me and said "Oh good, the lights are back on, so let's see if you can help me with my arthritis again now". "What do you mean by 'The lights are back on', Peggy?" I asked. "You; you are clearly OK again now, the twinkle in your eyes is back; your eyes are smiling again, so maybe you can do something useful for me this time. You have not been much use to any of us over the last few months, have you?" I laughed and got on with the consultation as best I could.

The Impact of This Event

Peggy's comments, characteristically blunt and pointed, were both helpful and hurtful. Had I really been that bad? Why hadn't my colleagues said anything? But I guess Peggy was right; I was getting better. And I found it fascinating that she could tell just by looking at me and that it was the eyes that told her. We have so much to learn about ourselves as creatures of the soul as well as body and mind (5).

But I was slowly getting better, and gradually finding my way again. When I first started seeing patients again, I often felt completely overwhelmed by their problems, but now I was able to spend time with them without distress.

And, as described next, my work was starting to go in new directions.

The Need for a Change in Career

I was badly damaged by my time as a hostage and suffered a lot for several years. But life needed to go on; I needed to work. I had responsibilities to my family and work colleagues, and I was still relatively young (45). Clinical medicine and research were the only skills I could use to earn money. But I just did not know what to do with myself. I looked at jobs in other countries (including Pakistan, to the horror of my family); I was searching for meaning and purpose. In retrospect, I was trying to deal with the cognitive dissonance between my science and my experiences, which was causing anxiety. I struggled with my clinical work, which I could no longer do properly. I took the jobs of Research Director and then Dean of the Faculty of Medicine in Bristol under some duress and out of a sense of duty (the University had continued to pay my salary while I was "away" and had been very supportive of my wife and children). But I was no good at those jobs, which I disliked. I did not know what to do next.

Memory can be fickle. It is now over 30 years since I was taken hostage, and I am well. I have largely forgotten how I felt in the 1990s. But I recently re-read an interview I gave just a few years after getting back, which reminded me of just how angry and "messed-up" I was at the time*.

This interview is quoted in Stephen Davis' book "Operation Trojan Horse" (1), where he erroneously says that I gave it 15 years after the event; I have checked my records and found that this interview took place in the mid-1990s.

Here are some of the things I said to Stephen Davis:

"I was in the prime of my life when I went out there, I had been appointed as a professor just two or three years beforehand ... and I never got back to that ... also I was practicing medicine fairly full on then. I've never been able to do that since I got back ... I do a little bit but I can't handle seeing patients much. So, my trade, if you like, has been shot to bits by this ... I can't practice my trade because I'm damaged".

"My wife's and my daughters' lives were irrevocably changed by this. That's unacceptable. My father died and I feel guilty for that ... this strange guilt response brought on by something very extreme. And this was extreme".

"I've never received an explanation or an apology from anyone ... I'm angry about that".

Clearly, I was indeed "messed up" and angry back then!

In retrospect, it is interesting to reflect on why I found it so difficult to do routine clinical work on my return. I had always found seeing a lot of patients exhausting but, in the 1990s, even seeing one or two left me emotionally "rung out". It took me a long time to figure out what was going on. Basically, I was being too empathic. I connected with and felt all the pain and distress of my patients, and, if they were empathic in turn, then we entered a sort of "folie à deux" – cycling each other toward despair. Empathy is usually lauded as a good thing for a doctor, but I slowly learnt that what we need is compassion, not empathy. As the psychologist Paul Bloom argues in one of his books – the ideal consultation takes place between a compassionate doctor and an empathic patient (6).

However, apart from clinical work, there were two activities that I could still do upon returning from Iraq: things I still seemed good at, and things that others wanted me to do more of.

The first was writing about rheumatology. While in Kuwait, I wrote a student booklet on how to examine the musculoskeletal system. This was published by the Arthritis Research Council (ARC, a charity now known as "Versus Arthritis") and was well received. Before I was taken hostage, I had started co-editing a major new textbook of rheumatology, which had been progressing (slowly) in my absence. My wonderful co-editor (Jack Klippel) and publisher (Fiona Foley) were very kind and patient with me and managed to persuade me to come back on board with the project. I did, and the successful product (7) is a source of pride to me.

The second thing I could do was carry out research into osteoarthritis (OA). Prior to being taken hostage, I had established myself as a world authority on this very common but ill-understood disorder. There was still OA research going on in my rheumatology unit when I returned to work, and the international OA research community welcomed me back generously. So I resumed investigating OA as soon as I could, and derived satisfaction from that work. But there had been a shift in my perspective. I was less interested in the disease mechanisms and searching for cures; I now think that a futile pursuit. Rather, I wanted to understand the symptoms and suffering and how to control them. Pain, stiffness and physical disability result from OA and they were not being investigated much. So, that was my new focus; I altered the priorities of some ongoing projects to center more on pain and started new research on this and the other symptoms of OA.

I managed to keep my writing commitments and my osteoarthritis research going during those first few, confusing years after my return to work. They were an outlet for my curiosity, conscious of the spiritual side of life, of the importance of human interactions, and of the centrality of caring and compassion in health care. Furthermore, I found that I did not need to drive myself as hard as before: I had already proved myself. My father was no longer alive, so I did not need to seek his approval. I was free to move on, as and when the right opportunity arose.

REFERENCES

1. Davis S. *Operation Trojan Horse – The Most Shocking Government Cover-up of the Last Thirty Years.* London: John Blake Publishing, 2021.
2. Long J, Perry P. *Evidence of the Afterlife: The Science of Near Death Experiences.* Harper Collins, New York, 2011.
3. van Lommel P. *Consciousness Beyond Life: The Science of Near Death Experience.* Harper Collins, 2011.

4. Murray H, Merritt C, Grey N. Returning to the scene of trauma in PTSD treatment – Why how and when? *The Cognitive Behavioral Therapist* 2015; 8: 1–12.
5. The Bible: Proverbs 30:17: "The eye is the window to the soul".
6. Bloom P. *Against Empathy: The Case for Rational Compassion.* Ecco Books, 2016.
7. Rheumatology Eds Klippel J and Dieppe P. First Edition London: Mosby, 1994.

Section Two

Investigation

3

A New Beginning and Placebo Research

In 1997, I resigned from my jobs as Research Director and then Dean of the Faculty of Medicine in Bristol after four years of service (I had been asked to do five) and was once again free to think about future jobs. After a few months of futile searching, I got lucky and was appointed as Director of a new Research Collaboration, to be funded by the Medical Research Council. This exciting new initiative, the "Health Services Research Collaboration" (HSRC), was to be based in Bristol, but involved inter-disciplinary research with seven other UK universities. I knew next to nothing about Health Services Research, (which explores the best way to deliver efficient, effective and acceptable health care), but it was thought that my extensive experience in research and management would allow me to co-ordinate activities and run the unit successfully.

Several other things were changing in my life in the late 1990s. Our daughters left home, and my wife and I moved house. We really were beginning again, indicating that we had healed from our trauma. I was in that new job (and house) in Bristol for 11 years (spanning two five-year cycles of research funding) for the HSRC.

A NEW JOB: HEALTH SERVICES RESEARCH

This new work challenge was hugely satisfying for me. For the first time in my life, I was working with health researchers who were not medical – they included sociologists, economists, psychologists, statisticians and epidemiologists. They helped broaden my thinking about health and research and opened up new opportunities for my own work on

DOI: 10.4324/9781003461814-5

osteoarthritis (OA) and placebos. My osteoarthritis research became led by questions posed by our patients, including "When in the course of arthritis is it best to have a hip or knee joint replacement?" And my long-standing interest in caring and the sort of response that Wykeham could achieve with people like his patient Doris (Chapter 1) had led me to want to understand more about how kindness and compassion might work. The obvious answer, according to biomedicine, was the placebo response.

Fortunately for me, an ex-trainee, good friend and excellent academic, Professor Mike Doherty of Nottingham University, was interested in collaborating with me to do research on placebos in OA. That was how my serious work on placebos got started.

What Are Placebos and Nocebos?

The word placebo is derived from the Latin "I shall please". The word is used to describe interventions that have no known value but are used to please or appease. Because of the dominance of biomedical and pharmaceutical thinking, we now tend to equate placebos with the inactive "sugar pills" used as the comparators of "real" medicines in drug trials. The general belief is that any benefit that might come from these "sugar pills" is all about the expectations and suggestibility of the person who gets better when given them – that, I now believe, is almost certainly wrong. And, strangely, things like giving someone a piece of cake, or a hug, to reduce their suffering or to "please" are not thought of as placebo treatments; I think they should be!

Nocebo is sometimes called "placebo's evil twin". It is about getting worse when given a dummy or sham treatment and is again thought to be about expectations (in this case, negative rather than positive), suggestibility or conditioning.

Personal Experiences of the Power of Placebos and Nocebos

I have seen lots of patients and relatives in whom placebo or nocebo effects seemed to have been hugely important; here are three examples:

"I Need My Usual Tonic, Doctor"

Soon after qualifying as a doctor, when doing junior posts in and around the London region in the 1970s, I did some work for general practitioners to cover their need for a day off or a short holiday period. One day, while I was doing one of these sessions, an older lady, smartly dressed and well spoken, came in to see me, and asked: "Can you prescribe me my usual tonic please doctor?" I looked through her file; she was in her 80s and seemingly very fit for her age. There was not much of note in the folder, except for a few entries saying, "seems fine, tonic prescribed".

"What is the tonic for?" I asked her.

"Well, to build me up, I think, doctor, and it keeps me going; I could not do without it. Doctor Smith always gives it to me".

"What would happen if you did not have it, do you think?"

"Well I don't know doctor, I am never without it, and I do not intend to be without it. You see I come in every few weeks to have a chat with Doctor Smith, and he checks me over, and he then prescribes me my tonic because he says that is what keeps me going so well".

I asked her if I could see the bottle, and I looked it up in "MIMS", the book that we all had with us that listed all the things we could prescribe, the doses to use and suchlike. Her tonic was in there all right, but it had no active ingredients in it of any note, apart from iron.

"You do know that there are no active drugs in this tonic, don't you?" I asked her.

"Well of course doctor, I don't like to take drugs, but I do need the tonic".

I wrote the prescription for her. She thanked me and asked me if I could make sure that she had another appointment with Dr Smith quite soon because she needed him to check up on her, as usual.

This lady clearly needed her dose of placebo and her talk with the doctor to keep her well. In those days, tonics were regularly prescribed and widely consumed, in the full knowledge that they had no useful active ingredients in them. And that was fine, I think; they never did any harm and often resulted in great benefit. But they have been banned now because it is thought that giving people a medicine that you know has no active ingredient in it is unethical and a form of deception. That seems a pity.

My Mother's Knees

My mother was in her late 80s and living alone when my wife and I asked her if she would like to join us on a trip to France to spend Christmas with our good friends who live there (whom she knew). She was a little hesitant at first, saying that her arthritic knees were a problem and she did not know if she could manage the traveling. But then she asked me, "Maybe you could give me something for my knees, Paul?"

In general, it is not a good idea to treat close relatives, and I was a bit nervous about giving her anything, but then I decided that, if I used something really safe, with a lot of positive suggestion, it might work. So I got some low-dose ibuprofen, making sure that it was a variety that was in brightly colored tablets* and I suggested she try them, telling her, very positively (and truly), that we used this medication a lot in our hospital practice, and I thought it should help her.

Ibuprofen is a mild non-steroidal anti-inflammatory agent, with analgesic activity; it is very safe in low doses. It is widely used for aches and pains and arthritis and is now available over the counter. It is made by many different companies, so there are all sorts of different tablets, capsules and formulations on the market.

It worked wonders. She told us that it had cured her pain completely and that she was able to walk so much better; she was delighted and enjoyed her Christmas in France. On our return, she asked me to get her some more of this wonderful medicine, and I did. All was well until a few weeks later when she ran out of the tablets and went to her GP to get some more. He saw that it was ibuprofen and prescribed it for her. She got her prescription from the chemist, but the new tablets did not work. She rang me up and we discussed it. The new tablets were ibuprofen as far as I could ascertain, but they were a different make and a different color. I tried to persuade her that they should work like the ones I had got, but they did not; her knees became a problem again. Her GP consulted with me, but neither of us could see a way out of the problem as the brightly colored ibuprofen tablets were no longer available.

She never found another good treatment for her knees.

My mother had clearly responded to me rather than the ibuprofen; it was my reputation and assurances that worked for her: only her son's special medicine was going to be effective for her, and once she could see that it was something else, she lost the response. It is well known that color affects the placebo response; so I think the "trick" here was a combination of a tablet with a bright color that my mother had not encountered before, alongside the positive suggestion provided by her son, the doctor.

"All Tablets Make Me Sick, Doctor"

"Caroline" was a rather sad-looking lady in her 60s, suffering from a relatively mild inflammatory form of arthritis, which nevertheless gave her a lot of pain and stiffness. She was referred to me by her GP who said that she could not find any form of medication that helped Caroline and that all the tablets she had tried made the patient feel sick.

I did my best for her, suggesting some physiotherapy, changes in lifestyle and other approaches that did not involve drugs. But she would have none of it and said that she wanted me to find her a drug that did not make her sick.

So I tried one that she had not had before. But sure enough, it made her feel sick. I thought about this for a bit and then came up with a rather sneaky idea, one which I am not too proud of in retrospect. I prescribed an anti-emetic* drug, telling her (truthfully) that it was a tablet designed to prevent sickness, and that I hoped it might also help her pain and stiffness (although there was no reason that it should, other than a placebo response).

She came back to see me a few weeks later, telling me that these tablets (the anti-sickness medication) had made her feel sick, just like all the others.

At that point the penny dropped: she was conditioned to react in this way to any tablet; a conditioned "nocebo" (negative) response. I moved on to the prescription of ointments that she could rub onto her painful joints, and they helped.

Anti-emetic tablets are designed to treat nausea and sickness

This lady's case illustrates the potential negative effects of expectation/suggestion and conditioning. She had come to expect (know) that all tablets caused sickness, although she was still hoping that she could find one that would not and that might work for her.

These stories are examples of the positive or negative effects of consultation and the use of prescriptions of drugs with little or no active ingredient, which produced so-called placebo or nocebo effects, respectively. Cases such as these were teaching me that placebo and nocebo effects are very complex and dependent on the prescriber, the patient and the context in which the medications were being given. It still did not seem to me to be about expectation, suggestion and conditioning alone, and I thought the subject needed further investigation. I thought it might be about connecting with people in some inexplicable way (as Frank and I had done in Iraq) and/or having a spiritual element to it.

Research on Placebos in Osteoarthritis (OA)

The first thing Mike Doherty and I wanted to know was just how good placebos were for pain relief in OA, compared with the standard medications and physical interventions we recommend. With the help of a statistician working with Mike Doherty (Weija Zhang), we were able to find out (1).

Using published trial findings, we were able to compare the pain relief that came from a test treatment with those of a placebo AND no treatment at all. The data showed, unequivocally, that placebo treatment is of great benefit. Indeed, we subsequently estimated that about 70% of the pain relief achieved from any treatment could be attributed to the placebo effect alone.

The effects are shown graphically in Figure 3.1.

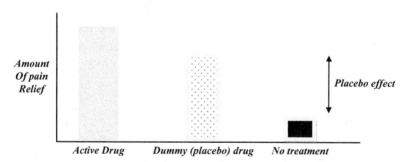

FIGURE 3.1

A diagrammatic representation of the comparative effects of an active drug, a dummy drug and no treatment at all, for pain relief in arthritis. The hatched bar (left) shows that an active drug can produce quite a lot of relief. The dotted bar in the middle shows that a dummy drug, or "placebo" (a tablet that looks exactly the same as the real drug, but has no active ingredient in it) produces nearly as much relief. The filled in bar on the right represents the small amount of improvement if no treatment is given at all (this small improvement is probably due to the effects of having your symptoms observed and measured in an experiment). The placebo effect is the difference between the relief achieved by a placebo and that of no treatment (the arrow).

So, placebo treatments are very effective for pain in arthritis, and the placebo effect accounts for the majority of the value of any of the pain relief treatments we use. Amazing!

As we were doing this work, an American group in Texas was looking at dummy or sham surgery (rather than dummy drugs) in the treatment of OA. A trial, led by orthopedic surgeon Bruce Moseley, compared the effects of a surgical washout of the knee, with sham surgery, in which a small incision was made in the skin over the knee (the same as that which would occur if you had a washout), but with no procedure being carried out. At the time, knee washout was a popular treatment for knee arthritis; I had been doing it myself in Bristol, as it seemed to relieve the pain very effectively. But the trial showed that the sham washout procedure was just as effective as the real procedure (2). I visited the group in Texas and saw films of delighted patients, who had undergone the sham procedure, telling the team how pleased they were with the improvement in their knee, and demonstrating how much better their function was.

Subsequent research has confirmed Moseley's findings, and trials of sham surgery in a number of other conditions, notably some forms of back pain, have demonstrated just how powerful sham surgery can be. But how can that be?

As mentioned, the accepted theories to explain placebo responses are expectation/suggestion or conditioning. These ideas presume that the response is mediated in the patient's brain, either as a response to their expectation of a good response or because they have been conditioned (like one of Pavlov's dogs) into responding in such a way. I was skeptical that such responses explained the whole amazing placebo/nocebo story and was on the lookout for different ideas to explore.

Different Ideas about Placebos and Nocebos

There is good evidence in support of both the expectation/suggestion and conditioning theories for some placebo effects. For example, we know that you can condition people to respond in a certain way to a tablet, and we know that giving an intervention with strong suggestions of what it might do increases the chances of those things happening. But my work with patients and my reading, as well as the extraordinary conclusions from our systematic review about the power of placebo for pain relief, made me feel sure that there was much more to it than that. And I found that there were many other ideas and theories around. Some of them are outlined below.

Finding New Meaning for Illness

One of the Americans best known for work on placebo effects is the anthropologist, Dan Moerman. He generously agreed to meet with me on one of my visits to the USA. Dan thinks it is all about finding meaning and wants us to rename the placebo effect as the "meaning response". This is subtly different from suggestion: it is more about an individual's understanding of their illness, its meaning, and their concepts of what sort of intervention might help them. Dan Moerman has a lot of fascinating research evidence to support his ideas, much of which is summarized in his academic papers and book (3, 4).

Power, Performance and Ritual

Many authors have written about the importance of power, performance and ritual in medicine. Ted Kaptchuk, a leading US placebo research scientist, wrote an important essay in 2011 in which he compared Navajo Indian healing ceremonies, acupuncture treatments and conventional biomedical encounters, pointing out that each involved similar sorts of power differential (the powerful healer treats the powerless subject), performance and ritual (5). He suggested that these factors were responsible for the placebo effect of each treatment.

My colleague, Dr Sarah Goldingay, of Exeter University is a performance scholar who takes a similar view. So, together, we pursued the idea that context, power, performance and ritual were important in mediating the placebo response, and published our views on how this sort of approach to placebo might aid our understanding of symptoms and their response to treatments in osteoarthritis (6).

Activation of the Nurturing Response

In the early 2000s I went to a seminar in Bristol given by Dr Steven Porges, a well-known American neuroscientist. He had developed a novel theory about our autonomic nervous system (the control systems that manage our heart rate and digestion and so forth, of which we are largely unaware). We have known for a long time that one thing this system does is to activate what we call the "fight or flight" response – our automatic response to fear – which includes changes in heart rate and blood flow throughout the body, as well as the release of certain hormones like adrenaline. What Dr Porges had uncovered was that there was an opposite type of response, mediated by the same autonomic nerves – which he called the "nurturing response" – activated by phenomena like seeing a young baby smile, and resulting in relaxation. This is his rather complex "polyvagal theory" (7). I had not come across this idea before going to his seminar, and I was excited by it. Afterwards, I asked him if it might help explain what was going on in the placebo response, and he said he thought that, yes, it might, and invited me to discuss this with him when I was next in the USA, which I did. I thought it's possible that activation of the nurturing response, allowing us to relax, listen properly and think positively, might play a role in placebo responses, and that, equally, activation of the "fight or flight" response might be a part of nocebo responses.

Validation and Invalidation

Around the year 2009, I was invited to give a seminar about placebos to the Psychology Department at the University of Exeter. Toward the end of my presentation, I said that one problem I had with undertaking further research on the phenomenon was the paucity of good theories to explain it. During the discussion one of the professors, Tom Lynch, said that he had a theory that might be relevant – the theory of validation and invalidation. He suggested that the key to placebo might be validation of the patient's problems by the physician – in other words, conveying genuine understanding of their problems. In contrast, invalidation might activate a nocebo response, he thought.

Tom Lynch and I were able to get funding for a PhD student to work with us on these new ideas about placebo. We appointed Maddy (now Dr) Greville-Harris, who did a great job over the three years of her PhD project with us and taught me a lot. She had her PhD thesis accepted in 2013 (8).

Using different experimental techniques, she was able to show that validation (feeling you have been fully understood and accepted) was beneficial and could activate the "nurturing response" of Steven Porges, whereas invalidation was highly damaging and had the opposite effect, activating our "fight or flight" response.

An "Oh My" Moment and the Nocebo Response

One day, while Maddy and I were discussing her findings together, we had an "Oh my" moment. We suddenly realized that the negative effects of invalidation were much more powerful than the beneficial effects of validation. In other words, "bad is more powerful than good" (9). Teachers have known this for ages – to negate the effects of one criticism of a pupil you will need to provide them with about five plaudits. We had stumbled on the huge importance of "placebo's evil twin" – the nocebo response. Working with patient interviews, Maddy was able to show just how easy it was for doctors to unwittingly invalidate a patient and make them much worse. The doctor might be trying to be reassuring by saying, for example, "I cannot find anything serious wrong with you". But this might be construed as "He thinks I am a fraud and does not understand how much pain I am in" by the patient, making matters worse, not better. As Maddy says in her thesis abstract, the problem is that "*doctors are more interested in understanding their patients than in communicating understanding*".

I believe this finding has major implications for medical practice and education. We need more teaching about how to avoid doing harm by inadvertently invalidating our patients' symptoms. It helps to listen carefully, to say things back to the patient and ask them how they feel about what you have said. But the key to avoiding nocebo effects of a consultation is to be able to validate the patient's experiences – making sure that they know you believe them – which means you must believe them. And you must be compassionate.

Connection, Metaphysics and "Telecebo"

While not dismissing the importance of expectation, suggestion and conditioning, I now had a lot of different ideas about what placebo and nocebo responses might be about. But I still did not feel as if things like meaning, ritual, validation and the rest quite explained it all for me. I was very conscious of that sense of connection that you sometimes get when interacting with other people, and I thought that must be important. But what is that sense of connection? Another important US academic doctor working in the field of placebo (and healing) is Dr Larry Dossey. In 2016, he published an important essay about telecebo (10), proposing that good intention was critical to activating placebo responses, and that this could even work at a distance – hence "telecebo". He linked this conjecture to distant healing (healers being able to help clients who are a long way away from them). I loved that idea, but it raised as many questions as it answered for me and others, because, to me, it meant that these phenomena were no longer explicable by materialistic science alone.

Nomenclature and Reframing the Placebo Response

One of the stumbling blocks to understanding placebos is the nomenclature. The idea of a "placebo response" is an oxymoron – you cannot respond to "nothing". A number of different terms have been proposed to improve upon "placebo", as shown in Table 3.1.

These different terms obviously reflect their authors' preconceptions as to what is most important in facilitating a positive response to an intervention with no active ingredient in it. Many stress the importance of interactions (participation effect, interpersonal healing), whereas others emphasize the context (context effects, social situation, life world).

TABLE 3.1

Some of the Alternative Terms for Describing the "Placebo Response"

- Context effects
- Remembered wellness
- Meaning response
- The relaxation response
- A social situation, not a substance
- Medically significant responses to the life world
- Participation effect
- Interpersonal healing
- Belief activation
- HEAL (holistic elements activating life force)

Some people, like Dan Moerman, have tried to reframe the idea – his term being the "meaning response". Shamini Jain, a medical scientist from the USA, has introduced the term HEAL (holistic elements activating life force) (11). She puts the emphasis on therapeutic relationships as well as ritual, expectation and conditioning. Much as I respect her work, I am unhappy about the acronym "HEAL" which might lead us to think that healing is all about the placebo response. Maybe it is, but I don't think so.

Other insights have come from psychology and psychotherapy, where treatment is often about the relationship between the therapist and the client. One person who put much emphasis on the importance of that relationship was psychologist Carl Rogers, who talked of the critical importance of "unconditional positive regard" of the therapist for the client (12). As we shall see later, this is similar to the beliefs of many of the healers with whom I have worked, who believe that "unconditional love" for the other person is the key to healing.

"CAM", PLACEBOS AND HEALING

The emerging field of "Complementary and Alternative Medicine" (CAM) was another area that I was interested in at the time. My interest was piqued in part by many of my medical science colleagues dismissing it all as "just a placebo". I was not so sure. There are a huge number of interventions that are used to improve health, but which are not used within mainstream biomedical practice. Many of them are ridiculed by the medical profession, in spite of the fact that they have been helping people for centuries – long before the rise of modern medicine. Indeed, the term "Complementary and Alternative Medicine" is itself somewhat dismissive. Later in this book, I will use the example of homeopathy to illustrate the fact that I think that many of these interventions may involve healing.

Medical Science and the Dismissal of CAM

The general argument given by medical science against CAM interventions, such as acupuncture or homeopathy, is to quote the fact that most randomized controlled trials (RCTs) do not show them to have much effectiveness (which is true).

My colleague Charlotte Paterson, who was working with me in the Health Services Research Collaboration, wondered if that might be because of the design of the RCT, rather than the fault of the interventions. Her hypothesis was that the effects of many CAM treatments might have a lot to do with the context in which they took place, and factors like the interactions between therapist and client. The randomized controlled trial (RCT) is designed to get rid of such influences so that the "pure" effect of the intervention (usually a drug) can be studied.

Charlotte and I published a paper about this in the *British Medical Journal* (BMJ) (13). We argued that interventions to be tested by RCT tend to be divided into their characteristic or specific effects (what a drug is supposed to do to the body, for example), and their incidental effects (which include numerous non-specific factors, including placebo effects). However, complex interventions (those in which benefits might come from more than one single element) should not be tested by simple RCTs alone, as they deliberately "control" out the non-specific/incidental effects that might be all-important.

I think this contribution of Charlotte's is an important one. There is now a lot more concern about how best to test complex interventions, but I don't think the medical profession is as concerned as it should be about the dismissal of CAM therapies on the basis of the results of RCTs alone.

My Conclusions About Placebo Responses

I came to the conclusion that context effects, ritual and interpersonal interactions were all key to placebo responses. In addition, it seemed critical that patients felt safe, cared for and validated if they were to respond well to any intervention.

And, as with all other aspects of health care, it seemed likely that some therapists were probably particularly good at activating a placebo response in their clients (and there is some scientific evidence to support that idea). Similarly, some patients/clients are probably more likely to be good responders than others, according to their differing levels of understanding and interpretation of their illness. One size does not fit all – even when it comes to placebo.

But two BIG questions remained unanswered:

1. Are therapeutic responses to CAM interventions explained by placebo responses?
2. Is healing a form of placebo response?

My thoughts about these questions, prior to me doing my own serious research on healing (described in the next few chapters), ranged between "yes" and "no" – it seemed likely to me that placebo responses were an important element of many CAM and healing interventions (just as they are in biomedical treatments), but that other things were probably going on as well.

Some years later, Dr Emmylou Rhatz and I wrote a discussion paper about this (14). We hypothesized that the placebo response is an important part of CAM and healing interventions, but that, in addition, **something else** is also going on.

Shifting My Research toward Healing

My government-funded Health Services Research Collaboration was closed down after 11 years, as part of a major restructuring of UK health research funding. I had learnt a lot about research methodology, continued with my research on osteoarthritis and launched my research on the placebo response. I was now in my 60s, my children were independent and I no longer had a lot of financial worries. So, it was time to "*go for it*" and start serious research on caring and healing, whatever the professional consequences.

I was fortunate to get a position in Exeter in what was then the Peninsula Medical School, on the understanding that, as long as I did some teaching and helped the school out in a few other ways, I could do what research I liked – I could even do research on healing!

REFERENCES

1. Zhang W et al. The placebo effect and its determinants in osteoarthritis: Meta-analysis of randomised controlled trials. *Ann Rheum Dis* 2008; 67: 1716–1723.

2. Moseley B et al. A controlled trial of arthroscopic surgery for osteoarthritis of the knee. *New Eng J Med* 2002; 347: 81–88.

3. Moerman DE, Jonas WB. Deconstructing the placebo effect and finding the meaning response. *Ann Intern Med* 2002; 136: 471–476.

4. Moerman D. *Meaning Medicine and the Placebo Effect.* Cambridge: Cambridge University Press, 2002.

5. Kaptchuk TJ. Placebo studies and ritual theory: A comparative analysis of Navajo, acupuncture and biomedical healing. *Phil Trans R Soc B* 2011; 366: 1849–1858.

6. Dieppe P, Goldingay S, Greville-Harris M. The power and value of placebo and nocebo in painful osteoarthritis. *Osteoarthr Cartil.* 2016; 24: 1850–1857.

7. Porges S. The polyvagal theory: New insights into adaptive reactions of the autonomic nervous system. *Cleve Clin J Med* 2009; 76 Suppl 2: s86–90.

8. Greville-Harris M. '*Does feeling understood matter? The effects of validating and invalidating interactions*'. PhD thesis, Exeter University. 2013.

9. Greville-Harrris M, Dieppe P. Bad is more powerful than good: The nocebo response in medical consultations. *Am J Med* 2015; 128: 126–9.

10. Telecebo DL. Beyond placebo to an expanded concept of healing. Explore: The Journal of Science and Healing 2016; 12: 1–12.

11. Jain S. *Healing Ourselves: Biofield Science and the Future of Health.* Boulder: Sounds True, 2021.

12. Rogers C. *Client-Centered Therapy* (3 ed.). Boston: Houghton-Mifflin, 1956.

13. Paterson C, Dieppe P. Characteristic and incidental (placebo) effects in complex interventions such as acupuncture. *BMJ* 2005; 330: 1202–1205.

14. Rhatz E, Dieppe P. Placebos, CAM and healing: P+X+Y. *Int J Complementary Alt Med* 2016; 4: 114–116.

4

Learning about Energy Healing

I worked full-time at the Medical School in the University of Exeter for 11 years. During that time, I pursued several different research projects on healing, many of which are discussed in the next few chapters of this book. They do not follow any logical order or progression, as several different strands of my research were going on at the same time. So, whereas the first three chapters of this book have followed a chronological path, the next few do not.

Research of this sort is a "messy" business. It does not go in straight lines but involves the pursuit of many different approaches at once. It is driven by curiosity. I was very curious about the nature of healing. I wanted to understand what people who called themselves healers did, and what they achieved. And I wanted to know "why and how?" But being able to do such research depends on funding (health research is expensive) and opportunity. I was fortunate enough to obtain a fellowship from the new UK National Institute for Health Research, which came with some funding to pursue research work of my choosing. In addition, around 2002, I was appointed as a scholar of the Institute for Integrative Health in Baltimore, USA (now the Nova Institute for Health of People, Places, and Planet). This wonderful Institute supported some of my healing research financially, and has been a source of much-needed intellectual help and validation. Many other members of the Institute are interested in healing, and we meet regularly.

In addition, my research was opportunistic. My curiosity led to my talking about healing with a variety of people in many different settings. For example, I vividly remember one important conversation with a stranger on a train – who knows what might have transpired had she not needed to get off the train long before I did! If my gut (intuition) told

DOI: 10.4324/9781003461814-6

me that the person or the idea was worth following, I would go for it. I was weaving a web of different ideas and concepts that I could look into (research).

HOW CAN ONE RESEARCH A SUBJECT LIKE "HEALING"?

I was trained in medical scientific research. This involves the collection of reproducible evidence – findings that can be duplicated by others. Although driven by curiosity, it often starts with the formulation of a hypothesis, a supposition or premise about what might be the case, followed by the development of some experiments to see if the hypothesis is upheld by observation. There are three main approaches to such work:

1. Secondary research: searching for data from all relevant literature, and analyzing and perhaps combining such data. Then you know what is already known about your subject/hypothesis.
2. Primary quantitative research: measuring things, with or without an intervention, to see if reproducible measures and changes can be found to explain something. This is the most common form of medical research, and includes approaches such as randomized controlled trials (RCTs) briefly discussed in the previous chapter.
3. Primary qualitative research: this includes things like observing what is happening in different situations, hearing what people have to say about something and capturing behaviors and reactions of people in different situations. Such research methods have come from anthropology and the social sciences rather than disciplines such as chemistry or physics, which underpin biomedical science. Qualitative research is often about the generation of ideas and hypotheses rather than trying to prove something.

You can also mix things up, doing what's called "mixed-methods research", for example, conducting qualitative interviews with people who are involved in an RCT.

Whatever type of research you are undertaking, it is critical to follow good practice guidelines and to make sure that your work is ethical and acceptable to all. Fortunately, my previous job, as director of a large government research institute, had resulted in my being well-trained in those things. In addition, I had experience of many of the large number of different methods involved in all three types of research project. So, I thought I could do the work "properly".

The obvious place to start was to look at the literature. So, with the help of some research assistants, I started out on secondary research on healing. But that proved to be incredibly difficult. Healing is not a well-defined, encapsulated concept, but involves a large number of different experiences, practices and ideas derived from a bewilderingly large spectrum of cultures and disciplines. We found some helpful work published in the nursing literature and a number of other valuable contributions within the conventional sort of health and scientific journals I was familiar with, as well as many books on the subject. However, it was clearly going to be impossible to do any sort of systematic review of the existing literature – the usual starting point for medical research. Having said that, the attempt to get a grip on some of what had been written previously was an important and valuable step for me.

The next step I took was to try to contact healing organizations and individuals to see if I could talk with them to get more of a sense of what sort of field I was playing in.

Early on, I made contact with two important UK-based organizations that helped open the door to healers and healing practices for me. One was the "Doctor–Healer Network" (DHN), the other the "Confederation of Healing Organizations" (CHO). Each has a website. My contact with each of these groups has proved invaluable to my work.

The "Doctor–Healer Network"

I first joined the DHN in the 2000s, when they held irregular face-to-face meetings in London. It was a bit of a slog to travel from Exeter to London for a couple of hours on a Sunday afternoon, but I did so on several occasions and found it very worthwhile.

I met several healers as well as a few other doctors who were interested in healing, and I was able to listen to healers talking about their work and see them demonstrating how they went about trying to help another person heal.

Two things struck me particularly forcefully:

1) Everyone involved was very humble, kind and helpful
2) I, as a doctor wanting to learn more about healing and do research, was accepted warmly by the group, and I was not alone.

I remember my very first meeting particularly well. I was welcomed by the small group of about 15 people in the room. We were waiting for the speaker to arrive, but he or she never turned up so, after a while, the chairman suggested we sit in a circle together and discuss our views on healing. Everyone was invited to introduce themselves and say what they did. Most were self-professed healers, without a biomedical training, and talked about a variety of practices and concepts that I knew next to nothing about, including energy healing, channeling, crystal healing and shamanism. There were a couple of other doctors there who, like me, seemed keen to learn. When it came to my turn to introduce myself, I explained that I was an academic doctor keen to start a research program on healing. The chairman seized on this, saying how important he thought it was that people like myself did some serious research on the subject.

He then suggested that I might want to ask the healers in the group some questions to help me with my research. I was, of course, totally unprepared for such a request, but took my time and tried to collect my thoughts. "Well", I said after a while, "I wonder if those of you who are healers could tell me about some of the key factors in your work that you think facilitates the healing process?" They were not shy to respond. One of the ladies in the group launched into a long explanation of the power of crystals, another spoke of the importance of centering yourself and being in the right frame of mind. They were keen to explain how powerful their differing approaches were, and the discussion became somewhat diffuse. After a while, the chairman intervened and said "I am not sure that any of us have really answered Paul's question yet, so maybe I could have a go at it. Paul, you asked us what factors can facilitate a healing response; well, I think the answer is very simple – unconditional love for the other person". After a short pause, another healer chimed in: "Yes, I agree. You see, Paul, the key thing is to let go of your own ego, leave that outside the room, and then channel unconditional love for the other person, whoever they may be". Others agreed with this, one adding that you needed to be able to love yourself and be healed of your own problems before you could effectively channel the unconditional love that is the universe, to allow healing to occur in another.

I was very grateful, moved and humbled by these comments, noting them down on the train back to Exeter. I knew that I had to explore these ideas further.

The "Confederation of Healing Organizations" (CHO)

My important link up with the CHO came via a chance meeting with a member of their board. She, like the DHN people I had met, was excited by the idea of an established medical academic doctor investigating healing. She helped and encouraged me a lot. After a few years, I was asked to become a member of their Board of Trustees myself and was privileged to be able to serve this charitable organization for several years.

The CHO is an oversight organization that helps both individuals and other groups and organizations involved in healing. As their website states: "*The CHO is the leading charity advancing the practice of Healing: promoting its benefits as a recognized, complementary therapy by providing education, research and information to a wider audience of healing and health care practitioners and society as a whole*". It certainly helped me in those ways, as I attended some of their educational events, was able to access their information and, through them, meet with many healers.

So, I decided I needed to learn more about healing, particularly what was being called "energy healing", as this seemed to be the dominant healing intervention being used in the UK.

The first thing I did was to interview an energy healer whom I had been able to contact through the CHO.

Talking to an Energy Healer

My early insights into the world of energy healers came through this interview, done at a time when I was still very naïve about the subject. But, even now, I think it is one of the most informative conversations about the subject that I have ever had. I am going to quote it at length, as I believe it provides an excellent introduction to the nature and practice of energy healing. I shall call the lady concerned, "Fiona"; she is an experienced energy healer in the UK, who has provided healing in National Health Service hospitals in the past. She became a good friend and mentor to me on my own journey into the world of healing and healers.

This is an edited version of that interview, which I recorded:

Me: *What is healing?*

Fiona: In my own opinion, healing is about a type of energy that we are all a part of, that healers tap into and channel to others who are in need. It is something that does not cure those recipients, but it helps kick-start their own healing processes. So, the analogy I often use is that it is like the battery being topped up.

Me: *Do you have anything else to say about that energy?*

Fiona: It is something that people of faith believe in, that they describe as divine, something higher that is a source of that energy. And sometimes the way I see it is as different levels of energy or different levels of existence. Different healers believe in different entities, such as spirit guides, while others work more on an energy and science base.

Me: *And you?*

Fiona: A bit of both, a bit of everything, I think. It depends on who I am talking to at the time. For example, if I was in an NHS setting, it would not be about faith and the spiritual stuff, it would be much more about the energy and science basis.

Me: *Can anyone tap into this energy?*

Fiona: Yes, I believe so. I think the ability improves with experience. I think I am a better healer now than when I first started. You need to be able to open yourself up to giving without any conditions; it is about unconditional giving, it is unconditional love in the end. One of the hardest things that healers have to learn is to love themselves, because, if you cannot love yourself, how can you give to other people?

Me: *I'm trying to get my head around what unconditional love means in this context.*

Fiona: You only have to look at an animal to know what unconditional love is; you do not have to love them back. I think that is what healers are giving, they are giving of themselves. The majority of healers in this country are giving, not for money, but for love; they are not charging people. It is like the effect of the love given by a parent who sees their child hurt; the first thing they want to do is give that child a cuddle and comfort and, within seconds, the child feels better.

Me: *But you are not cuddling, so how are you giving loving comfort?*

Fiona: You are giving it energetically. You open your mind to that person. Each healer will tune in to their energies, their different vibrations and let the energy do the work.

Me: *So what is the difference between this and caring?*

Fiona: There is a large element of caring within healing, and it involves a lot of listening. For example, as you listen you feel connected to the person. And you might feel their pain, that often happens to me (laughs) and you need to protect yourself. I have lots of ways of protecting myself against negative energies coming from others. And you have to want to do it, to listen, to open yourself up. You can feel energies from people, and in rooms; for example, if you go into a room where people are having an argument, you can feel – "WOW, negative vibes!" You cannot explain these atmospheres but you can feel them, feel the energy, positive or negative.

Me: *So is it like intuition?*

Fiona: Definitely.

Me: *Can you run through what you actually do when healing?*

Fiona: If someone was to contact me about wanting healing, then there is already a connection that has been made; they have asked for healing, and that is the start of it. I get a sense of where they are, what is wrong. Before they arrive for an appointment, I will have cleansed the room to remove any negative energy and dressed in my healing color. Purple is my healing color, others have different colors. So, I am creating my space in which to do something with energy. Then as they come through the door it is very much about making them welcome, helping them relax, general chatting to calm down any nervousness. I will explain that we are all made of energy, even the tables and chairs, that sort of thing, all vibrating in different ways, at different rates. And I explain that healing is about tapping into that, and that the body will use the energy as it feels fit. Then, I sit and chat first, take details like date of birth, a full medical history, and reasons why they have come to me. If they are still tense, I will get them onto the therapy couch and I may ask them to visualize something relaxing. I will ask them if they are OK with touch, and, if yes, I usually tune in around the shoulders and the head, feeling, sensing energy. Basically, I am putting out a feeler to ask what sort of energy is right for that person's healing. All that sensing of their energy happens in a very short time. I will have already explained what they might feel, including heat, cold, tingling, or possibly nothing. I then have a kind of routine, a kind of basic routine I stick with. It is to do with the chakras, I am kind of sussing people out, so I tend to go down the arms, down the legs, via the minor chakras, around the wrists and that kind of thing, down the back, the hips, the knees, ankles. I very often find people need clearing, a sort of unblocking to allow energy to circulate; and if they are blocked like that, I will often ask them to join in with that idea, to visualize the energy becoming unblocked.

Me: *So how do you finish the session?*

Fiona: Whatever is easiest for them. If they are very stressed, I might give them a few visualizations to use; and then basically detuning to make sure we are both grounded. That is important, because it would be all too easy to be away with the fairies. It is about being sensible and responsible, perhaps give them a glass of water because I have been taught that this will help the energy go around.

Me: *Are you hypnotizing them?*

Fiona: No. Actually, I had never thought of that. But I don't believe I am hypnotizing because, although I am the one guiding the healing, it is coming from elsewhere. It is not about me. I have seen healers go through that, their ego starts to get in the way and then they cannot heal.

Me: *How important is the ritual?*

Fiona: I think it is very important to me. But that changes depending on who I am with. If it is someone who is much more spiritually aware, then they would get less of the ritual, but there is always the ritual of tuning in and tuning out.

Me: *Can you give examples of what sort of human predicaments respond best?*

Fiona: What I am helping is people's wellbeing, their state of mind. I am there to help people cope, not to cure a physical ailment. But it is really strange, the way it can all turn around. And that very often happens as a healer, you suddenly understand why you are there, and things change. There are still miracles that can happen. For example, a lady came to see me at a healing weekend recently, with a terrible back, she could hardly move, and she went away still hobbling but saying that it felt very much easier. At the end of the day, she came back to me, and I just looked at her and she came walking in with this huge beam on her face and she just said, "It has gone, I cannot believe it, within minutes of seeing you, it went and I have had no pain for the rest of the day". And it stayed away.

Me: *What about barriers and facilitators to change?*

Fiona: Sometimes, people do not want to get better and that is a barrier to healing. And the way they are living, their circumstances at home, for example, can interfere with it. But the very fact that someone has asked for healing can facilitate a good outcome.

Me: *Thank you so much*

So, What Is the "Energy" That Fiona Was Talking about?

Fiona's explanation for her healing was that of "energy" channeling (movement to and from and around the body) and balance. Such ideas are largely alien to science, because no such energy can (as yet) be measured or explained in materialistic terms. But the idea is as old as healing itself and shared by many different cultures and practitioners throughout the world. For example, in ancient Indian practice, the term "prana" is used for the natural energy in the body, which needs, according to their philosophy, to be in balance. Similarly, in Traditional Chinese Medicine, the "Chi" energy needs to be able to flow appropriately in the body, without blockages. Traditional Chinese medical practices, like acupuncture, are about balancing the energy flow, and much of Indian Ayurveda is about balancing energy in the body.

Today, in the West, we sometimes use the term "energy medicine", the subject of a recent edition of the journal *Explore* (1)

In his introduction to this special edition of the journal, Dean Radin notes that energy medicine is sometimes defined as "a branch of integrative medicine that studies the science of therapeutic applications of subtle energies ... to assess and treat energetic imbalances, bringing the body's systems back to homeostasis"; but he goes on to say that the problem with

TABLE 4.1

Some of the Terminologies and Techniques Used Within the Many Different Types of "Energy Healing"

• Reiki
• Johrei
• Spiritual healing
• Crystal healing
• Therapeutic touch
• External QiGong
• Biofield therapy

this is that these subtle energies cannot be measured, and are not what any modern physicist would regard as energy.

There are many different varieties of energy healing, as discussed by Levin (2) and shown in Table 4.1.

In the US, the term "biofield therapy" is often used as an umbrella term for all these different approaches. There are a lot of overlaps between the categories; for example, a Reiki healer may also use crystals. And there are also many commonalities, as discussed later. Other categories sometimes included under the generic term "energy healing" include acupuncture, homeopathy, shamanic healing, thought field therapy, emotional freedom therapy and others, as energy changes are thought to be associated with each of these therapeutic practices. There are also a variety of other idiosyncratic techniques championed by individuals, who tend to name them after themselves. In addition, many healers, like the ones "Fiona" quoted above, just call themselves "energy healers".

The common belief is that we can heal ourselves, or be healed with the help of others, through a rebalancing of energy in the body or a channeling of energy from outside. This is often linked to the theory of chakras (energy centers) in the body. Skeptics often deride these beliefs and practices as classic examples of "pseudoscience" but, as discussed later in this chapter, there is good scientific evidence that "energy healing" can have tangible effects on living systems. Furthermore, quantum mechanics and evidence for "non-locality" (consciousness existing outside the brain) provide a possible scientific basis for some of the ideas behind the ancient practices of energy balancing, as discussed toward the end of this book.

So, in answer to the question posed above ("What is the energy that Fiona was talking about?"), the answer is "I don't know". But that does not bother me.

ENERGY HEALING OF MY KNEE

Soon after meeting "Fiona", I had the opportunity to interview another energy healer in her own home. At the time, I had a lot of knee pain. Being a doctor, I had asked medical colleagues about it, been examined, and had X-rays taken. They said it was osteoarthritis of the knee joint and suggested that I should have a knee replacement done soon. I decided to put that off for a bit and see if the pain settled down on its own, as it can do.

So, I limped in to talk to my second energy healer, whom I shall call "Sharon".

She greeted me warmly when I arrived at her house. We started talking over a cup of tea together, without any recording going on; I asked her about herself and how she got into healing. It was a remarkable story. She had been happily married to a man in the services, who had retired at the age of 55. Soon after that, he developed cancer and was treated with chemotherapy, but the drugs made him feel worse, and they did not have much effect on the cancer. In desperation, they called on a local healer. Soon after entering the house, the healer looked at Sharon and said "You are a healer too, I see". That came as a shock to Sharon, but was, I now think, an example of one healer recognizing the sensitivity of another. Her healing had helped her husband's symptoms but not the disease, which killed him, so, in this case, as with many others, healing did not lead to curing (although I think it sometimes can).

After her husband's death, Sharon contacted a different healer for some help for herself, and this second healer said the same thing to her "You are a healer yourself, you know". So, after a while, she decided to find out more about healing, and went to some training courses in energy healing. She found out that, yes, she could do it, and then set up as a practicing healer in her own home, charging no money for her services.

We finished our tea, went into her sitting room where I set up the recorder, and I started the formal interview. She told me that, for her, healing was about accessing energy from the universe and channeling this to help people heal. She described using techniques such as foot massage and sound to help people relax, by "tapping into their vibrational energies".

Then she said to me, "But you need to experience this to understand it, Paul. Is there something that we can work on for you?" I told her about my painful knee and she said she was happy to work on it right now. I hesitated a bit, but then agreed, rolled up my trousers as instructed and sat back on her sofa as she put her hands on my right knee. She explained to me that she would ask the energy to flow and that no harm should come to either of us as a result of this.

Then, she closed her eyes, concentrated hard, and seemed to "disappear" from the room for a while; she was physically there, of course, with her hands on my knee, but the essence of Sharon seemed to be somewhere else. After a while, I felt warmth and a strange positive sensation (that I cannot describe) over the inside of my right knee (where the worst joint damage was). Sharon murmured that she could feel the energy flow as a tingling sensation in her hands and that good energy exchange was taking place. Then, she was quiet for a while, and I continued to feel an unusual sensation over the inside of my knee. My mind, however, was all over the place; (including feeling regret at leaving the recording machine on during this long silence). Eventually, Sharon opened her eyes and "returned" to the room. She took her hands off my knee, which immediately felt cool. She said she thought things would be better, but that the work was not finished, and she would like to do a bit more. I agreed. Again, she put her hands on my knee, closed her eyes and "disappeared". Again, I felt warmth and other strange sensations in my knee. Then she finished. She looked drained. She told me that my knee would be a lot better, but that it was not completely healed, that she could not do any more today but that I could come back another time if I would like to. I got up and walked around, without pain; my knee felt OK.

We completed the interview; I thanked Sharon and took my leave. As I drove away, I felt skeptical about the whole experience; how could that sort of treatment possibly do any good to my bad knee, which, as shown by X-rays, had severe structural damage? "I am a rheumatologist", I thought to myself "and I know that there is no treatment for the structural changes of osteoarthritis".

And indeed, over the next couple of days, my knee seemed to feel much the same. But gradually, over the next two weeks or so, my knee seemed to be troubling me less; pain was not much of an issue anymore. And for the next ten years, my knee caused me very few problems. I could not run, but I could walk and cycle well and had almost no pain. What did I make of that? Well, I think it contributed to the increasing cognitive dissonance I was experiencing: the conflict between my scientific understanding of what was, and was not, possible, and my experiences.

A few months before meeting Sharon, I had been visiting my doctor daughter and her doctor partner. I could hardly get up and down the stairs of their house because of my knee problem and they had both said to me, "Oh, for goodness' sake, go and get it replaced, will you?" I returned to stay overnight with them again a couple of months after Sharon's "healing". The stairs were no problem. They did not notice for a while, but then we all decided to walk to a nearby pub for a drink. As we marched along briskly, my daughter suddenly stopped, looked me up and down and said "You are walking fine now, did you go and get your knee replaced without telling us?" "No, I have had healing" I responded. She looked at me as if to say "Blimey, my father really has gone mad now" (she has a "look"). But then she stopped herself and said "You are serious, aren't you?" I told her a very brief version of the story as we walked on. "So, have you had another X-ray to see if the knee is structurally better?", she asked. "No, I am not interested in the X-ray, only the symptoms" I said. "But Dad, if you had it re-X-rayed and the X-ray showed the knee had returned to normal then – then all us doctors are in trouble aren't we?" By which, she meant that it would really challenge the biomedical, materialistic paradigm that all of us conventional doctors believe to be the only truth. And I think she nailed one of our key problems; we have no way of accommodating this sort of healing within our current scientific approach to medicine. Why did I not have another X-ray to see if it had improved? I think there were two reasons: first, I know that what you see depends critically on positioning and other variables that are difficult to reproduce from one X-ray to another. But secondly, I think I was frightened about the result – either way! I was finding all this "healing stuff" very confusing.

So, what happened? There are, I think, at least three possible explanations for my knee being better now for some ten years:

1) Energy healing helped improve my knee
2) This was a "placebo response" (Chapter 3)
3) It was the natural history of the disease – it went into a spontaneous remission

I really don't know which of these explanations is likely to have played the greatest part in my knee's improvement. Maybe it was a combination of all three?

LEARNING HOW TO DO ENERGY HEALING

These and other experiences with healers piqued my interest sufficiently to make me want to learn more. So, the next major event on my journey into the world of energy healing came when I decided to go on a training course over two weekends.

I was somewhat nervous when I arrived at the venue for the first weekend; it was an ordinary-looking 1930s house in a pleasant small town in "Middle England". There were eight of us in the group. We were a motley crew of very different people from a variety of backgrounds: a psychiatrist, a pharmacist, an accountant, an out-of-work laborer, a retired businessman, a housewife and counselor, a Reiki practitioner and myself.

There was a mixture of theory and practice on the course, which ran for two full days one weekend, and one-and-a-half days on another weekend a few weeks later. It was, for me, a massive experience that changed me and the whole way I think about things. For that reason, I am going to recount what happened in some detail.

Some Theory

We started with a few basics. "Julie", the course leader, explained that energy healing was about allowing energy from outside us to flow through us and into others for their benefit. It could also help restore the balance of the existing energies within another person.

She explained that, before you could help others, you had to heal yourself. We also needed to understand "karma": the spiritual principle of cause and effect, where the intent and actions of an individual influence (cause) events in the future of that individual (effect). Good intent and good deeds contribute to *good karma* and future happiness, whereas bad intent and bad deeds contribute to *bad karma* and future suffering.

Julie told us something about various organizations in the healing "business" in the UK and offered a primer on some of the terminologies they use. She told us that spiritualist healers were those who generally worked in churches and religious organizations. They had faith in God as the source of energy and healing and channeled this to others. This was usually accomplished with "hands-on" contact with another, and generally without any verbal communication with the "healee". In contrast, energy healers like herself worked with chakras and auras in people as indicators of their internal energy and energy flow, and they channeled energy from an external source as well. Furthermore, energy healers generally communicated verbally with their clients to help the flow of positive external energy and facilitated the rebalancing of energy, rather than just relying on God to do her thing. She mentioned Reiki healers as well, and said they did much the same sort of work, but used a ritualistic approach developed in Japan. She was a bit dismissive of them, as most were not properly trained, she said.

The concept of an external source of energy was central to all healing practices, Julie explained. It is all about channeling loving energy. This was something that we, as a group, discussed at some length with her. Julie used lots of words to try to explain it, including:

- The source
- God/godhead
- Faith
- Love
- Power
- Positive intention

You can use whatever words you like, she told us, according to your beliefs and experience, but it was really about sensing this energy, which we would be doing later. Healing, she continued, was a very individual experience difficult to put into words, although helped by metaphors. Perhaps the concept of chakras and auras, that we would be working with, was one type of helpful metaphor.

As a group, we tried to boil it down to a phrase, and the one to emerge was:

"A positive, loving flow of clear intent".

The First Exercise – Centering and Detecting Auras

Julie had explained that the energy within us is detectable away from the skin as "auras" which you can see or feel. Our first exercise together was to see if we could sense the aura of another person.

We needed to learn how to "center" ourselves, and then to feel the aura around the head of another. "*Get comfortable, feel your feet in contact with the ground, feel the roots spreading out from the soles of your feet into the ground, anchoring you to the earth and putting you in proper contact with the earth. Breathe deeply and calmly, still the mind, tune in to the person you are with. Then, standing behind the other person, with feet wide apart and connected to the earth, bring your hands slowly in towards the head, starting well away and feel the point of resistance that you come to*".

I did this, and, as I brought my hands in toward the head of "Ken", I did come to a point where my hands tingled, and I felt resistance. Ken said he felt me encroaching on his person at that time. Was that real or just the result of the suggestion of Julie telling me what to expect, I wondered?

The Second Exercise: Dowsing for Chakras

We moved on to chakras. Julie explained a bit about how she uses them in her practice. It was the common seven chakras system, derived from Hindu beliefs. She explained that the chakras represent aspects of the subtle body or the energetic body, which is sensed as channels of energy within the physical body. As such, the chakras represent the "nodes" of this energy channeling system within our bodies.

These seven paths of energy flow, from the lowest root chakra to the crown chakra at the top of the head, each manifests with a different color and a specific emotional meaning within our bodies. We went through them using a classical picture of the differently colored chakra system (Figure 4.1).

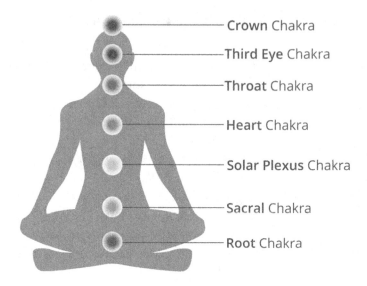

Crown Chakra

Third Eye Chakra

Throat Chakra

Heart Chakra

Solar Plexus Chakra

Sacral Chakra

Root Chakra

FIGURE 4.1
The seven classical chakras. Chakras are thought by many people to be the centers of circulating energy within the body, although others see them as metaphors.

And now we were to dowse (search for) these chakras using crystals on strings, which we attempted to do in pairs. One person lay on a couch, face up, while the other passed the crystal over them, along the line of the spine, from the top of the head to the groin. When I did this with "Bill", it swung mostly when over the point of his sixth chakra (the "third eye"). I am not sure what happened when Bill was "dowsing" me.

Picking Tarot Cards

Although shaken, I was still not convinced by the auras or the crystal swinging exercises, my skeptical scientific brain still held on to its preconceptions that this was impossible. And I certainly was not feeling as if picking Tarot cards, our next exercise, would mean anything to me. I wondered why we were being invited to do it, although Julie told us it was just another way of discovering things about ourselves, an essential step in becoming able to help others to heal.

So, she laid the Tarot cards, face down on a flat table and encouraged us to concentrate, get into it, look at them all, and see if there was one that seemed to be choosing us. I made an effort but was not convinced that there was a particular card I should choose (or that wanted to choose me); but eventually, like everyone else, I chose one. We then went around the group, showing the card that had "chosen us". There was a wide variety of them, and Julie commented on each. Mine was "Mountain Lion". I had no idea what that meant but, as I showed it to the group, there was a gasp; "Golly", said Julie, "that is one of the most powerful cards in the pack. That is a symbol of great power, Paul".

I remained unimpressed. But we repeated this exercise on the second day and, to my own amazement, I again picked "Mountain Lion". The "coincidence" discombobulated me (and some of the others)!

One-to-One Healing Exercise

One of our next exercises was one-to-one healing.

Again, we were paired up, the object being to channel healing energy to the person we were with. I was paired with "Bill". Julie went through what we should do, demonstrating and talking us through it: "*Center yourself with a simple meditation, as before, then call in the healing energy from above, through your own crown chakra, and prepare for it to flow out to the other person through the palms of your hands – this is pure love and nurturing energy, that you give to the other with unconditional love. When you are ready, place your hands on the subject's shoulders and say you are starting the healing. Then take your hands off them and try to sense them, feel with them and connect. Bring your hands towards them and feel the resistance of their aura, and then let the energy flow through the palms of your hands to the other person. You will feel the flow and know where your hands need to be for it to be most effective. Let it happen. You will know when it is over, and you can then take your hands away. Tell the other person you are finishing, sever the connection, then wipe your hands to cleanse them*".

We agreed that I was to try to be the healer first and Bill the "healee". Bill lay on the couch and I went behind him to prepare myself. As I did this, I felt a genuine and powerful sense of compassion for Bill, without really trying. And I was "in the moment"; I brought my hands toward his head and felt the point at which his aura stopped me. I moved down to the heart chakra and felt an intense tingling in my hands and a strong connection with Bill. Energy really did seem to be flowing between us – from "above", through me and into Bill. I wanted to stay there, letting this go on, but the other pairs had stopped and Julie asked me to disconnect. I did so, and wiped my hands as instructed, but the tingling went on for a while.

Bill burst into tears, and said he felt a powerful, meaningful change within him.

And then I did the same exercise with Rob. This time, we were told to "balance the chakras". I passed my hand over his body and detected a low point around the heart chakra and a high aura over the base chakra. I was able to be fully in the moment, to feel compassion, love even, for Rob, and a desire to rebalance his energy. As I passed back up to his heart chakra, something really extraordinary happened – there was such an intense feeling of flow, of connection with everything, of love and beauty, that I was almost overwhelmed. But I managed to stay with it, and my hands were tingling a lot, as with Bill. A rush of energy seemed to be flowing through us. I stayed there and it went on. Then, I moved my hands further up and the feelings subsided, I gradually "came back", disconnected and cleansed myself. I looked round to see several others of the group looking at me in awe. They said they saw a great presence and strength around me. Afterwards, Rob seemed relatively unmoved, but I was wrung out and exhausted.

Curiously, when we reversed the exercise, and others tried to channel healing energy to me, I felt very little, and neither did they.

But I was shaken by my experiences.

Distant Healing

Many healers believe that healing can take place at a distance, even across continents, and they practice "distant healing" to achieve that, often working in groups (in the belief that if several people try to send healing energy to the "target" person, there is a better chance of a good outcome than if one alone does it). So, Julie did an exercise in distant healing with us. She got all of us to sit in a circle and asked us to meditate together to allow us, as a group, to gather energy and channel it to others.

We dutifully did as suggested, and she led us through a long meditation exercise: "*feet connected to the ground, roots growing into the earth, anchoring us to the land, slow breaths in and out, in with leaves growing out of the trees above us – out with the roots going further into the earth. We are in a castle that protects us and we are safe as we receive energy and channel it to others; there is a canopy over the castle which protects us, but there is a gate through which our healing nature – nurturing and blossoming – enters into our being. And then we direct that energy to a space outside, to someone we love and wish well for, as long as they allow this, and we send it with unconditional love*".

We did this as a group, for what seemed like a long time, and we sent our healing energy to those we chose, with unconditional love. It felt good to me, but, of course, I had no way of knowing if it had any effect on anyone else.

I was reminded of the concept of "telecebo" (placebo effects at a distance) put forward by Larry Dossey and discussed in Chapter 3. I wondered if perhaps healing intention could work at a distance, however ridiculous I would have found such an idea in my early years as a doctor.

Reinforcement

The second weekend of the course began with rich discussions within the group about how the first weekend's activities had impacted on each of us. I was clearly not the only one to have been profoundly affected. Then we repeated some of the exercises, and I once again "experienced" amazing things – feeling auras and sensing energy flow.

The idea that I was powerful, particularly "Yang" powerful (more of a giver of energy than a receiver), was again raised. At one point, Julie took me outside, into the car park by the side of the house, and confided in me that I had a huge presence and great power, and that I needed to be "careful". I was not clear as to what I needed to be careful about, but I am now more aware of my potential "power" when I am with others. For example, I am aware of the fact that I can be the focus of attention within a group, even if I am not doing or saying anything. But, like so many of my feelings and experiences, I do not understand this and find it rather frightening – partly because it seems to be out of my control.

Throughout my life, I have been told that I have charisma (whatever that is), and that I am a natural leader – ideas I have always found difficult to embrace or understand. But now I was wondering if this was, at least in part, about my aura and ability to channel energy.

These weekends really did change the way I think about things! Since my return from Iraq, I had become increasingly aware and accepting of the spiritual components of life and of my being. I had begun to investigate healing from an experiential and a research perspective. Still, up to this point, I had found concepts like auras and chakra balancing ridiculous. Not any more. During these workshops, I had felt and seen the auras, and I had sensed energy flow between chakras. I had to believe!

But, still clinging to my science, I wanted to go back to the "evidence" and see if there was any support for such phenomena. And there is, as explained later in this chapter.

Did I try it, and help people heal? Well, I did heal a horse once, but that just made me feel even more frightened of my "power" and I have not become a healer.

HEALING A HORSE

Soon after my course on how to heal, I met up with an animal healer whom I shall call "Jane". She specializes in healing horses. I voiced some skepticism, and her response was to say to me "Well, come down to my farm and see for yourself". So, I did; I went to Jane's farm one Saturday morning. After greeting me and giving me a cup of coffee, she suggested we walk down to the stables. There, I saw three large horses, stomping around in their separate spaces. I have never liked horses much, I have never ridden them, never been with them. They frighten me a bit, as they are big, powerful animals that seem to behave in unpredictable ways.

"I am just going to give them some food" said Jane, "then we can begin". I watched as she fed some hay into the stables, talking to the horses as she went about her work.

"OK, Paul, I want you to work with this one here" she said, pointing to one of the meanest-looking horses. "Me? I thought you were going to show me how you did it". "Paul, healing is an experiential thing, you have to experience it. Working with an animal is just the same as working with people. You have been on the course with Julie, just use the skills you learnt there. Center yourself, then connect with the horse and we will see what happens".

I took a few deep breaths, and then embarked on the task. I concentrated hard, carefully centering myself, connecting with the earth beneath my feet and opening myself up, as Julie had taught me. When I felt ready, I created a "sphere" to include myself and the horse, as it stomped around in its stable. And an amazing thing happened – I did indeed connect with the horse in a very real sense; the horse and I were as one – we were the same being. It stopped moving about, its ears went down, it looked very still and relaxed, and, in some very strange way, it *was* me. I maintained the connection and, after a while, the horse started to falter on its feet. "Stop, disconnect" shouted a voice from somewhere. I disconnected. The horse "came to" and started moving around again, and its ears stood up.

I felt drained, and I had a severe stomachache. I had no idea how much time had passed.

"Sorry to stop you", said Jane, "but I was worried that the horse was going to fall over; it was so relaxed; did you see how its ears went down?"

"Yes, but what happened, you must have done that?" I said, not quite able or wanting to believe what had happened. "No Paul, that was all you, I kept right out of it. How do you feel?" "I feel exhausted, and I have a terrible stomachache". "Ah, yes, good, you see I chose not to tell you this before you started, but the health problem which that horse has is with its stomach and digestion, that's what you were healing, and you have taken some of the problems onto yourself".

She encouraged me to connect briefly with another horse, just to prove to myself that I really could do it, and I could. Amazing! "It's all about the energy fields", said Jane, "and, like Julie, I think you are a powerful healer".

We wandered back to the house and sat down. I gradually started to feel better; the stomach ache subsided. I had had enough, and I think Jane sensed that, and I thanked her profusely and took my leave. When I got home, I wrote notes about what had happened, which are the basis of this story

This was another profound experience, cementing my belief in energy transfer, connection, and healing. But it also frightened me. I had felt my own power and a huge flow of energy between me and a horse. I was (and am) concerned about what might happen if I tried to use this power without supervision.

EVIDENCE FOR THE EFFECTS OF ENERGY HEALING

Skeptics and materialistic scientists reject the data I have presented so far as "anecdotal", and ask for "hard evidence" of the effects of healing. What does that mean? In the world of medical science, there is an "evidence pyramid", shown diagrammatically in Figure 4.2. This illustrates the different types and levels of evidence, from individual case reports toward the bottom (i.e., considered the least reliable form of evidence) to clinical trials, then systematic reviews and meta-analyses (that assess results from all individual trials for a given condition or intervention and pool the data). The latter lie at the top of the pyramid and are considered to represent the "best" evidence (3).

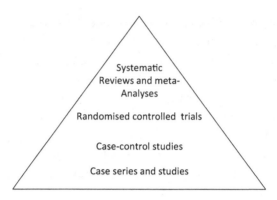

FIGURE 4.2
A picture of the "evidence pyramid" used in medical science (3).

"Hard Evidence" for the Value of Energy Healing

The evidence discussed so far is at the bottom of the pyramid, and thought by the biomedical community to be insufficient to answer the question "Does healing work?"

Both doctors and the general public often ask that question. They also ask it of any other form of complementary and alternative medicine (CAM). "Does it work?" we all ask. If you pause to think about this for a moment, it is rather an extraordinary question. It is totally binary: "Does it work – yes or no?" It takes no account of the fact that most things work for some people and not others, and that the response of any individual will depend on the context in which the intervention takes place. The context includes critical factors such as the people involved, the reasons for the treatment being used, the environment in which it is administered and so on. For most interventions, the answer is that it might work for some people under some circumstances.

However, let's go with the binary question for now – "Does energy healing work?" To answer that, clinicians call for randomized controlled clinical trials, a methodology that is essential to test whether things like drugs or vaccines *can* "work" but is less likely to be appropriate for interventions that involve an interaction between patient and therapist. As mentioned in Chapter 3, Charlotte Paterson and I showed that clinical trials will tend to underestimate the effectiveness of therapies like energy healing (4).

But a lot of trials have been undertaken, and they generally show a positive effect. The accepted way of trying to find out "the answer" to the binary question of "Does it work?" is to review all the good-quality trials and combine the evidence from all of them; this is a sophisticated statistical technique called meta-analysis. In 2015, Chris Roe and colleagues, from the University of Northampton, published a high-quality systematic review and meta-analysis of healing intention studies (i.e., studies in which intention was the only intervention). It showed that positive healing intention resulted in relatively small, but highly statistically significant benefits (5).

Roe and his team did a comprehensive search of English language literature for trials of healing intention and found many which they considered to be of a high enough quality to be included in their meta-analysis. They included 57 studies in which the target of the good intention was a human being, and 49 in which the target was an animal, a plant or an *in vitro* preparation. Interestingly, when the "target" of the healing intention was a plant or cells in laboratories, rather than humans, they found evidence of effectiveness as good as, if not better than, that for human studies. That means these findings cannot be dismissed as "just a placebo effect". As discussed in Chapter 3, placebos are thought to depend on properties of a sentient being, such as expectation. So, if a cell in a laboratory can respond to healing intention, we cannot call that a placebo effect.

A more comprehensive coverage of the scientific evidence to support the efficacy of healing can be found in a recent book by Shamani Jain (6).

What About Distant Healing?

As I explained earlier, healers believe that people can be helped by the channeling of healing energy at a distance, without the healer being anywhere near their client. Is there any evidence that such an extraordinary claim is true? Well, yes, there is also good scientific evidence that distant healing can be effective as well. The evidence here is harder to appraise in many ways. An introduction to the problems and the evidence is available in a paper by Radin and colleagues (7).

In addition, there have been several fascinating studies using brain imaging techniques, to see if one person's intention can influence the activity of another person's brain at a distance. And it seems that they can. One of the first examples of such a study was an experiment carried out by Jeanne Achterberg and colleagues, published in 2005 (8). They asked healers to identify a client whom they thought they could make a good connection with, and the recipients were then placed in an MRI scanner, isolated from all contact with the healer, who was many miles away, and the healer sent positive intention to them at random 2-minute intervals; significant effects on the scans were detected during the positive intention intervals compared to those in which no intention was being sent. Since then, numerous other studies have demonstrated similar effects, using a variety of different scanning techniques.

Returning to healing and placebo effects, as already mentioned, such findings led Larry Dossey to come up with the idea of the "telecebo" – placebo at a distance (9). The basic idea is that, because we are all connected through consciousness, thought by many to be the very essence of the Universe, our intentions can use that medium to affect others.

So, in conclusion, our conventional materialistic, reductionist scientific techniques have shown that energy healing is real and effective. But it is still not accepted by the medical profession, which continues to dismiss it as "quackery", "woo-woo nonsense" or "pseudoscience" because we cannot understand how it can possibly work. I can certainly understand that position. My scientific understanding of the world cannot account for many of the experiences described in this chapter. But I experienced them. My anxiety about it all remained, because of the continuing cognitive dissonance between experience and science.

But my curiosity remained intense. And, as explained next, I was talking to and learning from a lot of different healers.

REFERENCES

1. Radin D. Explore: The Journal of Science and Healing, 2021; 17 (I): 9–10 (Special Issue on Energy Medicine).
2. Levin J. Energy healers: Who they are and what they do. *Explore* 2011; 7: 13–26.
3. Murad MH, Asi N, Alsawas M, Alahdab F. New evidence pyramid. *Evid Based Med* 2016; 21(4): 125–127.
4. Paterson C, Dieppe P. Characteristic and incidental (placebo) effects in complex interventions such as acupuncture. *BMJ* 2005; 330: 1202–1205.
5. Roe C, Sonnex C, Roxburgh EC. Two meta-analyses of nonlocal healing studies. *Explore* 2015; 11: 11–23.
6. Jain S. *Healing Ourselves: Biofield Science and the Future of Health.* Sounds True, Boulder Colorado 2021.

7. Radin D, Schiltz M, Baur C. Distant healing intention therapies: An overview of the scientific evidence. www.gahmj.com/doi/full/10.7453/gahmj.2015.012.suppl

8. Achterberg J, Cooke T, Richards T et al. Evidence for correlations between distant intentionality and brain function in recipients a functional magnetic resonance imaging analysis. *J Altern Complementary Med* 2005; 11: 965–971.

9. Dossey L. Telecebo: beyond placebo to an expanded concept of healing. *Explore* 2016; 12: 1–12.

5

Some Other Healing Experiences

In the previous chapter, I described some of my experiences with "energy healing". This is one of the most dominant genres in use in the UK, along with the related practices of Reiki and spiritual healing. But there are many other types of interventions used by self-identifying healers to help their fellow humans (and other animals).

I have been privileged to talk to and witness the work of therapists who practice many different types of healing intervention and, in many cases, they have tried their approach out on me. I have also had the opportunity to witness traditional Chinese doctors working in China, and I have been treated in an Ayurvedic medicine center in India. Each of these ancient healing traditions believes that energy is an important component of health ("chi"" and "prana", respectively). However, I did not really get to understand either of them, perhaps because they are embedded in cultures quite different to mine.

In my own culture, in the UK, I have had direct experience with many other types of healing practice, as shown in alphabetical order in Table 5.1.

There are many, many more practices with which I remain completely unfamiliar.

Whether all of these can and should be classified as healing interventions, rather than, say, "mind–body treatments", is debatable, although, in each of the cases listed in the following table, practitioners whom I have talked to have claimed that their work has healing properties. Several may be variations on the same theme, perhaps different ways of channeling "energy". Furthermore, in my encounters with these interventions, I have been struck by the sincerity of all of the practitioners. Without exception, they cared for their clients and they were compassionate. Maybe healing intention is part of

DOI: 10.4324/9781003461814-7

TABLE 5.1

A List of Healing Interventions That I Have Experienced

- Acupuncture
- Angelic healing
- Aromatherapy
- Bone setting
- Crystal healing
- Emotional freedom therapy (EFT)
- Energy healing
- Eye movement desensitization and reprocessing (EMDR)
- Feldenkrais
- Forest bathing
- Gong baths
- Herbal therapy
- Homeopathy
- Hypnotherapy
- Kinesiology
- Mindfulness and meditation
- Pilates
- Pyramidology
- Reiki
- Shamanism
- Tai Chi
- Visualization
- Yoga

their "secret" – just as I was told at my first meeting with the Doctor–Healer Network?

As with Traditional Chinese Medicine and Ayurveda, some of my UK-based healing experiences have left me puzzled. But three experiences have had a particularly strong impact on me and my nascent understanding of healing, as described below.

SHAMANIC HEALING

Shamanic healing is old, widely practiced and takes many different forms, depending on culture, time, context and country. A shared central belief is that contact with the spirit world can facilitate healing.

The lady I have worked with (whom I will call "Anna") lives in England and has a practice based in nature. She uses aspects of shamanic healing, as well as Celtic "New Age" healing approaches. Her practice had developed from her own unique experiences and understanding of the world.

There is something about "coincidences" in this world; "synchronicity" is what Jung called it. I first met Anna at a meeting about two years before the events described here. We were both helping to facilitate a three-day residential workshop, and we had got on fairly well. We had taken each other's email address when we left the workshop, promising to be in touch, but had not been in contact for some 18 months thereafter.

Then I got an email from Anna. "We need to meet and talk" it said. "OK, when and where?" I responded, and she replied that she was based in a town some 80 miles away from where I was living. But – "coincidence" – I was going to that very place in two days' time for another meeting. So, I told Anna about this, and she said "OK, I will come to your meeting place at the time at which you are supposed to finish, and then we can meet and talk".

Experiencing the Work of a Shaman

When we met, she wanted to know a lot about me. She said that she had been "directed" to contact me and to give me the opportunity to go on a shamanic nature and spirit healing journey with her. She now spends her time working with people in this way, she said, and the spirits had told her that I should be one of her clients.

I agreed, so we set up a time a couple of months in the future, which was convenient for each of us. She told me to arrive at her house at 10.30 in the morning, ready for a four- to five-hour session with her in the woods, and I was to bring warm clothes, a cushion and a rug, as well as a notebook and waterproof boots.

I arrived on time, and she led the way into woodland close to her house, and then up a hill to a clearing in which she had a fire pit. She asked me to look around while she tended to the fire, explaining that she had opened this sacred space for me on the previous day. She soon had the fire going. There were four stones around it, and she sat on one, explaining that it was the "north" stone. She invited me to put my cushion on the stone to her left, the "east" stone, and sit there. We did a short centering meditation, after which she asked me a number of questions about various aspects of my life and preferences (which season of the year I preferred, which element (fire, water, wind, earth), which senses, those sorts of things). "Speak to the fire", she said as I answered. I did, and I found it easy to be open and honest when speaking to the fire, rather than to another person. That fire in the woods was magical. It was a blustery, showery day, and gusts of wind blew the flames here and there, and the smell of the smoke mingled with that of the wet woods around us; it was wonderful and I sat talking to the fire somehow mesmerized by the flames.

We broke for a rest, and she instructed me to go in whatever direction the woods drew me, to find a place that was important to me and spend time on my own there. I immediately set off in the direction of "west" (I don't know why) and found a strange depression in the ground, which was definitely "my place" – it seemed to speak to me in some way. I was there for a while, feeling very relaxed and tranquil; just "being".

When I returned, Anna seemed to be in a trance-like state at the fireside, but she soon roused herself, and we got back to "work". "I use the Celtic medicine wheel in my work", she said, "with its different emphasis on things at different compass points. Where is the right place for you to sit?" I was still sitting in "east" but I "knew" at once that this was not right for me and I immediately got up and went to sit in "west". As I sat down there, I felt better than I had when sitting in "east" – "west" was the right place for me.

We talked some more ("speak to the fire"), and she asked me quite a lot about my childhood. "This is not therapy", she said, time and time again, perhaps aware of the fact that it seemed a lot like a psychotherapeutic session to my medical mind. But I was able to suppress the medical thinking.

Then we took another break, before getting to the "nub of the matter – what had I brought with me? – what did I need to ask the fire/nature/spirit about?" I explained that I felt somewhat adrift since retirement from academic medicine, and no longer knew what I was for. I have been a doctor, a father, a carer, a researcher and a teacher, but now I was none of those things.

Arriving at a Deeper Level of Understanding

"Speak to the fire, see what it tells you". So I did, watching the flames flickering and inhaling the smell of wood smoke; I let the fire find me the answers, and it did. As I stared at the flames, surrounded by woodland, with the sound of the wind in the trees, and birdsong, I had one of those "moments" of intuitive understanding of the answer to the question:

- Stop doing, start being
- Spend time in nature and find a special place
- Do not try to find a new chapter for your life, it will find you

This was a very significant experience for me, being guided in a sensitive way to spend several hours in the natural world without being distracted by everyday worries, thoughts and concerns. I was just "there" in beautiful woodland. That in itself proved to be a healing experience (akin to forest bathing) (1)*. Afterwards, I felt tired, but relaxed and refreshed, and the fire had "spoken" to me. And I have heeded its words.

Forest bathing. This practice is derived from the Japanese "Shinrin-yoku" and involves mindful immersion in nature, particularly forests, and feeling at one with trees.

Perhaps the new chapter that the fire spoke of has now found me. Perhaps it is writing stories like this about healing and publishing a book.

That session in the woods with Anna took place early in 2020, just before the COVID-19 pandemic hit us. One of the things the woods had told me that day was to find a special place in nature. During lockdown, we were allowed out for short walks. My wife and I had only recently moved to our current house in the middle of Bristol, a sizeable town in Southwest England, and did not know the area well. But we started walking, and we found a small woodland area with a stream running through it, just a five-minute walk away from the house. This has become my "special place" to commune with nature. It works. But what is *it*?

Conclusions about Shamans and Healing

I have spoken to other healers who use shamanistic practices. For most, the emphasis is on the spirit world, the natural world, the interconnectivity of everything and the need to open oneself up to the "other" and "hear" its guidance. Again, I am more struck by the similarities to energy healing, energy medicine and the like than the differences. One of the key things that seemed to me to be common to so many different healing practices was the theme of "connectivity" and, in particular, connection to the spiritual world.

If you would like to read more about shamanism, I would recommend the beautifully illustrated book by my colleague and friend, Christa Mackinnon (2).

"BONE SETTERS"

The concept of a "bone setter" is an old one, particularly well known in some African countries, in India and in Ireland, but little known in a lot of other cultures (3). Bone setters are people with an unusual "gift" that seems to enable them to sort out mechanical problems in the musculoskeletal system, and sometimes other disorders, just by putting their hands on people. They are often men, whereas many other ancient forms of healing practice seem to be dominated by female practitioners (such as "wise women"). Bone setters need to be distinguished from people who are good at manipulation of the body, such as chiropractors; bone setting, in the way I am using the term, is a quite different issue.

I have met with two different men who, I think, are genuine "bone setters" and been "treated" by one of them.

The Man Who Found He Was a "Bone Setter" Late in Life

I was told about this person by a colleague, and he very kindly agreed to talk to me when I contacted him. We met in London. He is well known in a different sphere of life, so I shall be particularly careful to preserve his anonymity.

He told me that he had no idea about his ability until a female relative of his developed a bad neck. As a gesture of kindness, he put his hands on her neck and suddenly "sensed" what was wrong through his hands and was able to let the bones re-align themselves into the correct position. He did not manipulate the neck in any way, he emphasized, just had his hands there while the body sorted itself out. His relative's neck pain went away. After that, he found he could sense what was wrong with the musculoskeletal system of other people, particularly spinal problems, just by putting his hands on that person, and sort of "see" in his mind what was abnormal with the alignment of bones and muscles, and, when his hands were on the other person, things often sorted themselves out.

He had no satisfactory explanation for this ability, which seemed to have surprised him as much as anyone else, but he was comfortable with it.

"Things Moved Around on Their Own"

I was contacted by a musculoskeletal therapist who had read some of my work on healing in the medical literature, and who wanted to come and talk to me about what was happening to him in his practice. When we first met, he seemed very nervous and talked in a fast and furious, unrelenting way about what was going on. In essence, he had found that, when he was treating people, things seemed to "move around of their own accord", without him doing any manipulations or massage, and that he sort of "knew" through his hands what was wrong and needed putting right. He wanted me to help him research the phenomena he was experiencing so that he could understand them. I was enthralled and told him I thought he might be a bone setter. This "threw" him; he had never heard of the concept and was clearly upset by what he seemed to see as a dismissive comment from myself. However, we got back on track, and I agreed to go to his practice to observe him at work, and perhaps try a treatment myself.

First, I observed him at work with some of his patients. His clinical approach was exemplary; I rather wished I had some of our medical students with me to show them how to conduct themselves with patients. This young man was a master: polite, respectful, gentle, caring, softly spoken but clear and firm, and fully "with" each of his patients. After some history taking, he would ask them to disrobe down to underclothes and then stand so that he could examine their posture; he would then run his hands up and down the spine before inviting them to lie on the couch. Then, he would simply put his hands on their feet and seemingly go into some trance-like state before gently progressing to some mild manipulative or massage procedure. His patients' limbs did seem to move a little when his hands were on them, without him seeming to do the "work".

Afterwards, we talked some more, even though he was clearly exhausted. He thought there was some energy flow going on in the body, perhaps through facial planes (the fibrous tissue membranes that enclose our muscles). He wanted to be able to measure the changes that occurred when he was treating people. I cautiously asked if he might treat me for my bad knee at some future date, on a strictly fee-paying basis. He agreed but did not want me to pay. I insisted, and we fixed a time to meet again. I was again having problems with the knee which had seemingly responded to the ministrations of "Sharon", the energy healer, some ten years previously.

When we met again, he was very professional, starting by obtaining signed consent from me, and confirming demographic details. He then got on with a fairly conventional history-exercise, taking in the nature of my pain and other medical problems. Then came the examination. He looked at me standing in my underpants, from front and back, noting things as he did so, such as "good posture", but some of the comments seemed a bit beyond what I would think he could see – "tight quads" sticks in my mind as one of them – how could he know that just by looking at me?

Then, it was on the couch, on my back, covered with a blanket, and he was touching me, not examining me in a medical way, just touching. He sat at the end of the bed, at my feet, and put his hands lightly on the outside of my right ankle. I shut my eyes and relaxed as best I could (I felt quite at ease). He stayed there for a bit, concentrating on the right ankle. I did not feel anything much. Then, he moved his hands to my right knee, and then one hand under my back, around, and one hand on the knee. He stayed there for a while. I sensed he was going into his sort of "trance-like" state that I had observed when I saw him treating others, but I could not see him. I felt that my right leg was rotating exteriorly a bit, but it was subtle. He said that "things were changing" but I was not aware of much. Then he changed sides, went to my left side and did the same things, but for a shorter time. His hands felt quite different on the left than they had on the right. They felt cold on my left, in comparison with warm on my right. I was now thinking that his hands on the right side had felt warm, and maybe as if energy was flowing, but that was not at all the sensation on the left – just "nothing" on that side. Again, I thought maybe he was "trancing", I heard some deep sighs from him. I was quite relaxed.

I don't know how long that went on for, but it must have been quite a while.

Then he said he was done; could I get up and put my clothes on while he made some notes on his computer? "I think it must be something to do with the right tibia", he said, "maybe an injury you might remember now or later or not at all". I remembered – "Yes, I had forgotten, but I did have a stress fracture of the right tibia when trying to run marathons years ago". "Yes, that was it", he said. "But how did you know, I did not mention it, I had forgotten about it", I ventured. "It is all about listening carefully", he replied, somewhat enigmatically. After a pause, the penny dropped for me. "Listening with your hands, you mean?" "Yes, that's what I do, listen through my hands". Amazing.

"I think it is all muscular, the treatment is to stretch those tight quads like this", he said, showing me. "Do it regularly for 30 seconds or so, but not for the first couple of days after today. And the back pain is muscular as well, and will do well with stretching exercises, but we will think about the back next time. Just do the knee stretches for now and see me again in a few weeks". It was all very clear and professional.

The next day, I was very aware of my right knee; it felt different, worse, and I was walking badly. A few days later, it was back to much as it was before.

I went to him again. He had invited me to join him for a coffee before he treated me, so that we could chat some more. He told me about a mystical experience he had had in childhood that had changed the way he thinks about the world. His grandmother had been a healer and had told him, when he was about 18, that he too was a healer. He had dismissed it at the time, and only recalled when talking to me about the fact that he might be a bone setter and that this was a form of healing.

This time, the treatment on my knee was more remarkable. As I lay on the couch, he sat at the end with his hands lightly touching my ankles, I felt my knee "expand", loosen and move around in a strange, indescribable way. Nothing was said as this was happening. For me, it was another of those inexplicable experiences that I have had within the world of healing and healers. Afterwards, he looked drained but happy – "Yes, there has been some real change in the knee for the better", he said. His practice is a longish drive away from where I live, and I had to take time to recover myself before I could drive back. I felt completely drained.

And my knee has been better since then, not completely normal, but better.

Bone Setting, Touch and "Hands-on-Healing"

One of the reasons for my interest in these phenomena is that I have always been fascinated by the importance of touch in human relationships. We shake hands or kiss each other as a form of greeting. Hugs are important to us. And we "treat" ourselves to massages. Touching each other seems to be a key part of our connecting with each other and communicating. "Healing touch" is a term widely used in the USA to describe the mode of healing that I am calling "energy healing" in this book (in spite of the fact that most of its practitioners do not touch their clients but rely on healing intention). But other healers, including Reiki advocates, do use touch a lot, alongside healing intention, and many people speak of "healing hands" to describe people who seem to have an ability to heal another.

Health care practitioners I have spoken to, including doctors and physiotherapists, have told me that they seem to be able to achieve a sense of connection with their patients through touch and that this ability can vary from day to day for them. In addition, there are many forms of therapy that involve hands-on treatments – massages, manipulations or simple stroking (called "effluage"). Touch with some pressure is also a part of many alternative therapies, such as myofascial release, reflexology (which involves the application of pressure to various parts of the feet) and acupressure.

All of this makes me wonder if bone setters have a peculiarly well-developed ability to connect with others through touch?

Conclusions about Bone Setters and Healing

The bone setters seemed to me to be working with something very similar to the "energy" that my interactions with energy healers had taught me about. Furthermore, both of those I met seemed to be very compassionate, sensitive men. I concluded that there were probably huge similarities among the varied forms of energy healing; perhaps these are in the manner by which the ability is manifested and the energy rebalancing is facilitated.

In addition, I was struck by the trance-like state that my therapist seemed to be in when he was treating me or one of his other clients – the deep concentration, slow breathing and apparent "distance" from the physical things around him. I have seen the same thing with many other healers when with their clients. They seem to enter another world, to be "in the zone"* perhaps, or maybe in some other type of altered state of consciousness.

*Being "in the zone" or a "flow state" are terms used to describe the altered state of consciousness that we are in when totally absorbed by what we are doing, in such a way that our awareness of everything else disappears. When in this state, people often feel highly energized and able to achieve things normally beyond them.

Another reason for the bone setter who treated me having had such a profound effect on my own journey was because he was (and probably still is) experiencing the same sort of cognitive dissonance about healing as I was. He was desperate to find a reason for what was happening, to be able to measure something physical to explain it. He had theories about fascia, about nerves and chemicals; he needed something within scientific materialism to make sense of his experience. Not understanding was a source of anxiety for both of us.

HOMEOPATHY

It may surprise some readers that I have included homeopathy as a healing intervention. The medical profession tends to designate it as a useless form of drug therapy.

I too used to dismiss homeopathy as nonsense, citing the usual criticism that it was impossible for medications to have any effect when they are diluted enormously, past the point where – in theory – there should be virtually no molecules remaining. But now, having spent time working with homeopathy practitioners, some of whom are also conventional doctors, I think of homeopathy as a healing practice. I will try to explain why, once I have told you something about my own experiences of homeopathy.

My First Exposure to the Homeopathic Method

A well-known doctor and homeopathic practitioner kindly invited me to sit in on one of his clinics. It was a great experience: I felt as if I was sitting at the feet of a master craftsman.

The first patient (who was new to his practice) was an anxious-looking middle-aged woman. He welcomed her warmly, asked if she was happy for me to observe (she was) and invited her to sit herself down and relax. He engaged her in some small talk for a while and, as that went on, she clearly started to calm down and trust him. Then, he asked about her problems. There were many of them, some medical, some social. He explored each one carefully, making a lot of notes as he went along. At times, she became upset when talking about her problems; he would then say something along the lines of "OK, let's just notice that". He might perhaps ask how something made her feel, and when she responded, he might say "Just stay with that for a moment if you can" as he looked carefully at her and gave her whatever time she needed. He explored her history of past illnesses in detail, eliciting her feelings about each one, as well as their other effects. He explored her social life in minute detail, wanting to know what things she liked doing, what an average day in her life was like, what she liked to eat and drink, and so forth. He really seemed to want to know everything about her, to be able to gather a picture of the whole person and her life in a way that I had not experienced before.

At times, it felt a bit like psychotherapy, except for the fact that no interpretation of emotions or symptoms was offered, and there was absolutely no sense of judgment about anything; on the contrary, it was entirely about noticing, understanding and accepting

The interview went on for a long time. He went through a long list of possible symptoms and issues after the patient had wound down from her first round of telling him about her problems. He thanked her often, and let her know that he really did understand what she was talking about. At one point, he paused, saying that both he and the patient needed a short rest, and explained to me that he was looking for patterns; "This is mostly about pattern recognition", he said. I was not sure what that meant at the time. Then, he continued, carefully noting, validating and recognizing everything the patient had to say about her life and her problems.

He looked carefully at her, but there was no formal physical examination.

Toward the end of the consultation, he said something like "Well, thank you so much, I think we should be able to find something that will help you". She smiled warmly at him. "I would like you to try this homeopathic remedy", he said, giving her a bottle containing some small tablets. "It contains diluted arnica* and I hope it will help you to heal; the instructions are on the bottle". Come back and see me in about a month and we will see what has happened.

She thanked him as the consultation came to an end, after well over an hour.

*Arnica is a plant in the sunflower family. Hugely diluted extracts of Arnica are commonly used by homeopaths.

After the patient left, I asked him why he had chosen arnica for her. "I am not sure", he said, "I was trying to get a picture of the pattern of problems in her life, and it just popped into my head that arnica might be right for her. It is about finding the remedy that is right for any given individual and that will activate the healing process within them. Sometimes, choosing a particular homeopathic remedy seems to be as much about intuition as anything else for me". "And how often will you see her?" I asked. "Oh, probably only once more", he responded, "I think it is important not to let people get used to these long in-depth consultations. It is easy for folks to get addicted to this sort of therapy, and I want to avoid that; the GP can take over when we are done next time".

Another Homeopathic Consultation That I Witnessed

This encounter was with a different practitioner. The patient was someone he had seen before, about three weeks previously. Before she came in, he explained to me that, since being bereaved a couple of years ago, she had been suffering physical, mental and spiritual pain. She had been given the diagnosis of fibromyalgia by her doctors, but they had not been able to find anything to help her, so she had come to see him, a homeopath, as something of a last resort. He told me that he had tried to get a complete picture of her problems when he had last seen her, and made a note of the severity of some of her key problems, before prescribing *Rhus tox**.

> **Rhus toxicodendron plants are well known for producing an itching, irritating or painful rash on contact, as well as joint pains. In homeopathic potencies, the Rhus-t remedy treats symptoms related to skin complaints, as well as joint problems.*

When she came in and after introductions had been made and everyone was settled, he started going through her key symptoms one by one, often noting "Oh, that's better than last time" or some such as she described them. She agreed with him that most things had improved. He asked her a lot about her response to the *Rhus tox*, and she said that, at first, it had made her joint pain worse rather than better, particularly her knee pain. He explored the knee pain in detail, in much greater depth than I, a so-called medical expert in knee problems, would have done.

After some 40 minutes, dominated by their both agreeing that things were much improved, he told her that he thought it best to go on with *Rhus tox* for a little longer, rather than trying to change treatment at this early stage. They agreed on this, and the patient then turned to me and said, "This homeopathy has already been so much more effective than anything the doctors did for me, you know".

After she had left, I asked him about the knee pain. He got a big homeopathy "tome" down from the bookshelf in the consulting room and looked it up. He showed me that it listed a huge number of different patterns and associations of knee pain, patterns (combinations of symptoms and features in the history of the disorder) that made sense to me as I read them, but which conventional doctors like me do not recognize.

He also showed me his book of remedies, a dense, large book containing very detailed information on a huge number of substances. He told me he often referred to this tome to help him decide on therapy. This practitioner seemed to work with these written manuals more than on the intuition used by the first practitioner.

A Discussion with a Group of Homeopaths

I had been invited to one of the regular meetings of a local group of homeopathic practitioners. They asked me to give a short talk on my research into healing, after which, I was told, they would like to have a longish period of in-depth discussion about healing with me.

So, I gave my short talk, in which I concentrated on the idea that the special type of connection that can occur between two individuals, between a healer and their client, might be the key factor in the induction of a healing response. I pushed my thesis that "focused attention with good intention" was at the heart of healing, a concept that had emerged from my analysis of interviews with healers. They seemed engaged and attentive.

This was followed by a long, fascinating group discussion, involving everyone in the room (about 25 homeopaths and me). They looked to me to moderate as it went along, which suited me just fine. As I told them, I wanted to learn more about homeopathy and to hear what they had to say about it.

The first discussion topic I embarked upon was *the consultation*. I told them how impressed I had been by the history taking, when sitting in with homeopaths, and that I found their approach wonderful. We discussed the fact that everyone was different and that conventional medicine's need to put people into diagnostic boxes that lead to specific interventions was naïve. "If you go to a doctor with problems, you often come out with a disease and not much else", said someone.

The second area of discussion was *energy*. Although this is a foreign concept to conventional medical practitioners, it was not to the homeopaths. They saw their remedies as being a vehicle for energy channeling to the patient to help them start to heal and achieve balance. This was talk that was very similar to that which I had heard from energy healers.

Finally, it was time to talk about their *remedies*. I reminded them that this was a source of ridicule among many scientists. They readily agreed, but told me homeopaths are taught that the serial dilution and succussion (shaking violently or tapping between dilutions) are key to the transfer of energy from the remedy to the patient; the remedies were their vehicle for healing. What they then told me was a revelation: you do not necessarily need to ingest the remedy, they said; you can simply put the name of it under a glass of water that you drink, or think about it when on the phone to a client, you can even use the remedies as a vehicle for distant healing. WOW! Just when I am opening up to homeopathy, they are telling me things that are way out of my comfort zone! Then, we talked about whether the use of the remedies gave homeopaths credibility or were a problem. I explained that I saw it as a problem and, given what they were telling me, wondered why they didn't talk more about energy and healing, and less about dilutions and succussion. They explained that talk of energy was seen as just as unscientific as talk of homeopathic dilution of remedies. A fair point, I thought. As this discussion continued, it was clear that we were all struggling with the gap between the materialistic world and what we all thought might be going on in the world of healing.

What I Took from These Experiences

I was hugely impressed by the two clinicians I witnessed at work. Their compassionate, sensitive history-taking was wonderful. Pattern recognition was the key to sorting out the problems of each of their clients. But the patterns they were detecting involved a lot of past experiences and social issues, as well as the current symptoms and signs, the latter being what all doctors like myself concentrate on. The second consultation centered on problems within my own speciality (rheumatology), but I was being taught about different patterns to the ones I knew about. Furthermore, each practitioner really seemed to connect to their client, and they made sure that they validated the client's experiences. This appeared to result in relaxation and trust.

The main message I took from the meeting with the group of homeopaths was that many of them are quite open to the concept that they are healers, working with energy, and that the connections they made with their clients could be a key element to their ability to help them heal.

Homeopathy and Healing

Homeopathy was developed by the German physician and empiricist, Samuel Hahnemann, at the end of the eighteenth century. He worked on the principle of "like-for-like" and did many empirical experiments to find out what dilutions worked for which people. A lot of them seemed to work better than most of the other remedies available at the time, and his approach soon became popular.

So homeopathy was based upon the idea that a substance which causes the same symptoms as the patient exhibits might also, when administered at a high dilution, provide a cure. That is its problem; the dilutions are so huge that hardly any molecules of the original substance are left in the remedy that is given to the patient which clearly makes no sense to materialist science.

But homeopathy as it has developed is much more than diluted remedies, and its philosophical basis goes far beyond the remedies. It is a "whole system" of health care, based on the concepts of individualization and universal energy. Its system of history-taking looks much more holistically at people than does conventional medicine. Many practitioners see the remedies as vehicles for energy transfer, rather than a physical cure, and the philosophy is about the activation of healing of the whole person, rather than the curing of disease. And there are now different forms of homeopathic practice, with varying philosophical principles.

Largely because of the ultra-high dilutions of its remedies, homeopathy is dismissed as "just placebo", or worse, by conventional science. Recent research cited to support this assertion is that some people are better at inducing the effect than others. I don't think homeopathy is just placebo, but I do think that some homeopathic practitioners are better at activating self-healing of their clients than others. Furthermore, I think they are "between a rock and a hard place" in their adherence to the use of "similars" (something similar to a toxin or poison that might be making you ill) and diluted remedies. To reject them might be to rid homeopathy of the vehicle which helps practitioners channel healing energy, whereas adherence to them means that they are stuck with poorly understood phenomena (in terms of Western science), which leave them open to ridicule within our materialistic culture.

My Conclusions

I think many homeopathic practitioners are skilled healers. Like other healers that I have talked to, observed in their clinics and worked with, their practices are holistic and compassionate, and they emphasize the development of a connection with the client/patient that centers on good intentions. But they have an explanatory model for the effectiveness of their work which is different from the biomedical one.

My understanding of homeopathy's use of diluted substances, as well as its guiding philosophy, were made especially clear to me by a book first published in 1900 (4). It was given to me by a friend who is herself both a philosopher and a homeopathic practitioner. I have also found the book on homeopathy by my friend Jeremy Swayne helpful (5).

We do not understand homeopathy, but that is not a reason to dismiss it. Trials do not show much efficacy, but that is not a reason to reject it either, because, as stated previously, trials are inappropriate for interventions that have to be highly individualized and depend on the relationships between therapist and client. Finally, I don't think we need to completely reject the idea that the diluted substances may themselves have efficacy, even though my own opinion is that the value of homeopathy is much more to do with its similarities to other forms of healing that depend on the individual practitioners.

Homeopathy is one of a huge number of interventions that have little or no support from science, but remain popular. In the UK, they are generally called "Complementary and Alternative Medicine" (CAM) treatments, a somewhat dismissive term. I have experienced others but have not been able to study them in detail. It would not surprise me if healing was an important reason for the popularity of many of these treatments.

ANIMALS AS HEALERS AND ANIMAL HEALING

Healers will often work on animals, as well as other humans. As outlined in the previous chapter, I have experienced that myself, when healing a horse.

And there is evidence that healers, using healing intention, can sometimes effect cures of disease in animals.

For example, William Bengston, an American scientist who has been studying healing for years, has a considerable amount of data to show that his form of energy healing can cure rats of cancer (6, 7); he and others have published a lot of carefully conducted scientific studies to show this. And Bengston's work is not alone: there is a considerable body of other scientific work on the ability of healing intention to help animals.

I have not studied this literature, taking more interest in the evidence that animals can help humans to heal. There is an impressive amount of literature available on these subjects as well, most of which is dismissed as anecdotal or pseudo-scientific by the mainstream scientific community, but I find it convincing.

In the West, lots of us keep cats or dogs as pets, or less often, a variety of other animals; they become much-loved members of our families. And there is compelling evidence that they help maintain and improve health and wellbeing, particularly in older people (8, 9).

Some think the reasons are simple, such as your pet dog increasing your exercise time, as it needs to be taken out for walks. But there may be more to it than exercise. Perhaps the intense, loving bond that many owners forge with their pets is important. I do not have a dog or a cat (because of allergies to fur, among other things) but many friends and relations tell me about the extraordinary, unconditional love their pets have for them, which is reciprocated.

Connecting with dolphins has a reputation for helping people to heal, and I have been amazed by my apparent ability to feel in contact with elephants when being with them in the wild on safari. In my opinion, there is no doubt that animals are sentient, and can connect with us and *vice versa*.

As with other types of healing, animal healing of humans seems to be about making these connections between living things and about love. Those of you who look after a cat or a dog or perhaps some other animal, such as a horse, will understand the love and connectivity that can take place between you. You have probably also experienced the extraordinary way in which the animal seems to be able to not only respond to but predict your thoughts and actions. Telepathic communication between animals and humans is well established, and there is strong scientific evidence for it, as Rupert Sheldrake and others have shown (10).

When it comes to animals healing people, cats are probably the most renowned for this ability. There are a lot of individual reports of remarkable cats in the literature and cats are well known for other abilities in their interactions with humans. For example, there are many reports of cats being able to predict deaths in hospices for the care of terminally ill people. Similarly, dogs and horses have long been used to help heal humans, and to improve their wellbeing.

Animals can heal us, just as we can heal them.

CONCLUSIONS

As Shakespeare's Hamlet muses, "There are more things in heaven and earth, Horatio, than are dreamt of in your philosophy". My experiences with healers and healing led me to agree: there is more in heaven and earth than I ever dreamt of in the first half of my life.

Whichever type of evidence I consider, it seems to lead to the same conclusion: that there is "something else" out there, beyond our materialistic sense of the world. There is an ineffable, spiritual mystery to the Universe. Some call this God; others, love or universal consciousness, whereas healers tend to talk of energy. And it seems that all living things are connected, or can be connected, in some way that is inexplicable to our current scientific knowledge. I *know* this for two reasons – first, my direct experiences of energy flow and connecting to other living beings, and second, the scientific evidence that I increasingly believe to be incontrovertible. Both the subjective and objective evidence tell the same story, but neither explains it.

I need to consider two major implications of that conclusion. First, what sort of a world am I living in? Second, how can we convince the medical profession to take healing seriously? Obviously, I do not have a complete answer to either question, but I do have some ideas.

What sort of world are we a part of? I find some ideas helpful to resolve the conflict between what I sense and understand from my "normal" materialistic stance, and what I experience with healers. First, those derived from quantum mechanics (which I cannot understand) that suggest, as Max Planck put it, "That consciousness is primary and matter secondary to consciousness"*; and, second, the related concept of "panpsychism" – which views consciousness as a ground substance of the cosmos, to which we can all connect (11).

I shall return to these themes toward the end of the book.

REFERENCES

1. Fries H. *Forest Bathing Retreat: Find Wholeness in the Company of Trees.* North Adams, MA, USA: Storey Publishing, 2018.
2. Mackinnon C. *Shamanism: Spiritual Growth, Healing, Consciousness.* London: Flame Tree Publishing, 2020.
3. Agarwal A, Agarawal R. The practice and tradition of bone setting. *Practical Advice* 2010; 23; 1:225.
4. Kent JT. *Lectures on Homeopathic Philosophy.* New Delhi: B Jain Publishers Ltd., 1997 (reprint edition).
5. Swayne J. *Homeopathic Method; Implications for Clinical Practice and Medical Science.* 2nd edition Saltire Books, Glasgow Scotland, 2013.
6. The Bengston Energy Healing Method® See https://bengstonresearch.com
7. Bengston W. *The Energy Cure; Unravelling the Mystery of Hands on Healing.* Boulder, Colorado: Sounds True, 2010.
8. McNicholas J, Gilbey A, Rennie A et. al. Pet ownership and human health: A brief review of evidence and issues. *BMJ* 2005; 331: 1252.
9. Hughes MJ, Verreynne M-L, Harpur P and Pachana NA. Companion animals and health in older populations: A systematic review. *Clin Gerontol* 2020; 43: 365–377.
10. Sheldrake R. *Dogs That Know When Their Owners Are Coming Home: and Other Unexplained Powers of Animals.* London: Crown Publishing Group, 2010.
11. Seagar W (ed). *The Routledge Handbook on Panpsychism.* New York USA: Routledge, 2021.

6

Lourdes, Belief and Healing

I ended the last chapter by suggesting that what you make of healing depends on what your worldview is, or what you believe. Many of us have a religious belief. Spirituality and religion intersect with healing. I have been able to explore some aspects of that in Lourdes, the Catholic pilgrimage site in France, famous for its miracle cures.

CLAIRE'S STORY

Claire was a very sick English lady in her 40s, whom I talked to in a hospital in Lourdes. She had multiple medical problems, resulting in bouts of near-terminal sepsis (infection). At home in the UK, she was being looked after by full-time carers and was generally in a lot of pain. Claire was a devout Catholic and this was her second visit to Lourdes. She had been told she was likely to have another episode of overwhelming infection soon and was unlikely to recover.

Claire had first come to Lourdes a year previously, in the hope that 'Our Lady' would allow her diseases to improve a bit. But she was so ill that she had to spend most of her time in bed in the *Accueil* (hospital), unable to join in the rituals, masses and processions, or to take the water or visit the Grotto. *"I was really poorly; I was on bedrest"*.

But one day, as she listened to the sound of the candlelight procession's singing of *"Ave Maria"* floating through the open window of her hospital ward, something remarkable happened. *"There was this lady sitting with me, just holding my hand because I was so poorly … and the sound of the service, the music was coming through the window … and I just felt*

DOI: 10.4324/9781003461814-8

this warmth come over me, wash over me, and it felt just like I was being
enveloped with it ... and just almost ... like ... being held. And it took
over my body and I felt just complete calm and peace ... and the pain just
disappeared into insignificance".

The effect lasted for several weeks after her return to England, and she
told me that she could reproduce the feeling of peace, joy and a lack of pain
just by imagining herself being back in that wonderful moment a year ago
in Lourdes. She was sure this was God's hand helping her.

Her tears as she told me this story were tears of joy, not of pain.

Her story touched me; this was clearly a very profound spiritual
experience linked to healing.

THE PILGRIMAGE SITE OF LOURDES

Pilgrimage sites, renowned for their healing properties, can be found all
over the world. Most are linked to a religion and, if someone recovers from
a disease after visiting such a site, religious leaders may pronounce that a
"miracle healing" has occurred, thanks to that person's faith in God.

Lourdes is in Southwest France. It is a Catholic Marian shrine that
became famous after a young woman, Bernadette Soubirous, saw visions
of the Virgin Mary in a grotto there, in 1858. The visions gave instructions
that people should come in procession to the grotto, drink and bathe in
the waters there and build a chapel. Soon after Bernadette's visions, the
first miraculous cure of someone visiting the grotto and drinking the
water was reported. Other cures occurred, word spread and Lourdes and
its grotto started to attract pilgrims.

Literally millions of people visit Lourdes each year, many hoping for a
cure. Sick pilgrims, called the *"malades"*, often come in large pilgrimage
groups – some of them several hundred in number, with their own priests,
doctors, nurses and volunteer helpers. These groups can be organized
by churches or individuals, and they come from all over the world. It is
a beautiful place, nestled in a valley near the Pyrenees mountains, with
the river Gave de Pau running through it. Pilgrims center their activities
within the *"Domain"* or "Sanctuary of Our Lady of Lourdes" a fifty-one-
hectare site of carefully managed land. It is fenced off from the surrounding
town, and within it is the imposing basilica, built, as instructed, above

the Grotto where the visions of Our Lady of Lourdes appeared. Baths for immersion in healing holy water from the stream are nearby, along with taps where people can collect holy water for drinking or taking home. Mass is held in front of the grotto several times each day during the pilgrimage season. There is also a daily procession and mass for the sick in the new underground basilica, and a stunning evening candlelight procession accompanied by the singing of *"Ave Maria"* that Claire heard.

RESEARCH IN LOURDES

My work in Lourdes came about in a strange way in 2010, soon after I had moved to Exeter University. I received an email from a lecturer in the University's Department of Drama who said she had heard that I was an expert in pain, and she wanted to do research on pain relief resulting from religious rituals in Lourdes; could we meet to discuss a joint grant proposal? I thought this sounded distinctly unpromising, but I agreed to meet. During our long conversation over coffee, I was quickly captivated by this bright young woman's wit, intelligence and energy; I agreed to her putting my name on her research proposal. The grants being advertised by the University were for original inter-disciplinary research, and she thought that Drama and Medicine going to Lourdes together was perfect. I left thinking that I had found a new colleague with whom I could work well and have fun, but I was quite certain she would not get the grant, and that there would be no need for me to go to Lourdes.

But she got the grant, and a few weeks later this new academic friend from the Department of Drama, Dr Sarah Goldingay, told me we were off to Lourdes to make a film! So, I found myself in Lourdes with Sarah as well as Rob Alexander, a brilliant young filmmaker, and Dr Miguel Farias, an Oxford-based Portuguese neuropsychologist who had worked in Lourdes with Sarah previously.

The visit was facilitated by the wonderful doctor in charge of the Lourdes Medical Bureau, Dr Alessandro de Franciscis. Not only did he help and encourage us and introduce us to others who could facilitate our research and filmmaking, he also made sure that we became a part of what was going on in Lourdes. He had us take part in key rituals, even playing visible roles in some of them, and we were able to speak to senior figures in Lourdes. We were an integral part of what we came to call "the real miracle" of Lourdes, not just cynical spectators.

Highlights of that visit included the following.

Examining Cases Thought to Be Possible Miracle Cures

Dr de Fransciscis gave me, as a fellow doctor, confidential access to the records of possible and substantiated cases of miracle cures. One substantiated case impressed me hugely. A young man had developed an extensive bone sarcoma at the top of his leg. This is a highly malignant form of cancer that usually kills, and, if it does not, it is at the cost of surgical removal of a leg or whole "hind quarter", combined with a lot of nasty chemotherapy. The X-rays, showing the highly characteristic changes, were there in the file, along with histological confirmation of the diagnosis. That was "before Lourdes". A year or so after his pilgrimage visit, and apparently without any medical interventions, further X-rays were taken and there was absolutely no evidence of any cancer – his leg looked normal. That amazed me: that just does not happen, except that a handful of similarly unexplainable cases of spontaneous remission of cancer are reported in medical journals each year (1).

I was also invited to review a case that was being considered for possible ratification as a miraculous cure. It involved a rheumatic disease, and my host thought I might be able to help him decide whether or not to send it "up" to the Church authorities as a possible miracle. What a privilege and responsibility! I studied all the available documents very carefully. The individual had got better from a rare, ill-understood condition (that I was familiar with) after visiting Lourdes – that much seemed clear. But I thought that the improvement could have been due to a number of other factors operating in her life at the time. I discussed this with Dr de Fansciscis, and he agreed that it should not be taken further.

The Medical Bureau gets 30 to 40 possible miracle cases of this sort referred to them each year, but very few get ratified as miracles by the Church. There are only some 70 certified "miracle cures" on their books. In the early years, recovery from tuberculosis dominated these miracles, whereas now it is more likely to be unexplained remission of cancer.

Talking to People in an Accueil

The two "*Accueils*" (hospitals) in Lourdes are for the sickest pilgrims to live in during their visits. They are like big hospitals, with both large wards and smaller rooms for the "*malades*", as well as communal refectories and recreational areas. Pilgrimage groups often bring their own medical and nursing staff to look after their "*malades*" in these buildings. Friends and relatives sometimes join the groups as well.

I was given the opportunity to visit the *Accueil Notre Dame* and spend some time talking to people from one of the large English-speaking pilgrimage groups there at the time. I met some amazing people: doctors, nurses, relatives and friends of pilgrims, as well as some of the "*malades*" themselves, like Claire. I spent time just listening to their stories. There was a wonderful ethos of caring and compassion in those wards. In spite of my inability to believe in their Catholicism, I was very moved and impressed.

Talking to an English Doctor

We met an English doctor who was leading one of the pilgrimage groups. He was interested in the healing properties of Lourdes. He told me about the equality of Lourdes – everyone is of equal importance and worth, "*malades*" or not. And he explained that the Lourdes experience gave great help to many of those who came to assist, as well as to the "*malades*".

He provided me with a lot of insights, and this wonderful quote:

> "*These rich stockbrokers come from London for two weeks of their holiday time, to wipe the bottoms of sick people. And these visits seem to heal them – the stockbrokers – somehow, it helps them regain a sense of equilibrium*".

During my research visits to Lourdes, I came to understand the significance of this quote, through meeting people from many different walks of life who gave their time, often holiday leave, to help out in Lourdes, where they undertook menial tasks. Some kept coming back and told me that they were refreshed spiritually by doing this work.

Being a Part of the Procession

Each day, in the pilgrimage season, there is a large procession to the huge underground basilica, where a mass takes place. The procession is led by the clergy, followed by medical people, such as Alessandro, and other leaders of the Lourdes experience. One day, our host, Alessandro, suggested we join the procession and take part in one of the rituals at the beginning of the Mass being said for the *"malades"*.

A memory from that day stays with me. As we walked along the path from the upper basilica to the modern underground cathedral in the hot sunshine, people were kneeling down to the side of us and offering thanks to God and Mary. I saw one woman, a little way in front of us, who was kneeling on the pavement, crying her eyes out. As we approached, she stood up, looked straight at me and held my gaze; she was looking right through me, seeing everything. And I could see right into her tortured soul; we connected. Then she sank back to her knees on the paved surface, but pulled at my trouser legs, crying out and in tears, in a language I did not understand, as we moved on past her.

I had felt the same sort of connection and flow of energy with that lady as I had experienced when being taught how to do energy healing. Something very important passed between us, and I wondered if I had contributed to the healing of that tortured woman. But why did she pick me? This incident increased my ever-present confusion about healing and my so-called "power", and made me wonder if "energy healing" might be a part of what can happen in Lourdes.

Research "outputs" from this visit included the film that we had promised the University funding body we would make, as well as a publication (2).

TRYING TO UNDERSTAND THE LOURDES PHENOMENON BETTER

Other visits to Lourdes helped us move closer to an understanding of the dynamics we were witnessing, and of what we came to think of as the "real miracle of Lourdes": the change for the better that occurs for so many visitors, no matter in what capacity they arrive.

Firstly, one of the major insights for me was the description of a pilgrimage to Lourdes as a *"low-tech, high-touch intervention to improve health"*. A belief often voiced to us from those involved in the activities in Lourdes is that touch – both physical and metaphorical – is central to what is going on and that this is as important and beneficial to people as most medical technology.

Secondly, we realized that one of the major features of Lourdes is its *ethos of equality*. As the doctor I met had explained, everyone is equally important and valued, be they helper, "malade", priest, doctor, tourist or whatever. Some of the terminology (such as "*malade*") may seem difficult to us now, but it does not matter in Lourdes. While there, a sick person is in exactly the same place as everyone else – they are not a sick person, they are another valuable individual.

We also understood *the importance of rituals* in Lourdes. Many rituals and performances, some very powerful, occur there every day, which visitors not only witness but somehow become immersed in. Groups perform their own rituals in addition to the centrally organized ones, and the accompanying outpourings of emotion sometimes appear little short of mass hysteria or hypnosis.

We were also conscious of the *sense of hope and compassion* that infuses all daily activities – people come in hope, not just in expectation. And compassion is everywhere. Claire's story, for example, included the fact that another sick patient was holding her hand when she had her sudden "change". We heard of and witnessed many other simple acts of compassion between people during our times in Lourdes. Simple acts of kindness, such as helping someone in a wheelchair get to their destination, were "endemic" in Lourdes in a way that I have not seen anywhere else.

Then there were descriptions of people having amazing "moments" when in Lourdes – what might be called *transcendent moments*, as when Claire felt that sudden sense of warmth, peace and joy spread through her.

But what struck us most forcibly was "*the real miracle of Lourdes*", which many of the local authorities and Church leaders seemed to be agreed upon: the real miracle is the number of people who are changed for the better by their visits to Lourdes. Miracle cures are rare, but improvements in health and wellbeing are common.

Research on Transcendent Moments in Lourdes

Sarah Goldingay and I were impressed by so many things in Lourdes, and wanted to do more research to gain a deeper understanding of what is going on. It is difficult to get funding for such work, or indeed to find money to do any research on healing or caring. But we teamed up with two of our other "healing research" colleagues, Prof Sara Warber and Dr Emmylou Rahtz, and applied to the BIAL foundation in Portugal *(BIAL.com)* for money to fund a more substantive visit to investigate transcendent moments in Lourdes. Happily for us, our grant was funded.

Five of us (Emmylou, Sarah, Sara, Liz my wife and I) made an eight-day data-collecting visit to Lourdes in the summer of 2017. It was an intense experience. We were interviewing pilgrims, health care professionals and other visitors, and undertaking observational work (ethnography) in the hope of finding out if and how people's wellbeing improved as a result of visiting Lourdes, whether transcendent experiences contributed to such changes, and what triggered such "moments".

After an exhausting few days, both stressful and exhilarating, we returned home with a trove of potentially rich data, including some 60 recorded interviews, as well as a large amount of ethnographic data, drawings and photographs, all suitable for the qualitative analyses that we had proposed in our grant application. And as we analyzed the data, many other insights into the healing powers of Lourdes emerged, leading us to tentative conclusions about the pilgrimage site and healing there.

LOURDES AND HEALING

There is a small museum/exhibition within the Medical Bureau in Lourdes. It is tucked away and not advertised, so relatively few people go there. For me, it was helpful, as it documented some of the early history, including the first "miraculous cures", and explained the processes around documenting the miracles. But the best thing I saw there was this quote:

"Many marvels take place every day, in the spirit and in the heart"

I think that sums up what is going on in Lourdes. Yes, the place is known for its medical miracles, rare examples of disease remission attributed to direct intervention by God or "Our Lady". But for most of the clergy, doctors and other officials there, it is more about the many marvels or "mini miracles" that occur each day, about the people who are changed for the better, in spirit and heart as much as in body. As far as I could see, many marvels do indeed take place there each day.

Is that healing? I shall discuss the nature of healing in more detail later in this book; suffice it to say at this point that outcomes of healing interventions range from feeling a bit better to the disappearance of a disease process such as cancer. Within that broad definition, what we were witnessing in Lourdes certainly was healing, even if the "miraculous cures" for which it is renown were only apparent historically. And whether you attribute the healing to God, Jesus, The Mother of Jesus, Mary Magdalene (all of whom have a high profile in Lourdes) or to someone or something else does not seem important. I know very little about Catholicism (having been brought up in a Church of England home) or the stories about Mary Magdalene and the Mother of Jesus that are so prominent in Lourdes. But I found no difficulty in accepting that people there had a firm belief in their power and attributed any beneficial effects to these beliefs. As explained in my response to "Clive's" story in Chapter 1, different people give quite different reasons for their changes in health status, and I think we doctors need to be more open-minded about such things.

We went on to analyze the data we had obtained; this analysis was led by Drs Rhatz, Warber and Goldingay, with small contributions from myself, and articles and a book chapter have been written about it (3,4,5).

Facilitators of Healing

We concluded that there are multiple facilitators of healing at Lourdes. One is the *"therapeutic landscape"*, made up of its beautiful geography and architecture, within which the multifaceted daily interactions of the populace occur. Another is the *"prosocial behavior"* observed everywhere: Lourdes is not a place in which petty everyday issues interfere with our innate abilities to be nice to each other. Everyone there appears able to allow their better selves to guide their actions and give freely to others, thereby helping themselves to flourish (and heal) through giving. It is also a place of *caring exchanges*, where people take joy in altruistic behaviors.

Some people describe Lourdes as *"a thin place"* – somewhere where the boundary between the physical world and the "other", the metaphysical, or the divine becomes almost transparent. It seems a place in which the divide between different people falls away, allowing person-to-person connections that are easy, deep and immediately satisfying, even with others you have never met before.

TABLE 6.1

Lourdes as a Place for Healing Through Nourishing Exchanges (adapted from Goldingay, Dieppe, Warber and Rahtz (2))

Essential characteristics of places where nourishing exchanges can take place include: • Equality of all the people there • Feelings of safety when there • Everyone feeling cared for and loved by others/each other • Dominance of prosocial behavior. *The healing results of nourishing exchanges include:* • A positive whole-person interpretative response to the context • New meaning-making • Enhanced integration of mind, body and soul • Progress on an individual's journey to inner harmony.

Sarah Goldingay has coined the concept of *"nourishing exchanges"* to epitomize what Lourdes is about. We have concluded that healing comes from nourishing exchanges in Lourdes, as shown in Table 6.1:

RELIGION, BELIEF, PRAYER AND HEALING

My visits to Lourdes prompted me to explore the links between religion, belief, prayer and healing.

Lourdes is a place dominated by religious faith and prayer. Prayer is something that most pilgrims and visitors spend a lot of time doing while there, and nearly every visitor has faith in Catholicism. So, I needed to consider how important these factors might be in facilitating healing in Lourdes – and elsewhere. Although not a Christian myself, I was moved by the faith of those I met in Lourdes and how important it was to them, and I cannot dismiss the possibility that they are right and I am wrong, and that God is responsible for the positive changes we saw there.

Furthermore, prayer is something many of us without faith resort to in times of crisis. Once, early on in my incarceration in Kuwait, I had a severe panic attack, and found myself on my knees, praying for deliverance.

Praying for the recovery of a sick individual, so-called intercessory prayer, is one of the commonest responses to illness. It is probably the most commonly used form of "complementary or alternative medicine" (CAM). Several surveys have indicated that huge numbers of sick people and their relatives use prayer in the hope of improving outcomes. For example, a large American study carried out in 1998 found that about one-third of all adults use prayer when challenged by health concerns (6). In addition there are many case reports of remarkable "cures" resulting from prayer, sometimes described as miracles. They often result from people praying with the sick person; in other cases, one or more people pray for others at a distance, often without the subjects knowing that they are being prayed for. And I had been told that intercessory prayer had allowed me to heal after my rugby accident at the age of 16 (Chapter 1), so the subject is a personal one for me.

Looking at the literature, I found that there are a lot of scientific studies on prayer and healing, and a huge number of books on the subject. But what is prayer? It is difficult to define and can mean different things to different people, and varies widely among cultures and religions. Aldridge (6) suggests that there are three categories of prayer, as shown in Table 6.2

In Lourdes, each of these categories is prevalent. Many people spend a lot of meditative time on their own, often concentrating on the presence of "Our Lady". There is a lot of intercessory praying for the *"malades"* and regular church services at which liturgical prayers are said. Surveys have shown that praying for sick friends or relatives is extremely common (7)

Doctors and others may ask if there is any "hard evidence" that prayer can induce healing, other than case reports, in the belief that case reports count for nothing, as you can never be sure about what happened or why. So trials have been undertaken to test the power of prayer, but results vary, and my reading of the data is that there is no overwhelming positive or negative signal. And perhaps it is absurd to try to submit prayer to this sort of empirical test, in the light of the case reports and the firm beliefs of so many. Most religions include prayers for healing, but as Gaudia (8) has said, this seems to be treating your God in a strange way. You are asking the divine to intervene with the whole scheme of life on this tiny planet

TABLE 6.2

Forms of Prayer (after Aldridge (5))

- Meditative prayer: Time spent alone with the intent of achieving a presence with the divine
- Intercessory prayer: the person praying talks to the divine, often to worship, and sometimes to request help for others, as in healing prayers
- Liturgical prayer: formalized prayers within a specific religion used as part of religious rituals.

so that one person's illness can be improved. Why would a divine being do that?

Aldridge suggests that prayer is as much for the person doing the praying as it is for the person being prayed for and that it is basically part of the narrative re-construction that we need when existentially challenged by disease (the requirement to reinterpret the likely reason for illness and our individual life stories). Dossey (9) presents us with a different interpretation of the power of prayer; that its power comes from the positive intention of one or more people directed toward another, and that it is evidence for our ability to connect with each other in non-physical ways. Dossey does not need to invoke the divine for an explanation of the power of prayer. For him, it is about distant healing, a subject discussed in Chapter 4. Perhaps we need to think more about the power of positive intention rather than faith-based prayer *per se* as a key component of healing.

The Power of Belief

Belief, without any religious connotations, can have powerful beneficial effects on health.

A good example of this is what is called the "Healthy Adherer Effect" (10). People who do take their medicines, be they dummy (placebo) or active, do better than those who do not.

It has been shown, for example, that people who adhere to long-term treatments offered for heart disease (in other words, take the medicine exactly as instructed) survive longer than poor adherers. This effect is true for placebo treatments as well as for prescribed drugs (11).

One explanation offered is that those who adhere well to treatments may also pursue better health behaviors of other sorts. But this may not be the explanation. It may be about less easily definable things, such as "belief" itself. Belief is powerful. Take another example: voodoo deaths. If you believe you are going to die after being cursed, you often do (12).

Conclusions

As a scientist, my habit has been to look for a single "answer" to a question, such as "What is healing and why does it occur in Lourdes?" But I have learnt that this way of thinking can be naïve and inappropriate. A binary approach is unhelpful – the answer is not necessarily one thing *or* another

(God *or* not, for example); it can, as the saying goes, be "both and". There can be many different answers. I am now comfortable with the power of belief, faith and prayer, as well as the power of place and of "nourishing exchanges". Many other factors, as well, may all be contributing to explaining the 'true miracle' of Lourdes. Yet, I remain barely able to understand it.

REFERENCES

1. Rediger J. 2020 "Cured – The remarkable science and stories of spontaneous healing and recovery". Penguin Random House, UK.
2. Goldingay S, Farias M, Dieppe P. "And the pain just disappeared into insignificance" – The healing response in Lourdes – Performance psychology and caring. Int Rev Psychiatry 2009; 26(3): 315–323.
3. Goldingay S, Rhatz E, Warber S, Dieppe P. Nourishing exchanges: Care love and chronicity in Lourdes. In Hatala C (ed), *Routledge Special Collection on Religion, Spirituality and Health*, 2021. Routledge New York.
4. Rahtz E, Warber S, Goldingay S, Dieppe P. Transcendent experiences among pilgrims to Lourdes: A qualitative investigation. *J Relig. Health* 2021; 60: 3788–3806.
5. Dieppe P, Dieppe E, Godlingay S, Rahtz E, Warber S. Many marvels take place every day in the spirit and in the heart. *Bulletin de L'association Medicale Internatinale de Notre-Dame de Lourdes* 2021; 352: 42–51.
6. Aldridge D. *Spirituality, Healing and Medicine – Return to the Silence*. London: Jessica Kingsley Publishers Ltd, 2000.
7. McCaffrey AM et al. Prayer for health concerns: Results of a national survey on prevalence and patterns of use. *Arch Intern Med* 2004; 164: 858–862.
8. Gaudia G. About intercessory prayer: The scientific study of miracles. *Medscape General Medicine* 2007; 9: 56.
9. Dossey L. *Healing Words: The Power of Prayer and the Practice of Medicine*. San Fransisco: Harper San Francisco, 1993.
10. Ladova K, Vlcek J, Vytrisalova M, Maly J. Health adherer effect – The pitfall in the interpretation of the effect of medication adherence on health outcomes. *J Eval Clin Pract* 2014; 20: 111–116.
11. Horwitz R et al. Treatment adherence and the risk of death after a myocardial infarction. *Lancet* 1990; 336: 542–545.
12. Gomez E. Voodoo and sudden death: The effects of expectations on health. *Transcult. Psychiatric Res Rev*1982; 19: 75–91.

7

Healers and Their Clients' Understanding of Healing

As I pursued my healing research, I became aware of the fact that there were huge numbers of people practicing as healers in the UK (the estimate is around 30,000). Most medical practitioners never interact with these healers, but I was keen to talk to some of them to find out what they were doing. I was curious about how they went about their work.

INTERVIEWS WITH HEALERS

Over the past few years, I have had the privilege of being able to discuss these issues with about 25 practicing healers, nearly all in the UK. As part of a formal research project in the early 2010s, I recorded and transcribed long interviews with ten of them, and I have had less formal discussions with the others. I made notes soon after each meeting, and what follows derives from those notes or from transcripts of the recorded interviews. I met most of the healers in their homes or offices, but some meetings were in my university office or on neutral ground.

Most of those I met with were women, and the majority called themselves simply "energy healers", although a few identified as Reiki or spiritual healers. Two of them said they were crystal healers and another two were unwilling to pin their colors to any particular designation, saying they used a variety of approaches relating to energy. I found all but one of these people convincing and authentic. The one exception was someone who talked a lot about the number of fraudulent people in the healing business, and for this and several other reasons, including his apparent interest in money and fame, I thought that he himself was probably a fraud. After meeting him on several occasions and letting him "treat" me once, I thought he was not someone who deliberately deceives others; I think he believed in his own powers, but that he was not actually doing any energy channeling.

Here are some highlights, with *verbatim* quotes, of what I heard and learnt from the healers I interviewed (excluding the one man of whom I was suspicious).

Early Influences and Experiences, and Sensitivity to Others

The first thing that struck me about these conversations was that many of the participants had early life experiences that made them feel different and extra "sensitive" to others. Several had close relatives (mothers or grandmothers, principally) who were healers before them. Most said they were very sensitive to others; they might be called "highly sensitive people", defined by psychologist Elaine Aron as those who display notable sensitivity to various forms of stimuli (1).

Another term used to describe such people is "empath" because they exhibit a lot of empathy for others.

Some of the relevant quotes on this include:

> "At the age of about six, I could feel things in my hands. My mother taught me the meaning of these feelings and how to balance energy for people"
> "My grandmother was known as a healer by the people in our village"
> "My father could do strange things and was said to be a healer"
> "My sensitivity was always there ... from early childhood ... it scared the life out of me"
> "Since a child, I have been very sensitive to other people's moods and problems"
> "When I am with someone, really connected, I feel I am them; I don't know where I end and they begin"
> "I hear things, I see things, particularly related to other people I am with. I don't often mention that, because it would make people think I am crazy".

What Is Healing?

I asked everyone what they thought healing was. They all talked about it as a process that goes on between individuals, as something that one person helped another to do, rather than as a state, or something that applied to communities, to the world or to nature. It is perhaps not surprising that this was their interpretation of the word, given that they are people who try to help others heal, and that was the context in which I was talking to them.

I also found a great deal of consistency in the answers given. Nearly everyone talked of their healing ability being facilitated by some sort of energy balance, shift or exchange. They did not attribute it to any special powers or abilities of their own.

> *"Allowing the healing energy to work"*
> *"Making sure that all energies are as balanced as possible"*
> *"So it's all about energies, although I see it more as a vibration"*
> *"It's about a universal energy or force which we can all access to allow the body/mind to heal itself, and which can be actively channeled by others"*
> *"It is about energy balance and energy flow"*
> *"We are all vibrational energy; healing is about getting the vibrations right or synchronized"*
> *"It is about energy and raising the energy and directing its purpose – it is a mixture of their energy and some sort of universal energy, and it can be made to do good"*
> *"I see healing as channeling of energy from the 'source' ('God is too limiting a concept') to the benefit of another".*

The Outcome: What Can Healing Do?

I wanted to know what they thought healing did for people, what its outcomes might be.

They all voiced similar descriptions, relating to balance, harmony and related concepts, as reflected in the following quotes.

"(It allows you) to return to a state of natural health"
"Moving from a state of chaos to one of order"
"Someone finding more balance and harmony in their life"
"Returning to a higher state of awareness and connection with the natural state of being"
"The body has the ability to self-heal, or right itself, and the work of the healer is facilitating this ability"
"Finding balance and harmony"
"Deep within each of us, there's a sort of point of perfect energetic balance"
"It can help the person create an energetic environment for the physical body to respond to, to repair itself"
"Balance and coherence"
"Healing is 'letting go' of something that is blocking you"
"I think there is a clear distinction between medical treatment – cutting it out or giving drugs, and healing – helping the body sort itself out".

How Is It Done?

I also tried to explore what each of the healers I spoke to actually did to facilitate healing. Their answers seemed to echo what I had heard from the President of the Doctor–Healer Network, as described in Chapter 4: it is about loving intention.

Here are some of their answers – the ones that struck me with most force:

"By connecting with another in a real and meaningful sense"
"You need to be receptive and just let the 'magic' happen"
"Healing is 'love', you have let go of your ego and work with love for the other"
"Good intention for another and the subjugation of personal ego are critical issues"
"Cultivating a focus of intention – it's all about human intention"
"Anything done with the intention and effect of improving another's situation"

"There has to be focus and intent"
"I think probably it would revolve around the word empathy and
an energetic connection"
"It is about the interaction between healer and healee"
"I am just there, with and for them".

I am fascinated by these quotations, their consistency and the way they accord with what I had learnt from the healers I had interacted with, namely "Fiona", "Sharon" and "Julie". They seemed so straightforward, so consistent, so uncomplicated and real, and yet deeply profound. This all felt like the core of the matter.

My conversations with healers reinforced a conclusion I had come to relatively early on in my work with these gifted people, that energy healing is simply about:

"Focused attention with good intention".

As my work progressed, I expanded my ideas to *"being there for another, subjugating the ego, being receptive and concentrating on love and compassion".*

Can Anyone Be an Energy Healer?

I enjoyed ending my interviews with this question, and I received rather varying answers. Some said yes, anyone could do it if they tried and practiced. Others thought it was a gift given to very few. Between these extremes was the response that energy healing was something that most of us could do, but it was like playing a musical instrument – although most of us could learn how to do it, very few could ever become great musicians.

So, how do you know if someone is a "real" healer I wondered? I well remember the answer of one rather famous healer in the UK, someone who I think is the "real deal", for a variety of reasons, not least the remarkable stories told by many of her clients. "How can I know if someone is really channeling or rebalancing energy?", I asked her as we chatted together in a relaxed way, over a coffee. "Well *you* cannot" she answered "but I can, as I have the sensitivity to pick up energy changes in and around people". I feared that might be the answer. Most of us will never know if it is real or not, because we lack the sensitivity of the real healers.

But I now feel certain in myself that energy healing is real, and that I can do it and could be a powerful healer if I wanted to be. That is because of my experiences. But I am also a doctor, and I am not sure that I can be both a healer and a doctor. Trying to dance between two completely different belief systems and understandings of the world and use them simultaneously while trying to help another person is, I think, beyond me. And I am a bit frightened of my ability and apparent (to others) "power". I don't understand it and worry about the fact that misuse might lead to harm. Perhaps I lack confidence or don't love myself enough and cannot get sufficiently rid of my ego to be a healer?

I have discussed all these issues with a colleague, Prof Sara Warber. She is a primary care doctor in the USA who has also trained in Native American Healing, and who has been doing research on healing with me.

At one of our meetings with other colleagues interested in healing, Sara and I told the rest of the team that we had problems with the "doctor or healer?" issue. We said that we had each experienced moments of "connection" with our patients, that might be healing. The others jumped on this and asked us to discuss it together while they filmed and recorded the discussion.

We agreed, somewhat reluctantly, and almost immediately found ourselves in front of a camera and recording equipment. We had not had time to discuss what we might say, which was probably a good thing. Our colleagues called the short film that we made *"Approaching the Healing Moment"* and they have shown it to selected audiences.

Here is the transcript of most of that film:

"APPROACHING THE HEALING MOMENT": A CONVERSATION

(A filmed discussion between Drs Paul Dieppe (P) and Sara Warber (S))

P: *If I get to that point where I can hold the space between the patient and myself, I feel that I might be getting towards what a healer does. But I think healers are much more sensitive to using that space, and to dealing with energies in it than I am, because I have not been trained in how to do that.*

S: *I think I would agree, that, as a physician, you can approach that special moment, be in that moment, you can know when it is happening, and help it along; however, I think that maybe because we have to have our rational mind working, that tends to anchor us outside that place. If I go into that meditative grounded state, then I think I can be in that energetic healing place, I may feel it but, as you say, we have not been trained and I think healers can access additional energetic help; that's where they live, and can bring it to bear for the patient, in ways that are like what we do when we bring our biomedicine to the fore.*

P: *I agree the difficulty we have is that those concepts are so at odds with the biomedical thinking that keeps tugging us out of that space, and, of course, I am really much more comfortable with biomedicine.*

S: *Absolutely. It's much easier for us; like playing the piano – if you have learnt that instrument, you can make a beautiful sound with it.*

P: *And then someone gives you a saxophone. And that does not work, that's difficult.*

S: *But for people who play the saxophone well, they get soul music from the saxophone: yes, a brilliant analogy.*

…. (pause)
I'm trying to think universally, not doctoring, any kind of healing, and as you approach the healing moment … in some ways, it is about letting go. In Native American traditions, they talk about becoming the hollow bone, and that when you are the hollow bone, then spirit can flow through you, and do whatever it is that's needed for the highest good, and you actually don't want your intention, or yourself, or your thought in the way, you want to get out of the way.

P: *Yes, I think it's about getting out of the way. I think it is about letting go of your ego. And in this world that we live in, getting away from your own ego is very difficult. And, as doctors, we are taught in a way that expands our egos and makes us think we are important, and that we have power over disease. And all that has to go away. But I think there is another element to this. I think approaching the healing point, it is a moment of interaction,*

> *of connection, when both people feel they can trust each other enough to let go. So, I think there is a point of mutual trust.*

S: *Yes, mutuality; I like that. But, to me, the trust, although it can localize in people, I want to take it out of that localization, and understand that it is about the universe.*

P: *OK I agree with that. So, maybe what I am talking about is a necessary, but not a sufficient condition to activate healing, which requires something else which I do not understand.*

S: *Which neither of us understands. We think energy healers understand it better than we do, which is part of what we want to know. And I would take a step further to say that when that moment is reached, and experienced ... both parties are transformed. Both are healed.*

P: *Absolutely.*

S: *And we never talk about that in medicine.*

P: *No. And actually the beauty of it and the joy of it, the interacting with another person and their distress melting away, and you are no longer fielding another person's distress, or being burdened by a problem, you are somewhere else, that is joyful and loving and beautiful and OK.*

S: *Yes. And you are not exhausted by that, in fact, you are fulfilled by it.*

It seems that Dr Warber and I, each of whom had been studying healing alongside continuing with our biomedical practices, had reached some mutual understanding of healing, although each of us found what we were saying, unrehearsed or considered in advance, quite surprising!

Research on "Healing Moments" for Healers

When we discussed this further, we all agreed that there were sudden "moments" when healing could take place. We thought this needed exploring further with healers and their clients.

The opportunity came up when Dr Emmylou Rahtz and I were invited to do a presentation at a study day for healers taking place during a healing exhibition in the UK. We decided to show them the film and then ask the audience to tell us their stories of healing moments.

After screening the film, we distributed cards to participants, asking them to "please tell us a short story about your experiences of a healing moment". They were also asked to provide us with their age and gender, and a note of what sort of a healing practitioner they were, but we did not ask for any information that might identify them, and we kept no record of who was at the meeting, to ensure that the data were anonymized.

We collected 72 postcard responses from the audience of about 120; 75% of these participants were women whose ages ranged from 25 to 75, with a mean age of around 50. Most described themselves as healers, others said they were health care professionals or complementary and alternative practitioners; 32% said they had also received healing from someone else. Qualitative analysis of the stories showed that transformational change was the dominant theme, within which we found three constituent themes – connectivity, quiescence and control. We published the findings in "*Explore*", the journal of science and healing (2).

The three sub-themes of connectivity, quiescence and control were apparent in the video recording we made, as well as on the postcards. Here are some relevant quotes from postcard responses, published in the paper:

Connectivity:

> "*There is a sense of connection within a contained field*"
> "*There is a 'frisson'*"
> "*A point of mutual trust*"
> "*Something passed between us*"

Quiescence:

> "*My clients either fall asleep or feel deep peace*"
> "*A feeling of peace, stillness and benevolence*"

Control:

> "*A healing moment comes when we stop trying to change things and just let things happen*"
> "*From that moment, she took control of her own life and health*"

FIGURE 7.1
A model of key factors in sudden transformational healing processes.

From these data, Dr Rahtz produced a graphic to show how these different aspects of healing moments might fit together (Figure 7.1).

What This Taught Me about Healing

Clearly, the people surveyed were not likely to have been a representative sample of healers in the UK. But the majority of them had a story of sudden change to share with us. And these 72 short stories from healers seemed to confirm the fact that sudden transformational "healing" changes not only occur but are relatively common in the experience of healers. However, I also noted from this research that many of our participants recognized that sudden and gradual changes are not mutually exclusive and that some "healing moments" might be part of a longer healing journey.

Sudden transformational changes are well described in many walks of life, including the Bible (St Paul's epiphany) (3), in other spiritual writings (the work of William James, for example) (4), in psychiatry (where it has been called "quantum change") (5), in sport (suddenly being "in the zone") and in any number of songs, poems and other works of art, and we talk of "love at first sight". Clearly, human beings are susceptible to sudden life-transforming moments of change.

Furthermore, there seemed to be something spiritual or metaphysical in some of the stories; the idea that there was a connection with something else, outside of both healer and client. Again, this mirrors much of what we read about sudden transformations in other contexts.

Another learning point for me was the recurring emphasis put on connectivity between the two people involved in the healing (healer and client). Within Dr Rahtz's model, it seemed that the quiescence and control elements were necessary factors that allowed the connectivity, and that the transformational change stemmed from the connection made. However, that point was also made by Dr Warber and me in our filmed conversation, so it could be that we had "primed" our audience to respond in such a manner.

There is "magic" in the deep meaningful connections that are made between people in any situation, as we had also witnessed in Lourdes. They can be transformational and healing.

But, for many of us, healing is a long haul rather than a sudden event. That long haul may be interrupted by moments of change or insight, but, for many of us, it takes years to heal from trauma or illness.

"LONG HEALING JOURNEYS"

I was able to explore some of those long journeys with Dr Warber and others. The idea for this project arose at my first meeting with the Nova Institute for Health of People, Places, and the Planet in Baltimore (then known as The Institute for Integrative Health – TIIH), when I was appointed as one of their scholars. I talked about wanting to do a research project called "moving toward an understanding of healing", and one of the other new scholars (Dr Kurt Stange) said that he might be able to access data, collected by Dr. John Scott in the USA, that would help me with my project. Some months later, three US-based doctors and I joined up with Dr Scott to re-analyze some of his findings from a previous study.

Some years earlier, Dr Scott had interviewed people who had been identified by their primary care physician as having "healed" from the consequences of illness or life trauma. Our plan was to look at these interviews and try to understand the healing process from the perspective of the patients interviewed, as opposed to the physician and his or her ability to facilitate healing (the focus of John Scott's first analysis). The group of us studied 23 long, wonderful interviews and got together for a three-day intensive retreat in Vermont to try and bring our findings together.

We published the results in the *British Medical Journal* (6).

Many of the people John Scott had interviewed had been through extreme illness or trauma, including problems like drug addiction and sexual abuse, as well as serious chronic diseases. All had found their way through this to a state in which they were living fulfilling lives. They had got through it and been able to move on, and they had all done it differently with lots of bumps on their long roads to recovery – their healing took place in fits and starts over an extended period. We found three interrelated key themes within their healing journeys:

1. Making connections
2. Finding safety and trust
3. Acquiring resources and skills.

Here are some quotes that illustrate each of those themes:

Making connections

"Once I started connecting with people, I started healing"
"Family and friends was the most important part of it"
"The healing process is about connecting"
"I got close to my swim coach – I think that was a healing relationship"

But, for others, connections could be with pets, with your God, with nature and with creativity, as well as with other people.

Finding safety and trust
Several respondents commented that meaningful connections could not be made in the absence of a feeling of safety and trust:

"Trust is really important"

Acquiring new resources and skills
The connections made, in safety and trust, were facilitated by necessary skills and resources, such as taking responsibility and acquiring a positive attitude:

"You have to be positive"
"I have to take responsibility"
"Persistence was critical"
"I am still trucking away"

If people could make connections, then we found four emergent properties that were crucial to their healing:

- Hope
- Finding new meaning
- Self-acceptance
- A desire to help others

> *"Gradually, I came to believe that maybe I could live a normal life again"*
> *"I didn't want to feel just passive; I could be doing something for somebody else too"*

We developed a graphic to illustrate their journeys to that position, journeys that had their ups and downs, and often took place over several years. The graphic in Figure 7.2 illustrates healing as an "emergent property" – something that emerges from a varied lot of complex, antecedent factors in one's life.

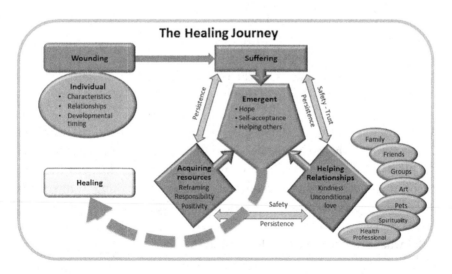

FIGURE 7.2
A graphic of factors involved in people's "Healing Journeys", derived from our research on their stories (Scott et al. (6)).

What This Taught Me about Healing

What healing seemed to be about for these people was regaining the ability to live a fulfilling life that often included altruistic work (for example, a couple of them had become counselors). To use another concept, originally from ancient Greece, healing for these people involved getting to a point where they could once again "flourish" – using the Aristotelian meaning of flourishing as living to the best of our ability, for the good of ourselves and others in society. And a critical element in their journeys was making meaningful connections with others, a theme I will say more about later in this book.

These people had disease, trauma and distress of the sort that I understood from my clinical work and personal experiences, and their journeys included a number of things that I could relate to directly. There were not many reports of allusions to any metaphysical or mysterious element in this type of healing. Perhaps that was because the participants had been recruited by doctors from conventional clinical practice.

I have been asked what I, as a doctor, think these findings taught me about how best to help patients who are suffering terribly, and need to heal.

Here is my answer:

- Be there for the other person with love and compassion
- Create a safe, trusting environment
- Be positive and provide hope
- Encourage connections with others
- Encourage self-acceptance
- Look for opportunities for them to help others
- Remind them to "hang in there".

As instructive as this study was, it was far removed from the world of people who call themselves healers, and those who go to them for healing. But there was one important similarity: connecting. This was the first major theme we extracted from the interviews: making connections with other people seemed to be critical in the facilitation of their healing journeys.

But what is it like to be the client – the "healee"?

THE EXPERIENCES OF PEOPLE WHO GO TO HEALERS

A project my colleagues and I undertook to try to further understand the perspectives of healers and their clients involved surveys in the UK.

Soon after starting to work on healing, Dr Sara Warber asked me to help her with a paper she had been asked to write, namely a review of the perspectives of healing practitioners, and was recruiting a small team to help her. We reviewed the literature and, in addition, I conducted a small survey of UK healers, asking them about their priorities for research. One of the most interesting things to emerge from this was that healers wanted to know more about the experiences of their clients, the "healees" – healers did not know much about what it was like for healees (7).

A few years later, we were able to have a go at answering the question that had been raised about the experience of the clients of healers. In collaboration with the Confederation of Healing Organizations in the UK (facilitated by Sue Knight), and with the help of Dr Rhatz (who led the study) and Sue Child, Dr Warber and I surveyed clients of UK healers (8).

We found that women outnumbered men as clients of healers and that the main reasons for their consulting with a healer included mental health problems (such as anxiety or depression) and chronic pain. Interestingly, the majority reported more than one problem – so-called multi-morbidity – which is seen as a problem for orthodox medicine that prefers to concentrate on a single issue.

The immediate experiences of being treated by a healer were interesting. We had responses from 278 different people, and the most common outcomes they listed are shown in Table 7.1.

TABLE 7.1

The Most Common Immediate Outcomes of Healing Reported by 278 Clients of UK Energy Healers (from Rhatz et al. (8))

Outcome	Numbers Reporting
A sense of relaxation	173
Improved well-being	141
Altered sensations	76
Less pain	40

(The figures add up to more than 278 because several respondents reported more than one main outcome.)

The finding that clients of healers report relaxation, improved well-being and less pain are in accord with a few other studies reported in the literature. However, the reports of "altered sensations, which included feelings of warmth and heat, and tingling or pressure, in addition to seeing colors", were particularly interesting. Here are a few illustrative quotes that we included in our publication:

- *"An all-over warmth. An intense warmth at left side of face and magenta lights"*
- *"Sensation of little bubbles rising up the back of neck and spine"*
- *"The heat was amazing ... I didn't want it to end"*

These sensations are also what I experienced when my knee was being treated by healer "Sharon", and "Fiona" also mentioned their occurrence when she administers healing to people. Other studies in the literature also report such sensations, but what do they mean? We speculated in our publication that they "could indicate that some genuine (energy) transaction was taking place between healer and healee". Other researchers, working in the USA, Germany and Norway, have also collected data from healers and their clients. There is a good deal of similarity between their findings and ours, even if language and interpretations vary somewhat. The consensus would appear to be that many people feel better, more relaxed and are in less pain or anxiety after healing than before it, and that these changes are often accompanied by odd sensory experiences during the healing process.

One American study came up with the appealing idea that such healing interventions resulted in what they call "unstuckness" (9).

What This Study Taught Me about Healing

This research project was not of a high scientific quality, for a variety of reasons discussed in our publication, but I did find it helpful and informative. It is very easy to dismiss healers, and the healing process that they and their clients describe, as "hocus-pocus" or "woo-woo nonsense" and doctors and scientists are prone to do that, from, I believe, a position of ignorance about healing. The finding that people feel better after going to a healer is easily written off as "just a placebo effect", but the occurrence of odd sensations during treatment, and the consistency of this finding among the few publications in this area, are less easily dismissed.

This study confirmed my increasing conviction that something real, metaphysical and rather wonderful can go on when two people get together with the intent of activating healing.

REFERENCES

1. Aron E. *The Highly Sensitive Person: How to Thrive When the World Overwhelms You*. London: Thorsons Publishing Group, 1996.
2. Rhatz E, Bonell S, Goldingay S, Warber S, Dieppe P. Transformational changes in health status: A qualitative exploration of healing moments. *Explore* 2017; 13: 296–305.
3. The Bible: Acts 9; 3–9.
4. James W. *The varieties of Religious Experience*. e-books, Salt Lake City: Project Gutenberg 1902.
5. Miller WR. The phenomenon of quantum change. *J Clin Psychol* 2004; 60: 453–460.
6. Scott JG, Sara L Warber SL, Dieppe P, David Jones D, Stange KC. Healing journey: A qualitative analysis of the healing experiences of Americans suffering from trauma and illness. *BMJ Open* 2017; 7: e016771.
7. Warber SL, Bruyere R, Weintrub K, Dieppe P. A consideration of the perspectives of healing practitioners on research into energy healing. *Glob Adv Health Med* 2015; 4 (suppl): 72–78.
8. Rhatz E et al. Clients of UK Healers: A mixed methods survey of their demography, health problems, and experiences of healing. *Comp Therap Clin Pract* 2019; 35: 72–77.
9. Koithan M et al. The process of whole person healing: 'unstuckness' and beyond. *J Altern Complement Med* 2007; 13: 659–668.

8

Public Views on the Nature of Healing

A key question at the front of my mind, throughout my own journey into the world of healing, has been: "What is healing?". Most conventional health care professionals tend to equate it with the repair of a wound or fracture, rather than anything more holistic. My colleagues and I wondered what people not involved in health care thought that healing was all about. Four of us took on this project: Drs Sarah Goldingay and Emmylou Rhatz from the University of Exeter, UK, Professor Sara Warber from the University of Michigan Ann Arbor, USA, and myself; Emmylou, Sarah and I designed the protocol and conducted data collection, and Sara Warber helped with the analysis of data.

INTERVIEWS WITH ORDINARY PEOPLE ON HEALING

We decided to find out what the word means to "ordinary" people in England. We thought we would ask them the question "What does the word healing mean to you?" The first time we had a go at getting answers to this question from members of the public was at the Eden Project, a visitor attraction in Southwest England. The Eden Project is a nature-based center, which celebrates our dependence on plant life. It includes huge "geodomes", in which climates of the tropical rainforests or the Mediterranean are maintained, and appropriate flora and fauna allowed to thrive. There are also some 30 acres of outside gardens and exhibitions for visitors to enjoy. We obtained permission to spend a day there asking visitors about healing.

DOI: 10.4324/9781003461814-10

We were not sure how best to go about eliciting answers, so we decided to try out three different options:

1. To ask for written responses on a piece of paper
2. To ask people to tell us their answer while recording what they said
3. To ask them to draw a picture to illustrate their answer and explain that to us orally

Three of us tried all three methods on the first day. The early results were fascinating. People were happy to give us a few minutes of their time, but they found it really difficult to write anything meaningful about healing down on a piece of paper or to verbalize an answer. When we asked people to draw a picture, however, amazing things happened! There would often be a giggle, followed by the phrase "I am no good at drawing", but that was soon followed by the production of some sort of an image. Sometimes, that image seemed as much of a surprise to the person drawing it as it was to us. We encouraged people to talk about what they were doing while drawing. They were saying things like "Well, I don't know, but I seem to be drawing a sun, and it is yellow ... yes, it has to be yellow; why? ... and ... oh, I see, that is what I think healing is, it is energy from elsewhere coming into us – yes, that's it, that is what I think healing is". It appeared as if the idea of an image allowed them to access aspects of their understanding that they might not have been immediately aware of, and to use metaphor to describe what healing was about in a way that was difficult for them to verbalize or write about.

This was a breakthrough in understanding for me: the language of healing is metaphor.

Images of Healing

I vividly remember some of the drawings I got from people that first afternoon – they were wonderful. For example, there was the rather disheveled-looking middle-aged man who looked at me very strangely, then took his bit of paper and a pencil off to a table by himself and made a drawing. He came back and showed it to me – a rough sketch of the earth with a sticking plaster on it (Figure 8.1), and some scribbled words beneath. "We need to heal the earth" he said, and sauntered off before I could ask him anything.

Sticking plaster on the Earth.

FIGURE 8.1

"Sticking plaster on the earth": A pencil drawing made by a member of the public asked for his views on healing.

Then, there was the family whom I approached. The parents said they would have a go together, but that their teenage daughter was much better at drawing than they were, so maybe she might do it too? The teenager said "Sure, I will have a go, but what do I have to draw?" "I want you to draw a picture of what the word healing means to you", I said. "OK", she responded; picking up a piece of paper and a few crayons, she moved away from me, while the parents fussed around, wondering what to do. The parents got nowhere, but their daughter came back with a wonderful picture of a heart being held in hands, as shown in Figure 8.2. "That's what healing is about", she said, and wandered off.

By the end of the day, we were thrilled by what had happened. But we knew that, if we were going to get such work accepted as good research, worthy of publication, we had to tighten up the methods and have a set protocol. We decided to use crayons, on the basis of their having a feeling of playfulness and joy, and to frame the questions as follows:

- Opener – "Can I have a few minutes of your time for some research we are doing?"
- *If yes*

Hands healing with love.

FIGURE 8.2
"Hands healing with love": A crayon drawing made by a teenage girl in response to the question what does the word healing mean to you.

- "I would like you to draw a picture for us, using these crayons and this paper, and to talk to us about your picture when you have finished it, and we will record what you say".
- *If yes*
- "OK, I am going to ask you a question, and I want you to try to draw the first image that pops into your head. Don't think about it too much, don't try to analyze the question, just go with whatever image you get, OK?"
- *If yes*
- "What does the word healing mean to you?"

We asked our participants to sign a consent form for the research to allow us to use the data, *after* doing the drawing, as we thought that doing it beforehand would have "primed" them (given them time to think about the answer first). The protocol worked well, and we were able to get a lot of drawings from a variety of different people in different sites, along with recordings of what they said or, failing that, notes made by us immediately afterwards.

We have used this method with health care professionals at medical meetings in different countries, and with groups of students, as well as other groups, and the results are always fascinating.

The main body of work has been with members of the public in the UK. We have collected data at a museum in Exeter, at a music festival, and at a health and wellbeing exhibition, as well as at the Eden Project. The data were rigorously analyzed and published in the *Journal of Complementary Therapies in Medicine* (1).

A Brief Summary of What We Found

The majority of people described healing as a process (rather than an intervention, an outcome or a state), although there were a few who thought of it as an intervention. Three main "models" of the healing process emerged from the data analysis:

1) Healing comes from a great external force. This was most often illustrated with pictures of the sun, and the word "energy" was often used (Figure 8.3);
2) Healing comes from other people, who may be health care professionals, healers or others, and who facilitate healing;
3) Healing comes from within; we have the ability to self-heal.

There was overlap between these three models. For example, the person who drew a sun radiating energy into life below, allowing it to heal itself.

The concept of healing as "wholeness" was often mentioned, sometimes illustrated by circles, and love by hearts. One respondent combined these ideas with energy flow in one illustration, as shown in Figure 8.4.

"Wholeness" can mean many different things to people, and we found it hard to know exactly what each individual was trying to convey. However, words like "integrity" and "completeness" were sometimes offered.

We published some illustrative quotes, and showed a few pictures in our publication; here are some of the quotes:

FIGURE 8.3
"Energy from above is shining down on the earth allowing all living things to heal". A crayon drawing from a member of the public trying to explain healing.

- *"I have drawn ... a physical sun but it could be like spirit or some sort of consciousness or a pure awareness ... seeing through the relative, and the absolute ... putting it into perspective"*
- *"A never-ending universal life force giving out rays to cover everybody and everything in a positive way"*
- *"Healing hands ... healing through massage and alternative therapies, that sort of thing"*
- *"The word healing to me meant a bit more than just being fixed"*
- *"Love is the best form of healing"*
- *"Healing means being in control of your own mind and your own destiny. I feel that we're all capable of self-healing"*

For me, those sorts of quotes, alongside the pictures, illustrate the sophisticated, nuanced and metaphysical nature of what the word "healing" means to people who are not involved in health care.

FIGURE 8.4
"A heart for love, a circle for wholeness and energy flow". A crayon drawing by a member of the public who brought together many of the themes expressed by others.

Some of the pictures and stories that accompanied them were very moving.

As already mentioned, I was particularly struck by the fact that many people did not understand the image that popped into their head. Most seemed to be able to interpret it as they went along with the drawing, but some never made sense of it.

For example, I was with a middle-aged man who started to draw a blanket after I had asked him what the word healing meant to him. As he went along, he said, "That's odd, the blanket seems to be in the garden, not in the house". He went on drawing, producing a lovely image, as shown in Figure 8.5, but finished by telling me he did not understand it, before moving on.

Others told long and involved stories that included several different themes. For example, a lady I spoke to drew a complex picture of energy both radiating from elsewhere, and moving between people, with plants and animals, as well as people, responding to this energy flow while basking in sunlight. She said that the healing energy is part of the Universe (it does not come from the sun, she assured me) and that this could heal all living things and make them whole.

I have been amazed by the way in which the use of drawing has encouraged an intuitive way of thinking about healing within people,

FIGURE 8.5
"A blanket". A crayon drawing of a blanket in a room, surrounded by plants, drawn by a man who did not seem to understand why this image came to him when asked to illustrate what the word healing meant to him.

helping them capture concepts that are hard to verbalize and to express ideas that they could not get out in any other way.

As I have said, metaphor seemed to be the language of healing. In addition to the idea of love (hearts) and wholeness (circles), we heard of energy (often represented by a drawing of the sun) and of growth (with pictures of plants growing).

Nature was present in lots of pictures and positive stories were told around them. Many people put an emphasis on interaction with nature facilitating healing or on us being a part of the whole natural world that was in need of healing.

A few of the responses were more consistent with a biomedical understanding of healing, rather than a metaphysical or spiritual one, particularly those done by children. For example, one youngster of about five or six years of age drew us the picture shown below of a cut on her leg and a plaster being applied (Figure 8.6).

One or two people drew an ambulance or some other specific medical image, most notably, a group of medical students whom I came across at the Eden Project. They were confused by the question. One drew a picture of a hospital, another a blood transfusion. I thought to myself that they, just like myself in the first part of my life, had been enculturated into biomedical/scientific thinking.

In addition, we heard one or two personal stories of illness, with accompanying pictures. One of those that struck me most forcibly was the woman who drew the picture shown in Figure 8.7, crying as she told us:

"My mother was dying. The nurse came and held her hand. That made all the difference".

What This Work Taught Me About Healing

I learnt an awful lot from this work. Perhaps the thing that struck me most strongly was that nearly every lay person that we have spoken to in this way (and they number well over a hundred) has been able to engage with the question. They have expressed some opinions about the nature of healing, usually in a spiritual or metaphysical sense. In contrast, most health care professionals, of whom I have asked the same question, have

FIGURE 8.6
"Wound healing". A drawing made by a young child sitting alongside her mother when both were asked what the word healing meant to them.

looked at me strangely, before mumbling something about the repair of wounds and the value of inflammation.

We cannot claim that our participants were representative of the population of the UK. Not everyone goes to museums or nature parks. The people who drew pictures for us may well have been more curious and enquiring than many others. Nevertheless, I found the findings exciting and encouraging. They reinforced my opinion that the medical profession could learn about healing from the general population, as well as CAM practitioners and healers.

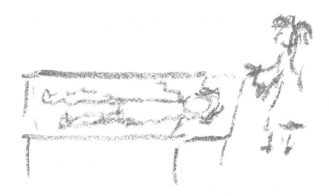

FIGURE 8.7
"My mother was dying and the nurse held her hand, which made all the difference". A drawing made by a distressed woman asked to illustrate healing.

The insight about metaphor also seems very important for those of us who wish to do more research into the phenomenology of healing. It means that we cannot easily use the "normal" scientific methods of the sort I had used when doing research into arthritis, health services or placebos. They are based on a purely materialistic view of the world, whereas what I was hearing was that ordinary people have a concomitant spiritual view of it. Our healing research needs to be based as much or more in the humanities than in the sciences.

Finally, there was the beauty of it all, not only the beautiful pictures but the wonderful, nuanced and sophisticated ideas that people expressed. As well as the beautiful privilege of being able to interact with strangers in this way.

Exhibiting the Material

Excited by our findings and the pictures we had obtained, we showed the work to colleagues and presented our findings at meetings locally, in addition to publishing some of it. Many people were interested. One such person was the Lead for Arts in a large hospital trust in the Southwest of England. One day, she asked me to develop an exhibition for her hospital, to be put up in about two years' time. Well, two years seemed like a long time in the future, so I gaily said "Yes, sure, no problem", and went on my way. I did not give it much thought for over a year. And then, suddenly, I was scheduled to put up an exhibition in the main hospital corridor/ gallery in some six months' time! I panicked; I had no idea how to do that. Fortunately, the Institute for Integrative Health (TIIH.org, now the Nova Institute for Health of People, Places, and Planet) agreed to help fund it, and I was able to recruit artist Deborah Weinreb to design and develop the fire-proof, linen panels (her idea) for the exhibition of pictures and quotations. We collected many quotations about healing, some from members of the public, others from reading or the internet. Deborah worked with us to sort these into themes for the exhibition. She did a fantastic job, and the exhibition went up on time.

The main themes were:

- The natural environment as a stimulus to healing
- Making connections
- The concept of wholeness
- Growth and rejuvenation

As shown in Figure 8.8, which shows the first few panels of the exhibition, we called the exhibition "How are you healing?"

The exhibition was on show at the first hospital for several months, before moving to a public exhibition space in another large general hospital for a further six months. Subsequently, it was shown at the Nova Institute for

FIGURE 8.8
"How are you healing?" A photograph of part of our exhibition shown in a hospital corridor. The exhibition, called "How are you healing?", was shown at medical meetings as well as in hospitals in Southwest England. It was sponsored by the Nova Institute for Health of People, Places, and Planet.

Health Headquarters in Baltimore, USA, at a Complementary Medicine meeting (also in the USA) and in an arts university in Finland. At each of these venues, we tried to interact with people viewing the work to get some idea of their response to it.

We were particularly keen to learn how hospital staff, patients and visitors reacted to our work. So, at each hospital, we put out feedback requests, in the form of cards with some simple questions and space for a general comment. In addition, we did observational work to see who looked at it and for how long, stopped some people who were looking at the work and sought their views, as well as conducted small focus groups with medical staff.

Our observational work was fascinating. Colleague Dr Emmylou Rhatz and I spent days just watching what was going on as people passed through the corridor which held our first showing, keeping notes on what we observed, and interviewing a few people who showed interest. Huge numbers of people passed through that space, and about 80% of them appeared to pay no attention at all to what was on show. Many were hurrying along, staring at their phone, or clearly thinking about something else completely. But 12% of those walking by paused to look at one or more of the panels, and 4% stopped for a while to have a good look at them. The people most likely to spend time looking at our work were patients and visitors, rather than staff, although a number of nurses were interested. Hardly any doctors took any notice.

The results from our interviews, feedback cards and focus groups reinforced our initial finding that, of members of staff, the nurses were most likely to be interested in the work and doctors the least likely (some porters, cleaners and other staff members were also fascinated). We obtained some interesting quotes from nurses, in particular, such as:

"It is wonderful to see something about healing in a hospital".

This quote seemed in accord with my view that hospitals do not generally think about healing; they concentrate on trying to cure.

Nearly all the comments, from interviews, focus groups, or written on feedback cards, were favorable.

Some commented on the artwork and content, for example:

- *"Lovely bright artwork"*
- *"It is great to see inspiring artworks"*
- *"Such thought-provoking words, full of healing in themselves"*

Others were very personal and moving, for example:

> *"I am a broken man who cannot be fixed. I sit here crying, and hoping for some healing. This exhibition has given me hope; maybe I will heal one day".*
>
> *"This exhibition has had a profound effect on me … it has been a comfort … It is bringing tears to my eyes and touching a deeper level than I can easily share".*
>
> *"I saw it first when I had just received a cancer diagnosis and it gave me hope and confidence to see such a holistic approach being expressed".*

Overall, we concluded that our efforts had been worthwhile. Even if only a small minority of those who saw it showed an interest, we clearly had a positive effect on some individuals. In addition, we wondered if we could help develop "healing spaces" in hospitals, alongside artists, by using work like ours on healing and talking about the subject openly.

However, our discussions and focus groups with doctors were less rewarding. Many appeared to have serious difficulty connecting with the concept of healing and could not find ways to understand the relevance, either to them or their work, of what we were talking about.

Healing may be a troublesome concept for the medical profession, but most of the lay people we spoke to had no such problems. It seems clear to me that we need to bridge this gap between the constrained, biomedical, materialistic view of the world which our health care professionals hold and the more spiritual, holistic and pluralistic world that most other people (and therefore the patients of the health care professionals) are familiar with.

That is what this book is about.

REFERENCE

1. Rhatz E, Warber S, Dieppe P. Understanding public perceptions of healing: An arts-based qualitative study. *Complement Ther Med* 2019 Aug; 45: 25–32.

9

Nature, Art and Healing

We have seen in previous chapters that healing involves transformative experiences, which can be triggered by many different things. We commonly associate such changes with interactions between people – the healer and the "healee", for example – or with spiritual events, as in Lourdes. But our research with lay people, outlined in Chapter 8, suggested that nature was another important factor in their understanding of healing.

My own transformational experiences have had more to do with art and nature, than anything else. Art, nature and healing are therefore the subjects of this chapter.

MOZART AND THE SEA

I had taken my family on a camping holiday to the seaside in Cornwall. One morning, I had to leave my wife and children on the beach and drive the car back up to the campsite to collect something. It was a short drive and I soon found whatever it was we needed, and I set out to drive back to the beach car park. I put on the car radio, and the second movement of Mozart's Piano Concerto #20 was playing; I turned the volume up. As I rounded a corner, the sea was spread out in front of me, with the blue sky above and the yellow sand at its edge. As I looked at that wonderful view, with Mozart's joyful music blaring out, I was suddenly transported to a place of pure love and joy. I was somewhere else, connected to the whole Universe, which was full of love. I don't know if I was still driving the car, or if it was driving itself; in a way, I was not there, I was "out of this world" and embraced by something infinitely more loving, beautiful and immense. It was wonderful; one of

DOI: 10.4324/9781003461814-11

those rare, spiritual, transcendent moments that stay with you forever, even though they do not last long. And it was triggered by a magical work of art by that genius of a composer, Mozart, along with a beautiful view of one of nature's wonders.

NATURE, ART AND HEALING

In this book, I have been exploring aspects of healing, based on a mixture of stories of my experiential knowledge and formal research. So far, I have described some of my experiences and research work with professional healers, who try to help others heal. But healing can take place without direct human interactions. Nature and art can both trigger healing. It can take place in the woods, when you are with animals, in an art gallery, in the theatre, and in many, many other situations, including with Mozart at the seaside.

The importance of both art and nature for healing were particularly well-known to many ancient civilizations and are still very important to some Indigenous people, whose healing practices make extensive use of them. For example, shamanic healing rituals in South America and elsewhere often take place in the natural environment, and involve drumming, dance and artistic adornment of those involved.

In addition, nature and art are both being used therapeutically in the West. There are some specific examples that fit the disease model of health in which we are embedded. We use dance to help people with Parkinson's disease, and we prescribe walking in woodlands for people with mental health problems (as part of the "social prescribing" movement in the UK). But, in our culture, we are more likely to discuss the value of nature and art in terms of their ability to help us improve our well-being, or make us happier, rather than to cure or to heal us.

If we do discuss the healing properties of nature and the arts, then we tend to badge them as "self-healing" measures. I do not like the term self-healing. In one sense, we could say that all healing is self-healing if it is about a transformational change within an individual. But I believe that healing is always relational: it is about connecting with something or somebody else. That connection can be with a bird, a tree, a painting or a poem, rather than another person, but it is a connection nonetheless.

There is another shared facet of the ability of nature and the arts to facilitate healing: in either case, it can involve an individual actively or passively. By this, I mean you can either do it yourself, or enjoy the works of others. So, you may be transformed by seeing or hearing the art of another, or you might be painting pictures or making music yourself. Similarly, you may marvel at the wonders of the natural world as you passively interact with it, or you might nurture animals, cultivate plants or create healing gardens yourself.

In this chapter, I will discuss nature and art separately and then try to weave the common threads between them.

NATURE AS A HEALER

What do I mean by nature? I mean the whole wondrous environment of this planet that we live in: its animals and plants, its coastlines and rivers, its deserts and woodlands – the whole, marvelous, living thing.

All of us have, from time to time, felt the sheer joy of being a part of our environment, to be surrounded by such incredible beauty and diversity. Sometimes, these moments of wonder are so intense, spiritual and otherworldly that they become moments of what the philosopher Patrick Curry calls "enchantment" (1): those magical, mystical, spiritual experiences that can be transformational and thus facilitate healing. I have had many moments of wonder and joy, and just one or two experiences of enchantment – including my "Mozart at the sea" moment.

Another of those "moments" took place in the natural environment.

A Walk in the Woods

I was staying with friends on Vancouver Island. One afternoon, we decided to go for a walk in a nearby woodland. It was a quiet, warm autumn day, with dappled light filtering through the trees. The woods ran downhill to a small river in the valley below, and streams meandered through the area we were walking in. We could hear the birds singing, the gentle rustle of leaves, and the trickling of the water in the stream. There was a heady smell of pine in the air. I loved it. I wandered off the path, away from my wife and friends for a while, just to "be there", alone, in this lovely spot.

That was when it happened: one of those fantastic, transcendent moments of enchantment and understanding, knowing that I was a part of something wonderful, something loving and something infinitely bigger than seems possible. I was an integral part of it all! It did not last long, although I don't know how long. But it was extraordinary: I "knew" that I was a part of a loving, beautiful, meaningful Universe.

In Chapter 2, I described the ways in which getting back in touch with nature helped me on my own healing journey after being a hostage. But the event in Vancouver was different and much more profound. Both types of experiences in nature, the walk around the lake with my wife after my release, and that transcendent "moment" in the woods on Vancouver Island, helped me to heal from my own trauma. They have been important triggers to my gradual change from a purely materialistic, scientific understanding and investigation of the world to a more spiritual journey; one that begins to recognize and accept the metaphysical dimension of healing.

I have also had the pleasure of working with someone who deeply understands the healing power of nature.

"All You Need Is Trees, Water, Stones and Animals"

"What you need to activate healing is quite simple, Paul", Fred tells me; "All you need is trees, water, stones and animals, and that's what we have in the Green Road".

Fred Foote is a retired military doctor (and an accomplished poet, (2)), who knows a lot about the need for healing after the trauma of military encounters.

His "Green Road" project is a wonderful example of a "healing woodland". He has seen a lot of damaged people during his time in service and at Walter Reed National Military Medical Center in Washington DC, where he has worked with war veterans faced with post-traumatic stress disorder, traumatic brain injury, amputation, and other life-changing injuries. Some patients also struggle with mental health problems such as depression, addiction and aggressive behaviors and, as often as not, the people Fred comes across have a mix of these problems resulting from their wartime experiences.

Fred noticed that the Walter Reed campus included woodland that was perfect for the development of a nature-based healing space. Encompassing a 1.5-acre natural wooded area with a stream and wildlife, it was well-suited to support the recovery of damaged veterans. It contained all four of Fred's core elements needed for healing:

- Trees – lots of them
- Water – a beautiful running stream
- Stones – lots of large old stones at the edge of the stream
- Animals – deer roaming wild, as well as birds and other small animals

He took me to see it. Walter Reed is a massive hospital complex, crammed full of daunting concrete buildings, and it is close to the city of Washington, DC. As we pulled into the multi-storey car park, it was hard to believe that there could be a healing space nearby. But just a short walk from the ward buildings, we entered the natural woodland area, the site of the Green Road. Fred organized the construction of a half-mile path through this natural area, which could be easily navigated by wheelchair users, the "walking wounded" as well as veterans without physical disability. Within this space, his team constructed a commemorative pavilion for lost colleagues, resting benches, a communal pavilion and a council meeting ring. It is a place for reflection, relaxation and restoration. As I wandered through it with him, I could feel myself benefitting from the beauty, simplicity and sense of compassion built into its design.

I had the time to just be "present" in that natural space. I sat on one of Fred's rocks, adjacent to the "road" going through the area. I listened to the birds singing and the babble of the water flowing through the stream below me. I breathed in the pure air and smelled the pines. I watched a deer stroll casually around the woodland surrounding me. I felt my body relax, my shoulders slump, my breathing slow and that constant hubbub of thoughts in my mind calm down.

It was a privilege to be in this lovely natural environment, which is pictured in Figure 9.1.

And perhaps Fred is right. Maybe what we need to activate healing is quite simple: trees, water, stones and animals. Maybe it is about making connections with these things, and within ourselves when surrounded by these natural elements.

Good research is being undertaken on the value of the Green Road. In a recent publication, the team showed that a 20-minute walk on the Green

FIGURE 9.1
A photograph of part of the "Green Road" at Walter Reed Hospital, Washington DC

Road resulted in significantly better outcomes than a walk of the same duration in a more urban environment. Participants reported feeling more relaxed, safe and calm when on the Green Road (3).

The Use of Nature and Natural Spaces in Hospitals and Health Care

One of the first studies to show that nature could help patients in hospitals was a famous trial published by Roger Ulrich in 1984, showing, as the title suggests (4), that having a view of nature from your ward improved recovery after surgery.

That finding led to a great interest in nature and healing and in hospital design. Healing gardens can now be found on the grounds of many hospitals.

In addition "nature" can now be given out as a prescription for mental health disorders and other problems in the UK as part of our "social prescribing" movement (5). This is because it has been shown, by Shanahan and colleagues, for example, that nature-based interventions (of which there are many) help improve health and well-being (6). A particular example is the "walk and talk" movement, showing that walking and talking with others in natural surroundings can have powerful beneficial effects on mental health (7).

Gardens and gardening play useful roles in rehabilitation in both hospitals and prisons. Patients or prisoners are encouraged to grow their own flowers and vegetables in these gardens, as such activities have beneficial effects on their health and well-being, as shown by Cooper and others (8).

THE HEALING POWER OF NATURE

The healing power of nature has been recognized by people of all cultures from the beginning of time. But, as I have said, our current Western narrative is about the wonders of the natural environment for improvement of health and well-being, rather than healing. There are a plethora of books about nature and well-being, such as those of Hardman and Williams (9, 10).

Many theories have been put forward to explain our love of nature, perhaps most notably the "biophilia hypothesis" a term first used by Erich Fromm in 1964, but made popular by the famous American biologist E.O. Wilson (11). Biophilia describes the innate affinity that humans have for all other living systems, or, as Wilson says "the connections that human beings subconsciously seek with the rest of life".

Then, there is Richard Louv's famous book about "nature deficit disorder" (12), in which he proposes that the converse is also true: not being in nature causes health problems, particularly in children. To date, this idea has not gained much traction within the scientific or medical communities.

Although nature deficit disorder may not be well supported by science, the scientific evidence for the value of our being in natural environments is massive and uniformly positive. Meta-analyses (combinations of all available relevant data) reveal large effect sizes for the value of nature for a variety of physical and mental disorders, as well as our general sense of well-being (13, 14) (i.e., on average, most people show statistically significant improvements in health in response to a nature-based intervention).

But what is "the natural environment", and how do we best make use of it for health and well-being?

There are several categories of nature, including:

- Urban green spaces, such as parks
- Water features, including lakes, rivers and the seaside
- Forests and woodland areas
- Open countryside and farmland
- True "wilderness", minimally disturbed by humanity

There are different ways of enjoying these spaces, including being in them, looking at them from a home or car window, watching nature programs on the television or looking at nature-related reels on Instagram and the like. Or maybe just having pictures of them in your home. In addition, there are multiple ways in which we use natural spaces – we enjoy them in our leisure time, choosing to go for walks in the park, or visit the seaside or we utilize them as interventions that should be harnessed to help others improve their health, well-being and healing.

When I say "we" in this context, I am speaking as a privileged white person who has always lived in the affluent West, who was brought up with access to natural spaces, and could visit the seaside. This means that nature is important to me. But that is not the case for everyone. Some people have had upbringings that led to them being terrified of open spaces and nature. Others, like me, find animals a problem because of allergies or early experiences (my first memory is of being knocked down by a huge dog, and the dog slavering over me – I have been frightened of dogs ever since).

So the healing power of nature, like other forms of healing, depends on culture, context and the individual.

The Value of Natural Spaces to Our Health and Healing

Conventional science has offered us two main types of explanations for the value of nature: the physical and the psychological.

Physical explanations revolve around two main ideas. The first is that it is about physical activity – we get out into the woods and walk more than we would have done otherwise, and that is why it is good for us. The second theory is that there is something chemical going on: trees and other plants secrete chemicals into the air (such as antimicrobial phytoncides) that do us good, and the air is different in natural spaces than it is in our homes, with more negative ions, for example. An overarching concept among some of those who believe in the physical explanations is that being in natural spaces improves our immune function.

Psychological explanations are many and varied. Some are relatively obvious, such as the idea that we feel more relaxed in open spaces than inside houses, whereas others are somewhat more complex, such as "attention restoration theory". This theory asserts that there are two main components to our attention – the directed component where we decide what to direct our minds to, and involuntary attention, where our interest is captured by something external that intrigues us. Nature, it is said, can capture our attention, and allow us to feel wonder, relieving the fatigue and stress that arises from persistent directed attention (15).

But perhaps the real explanation is a more spiritual one – about connecting with all living things on this earth, of which we are a part. Surprisingly, I have not found much literature on that idea, although there is some. The article by Kamitasis and Francis (16), for example, stresses the importance of a feeling of connectedness with nature.

Some healers I have worked with, such as the shaman mentioned in Chapter 5, and some of those interviewed by John Scott for his study of the healing journey (see Chapter 6), have emphasized connectivity with nature as an important part of their own healing. My own experiences, throughout my life, including when I was held hostage and during my recovery afterwards, have often included this sense of connectedness with nature. Sometimes, there has been a spiritual element to them as well.

What a Wonderful World!

It was late in a summer evening. I was lying in the grass near my friend's house in France, an isolated spot with very little light pollution. The smell of the grass was mixed with another sweet fragrance that I could not identify. I could hear some croaking of toads around the little lake some distance away, and some snuffling from the wild boar roaming the nearby woods. The area was alive. And I was looking up at the amazing clear sky above me. It was dense with stars, each one of them suns like ours, I supposed, with planets, and perhaps living things on some of those planets. Suddenly a shooting star shot across my field of vision. I was entranced. I was a part of something huge, mysterious, and wonderful. My goodness, I said to myself, this really is a wonderful Universe, beyond our understanding.

THE HEALING POWER OF ART

What is art? It is about the creation or enjoyment of beautiful things that have meaning to us and to others. It is about language (poetry, novels), sound (music), vision (fine art, sculpture), movement (dance), performance (theatre) and mixtures of all of these and other sensory experiences. Creative expression is something that is practiced by all cultures and is as old as humanity. It seems that creative expression is an essential part of being human – we need to enhance our lives through creativity and by experiencing the art of others.

Art changes the way we think about ourselves, and can change our whole perception of the meaning of life on earth. It is a part of our perennial search for meaning. Its ability to change both the search, and the meaning we draw from it, means that it is essentially transformational, and thus can be healing.

I have had a few wonderful experiences induced by art.

Connecting with a Work of Art

I was wandering around an art gallery somewhere in Europe, during my time off from a medical conference I was attending. I do not remember where or when. I had gone there without any particular agenda: there was no specific work of art I wanted to see. I was just idly enjoying the time, the space and the pictures. Until, that is, I came across a portrait of a middle-aged man that immediately captured me. I stood there amazed at what I was seeing. It seemed as if I could see right into the soul of that man, feel his pain and understand his problems. I connected with a man I had never known who was depicted in oil paints on a piece of canvas hanging on a wall! That was both amazing and wonderful.

So art, as we know, can be transformational, uplifting and meaningful. My further understanding of the power of art was aided by the opportunity to work collaboratively with an artist. Jaana Erkilla-Hill is a renowned

Finnish fine artist, who is now also a vice Rector of the Arts University in Helsinki. We first met in Exeter around 2015 and immediately started working together on the value of art and creativity for well-being. She then invited me to spend a two-month sabbatical working with her in Lapland in January and February of 2019 (when she was still working at the University of Lapland in Rovaniemi). That gave me an opportunity, for the first time, to work closely with professional artists.

Talking to Artists

During my time in Lapland I talked to a variety of different artists about the value of their art for health and well-being. As well as having many informal interactions with people there, I undertook in-depth interviews with 16 staff in the Arts Faculty, asking them about the value of creative practices to them, and encouraging them to compare such activities with the value of being in the natural environment, or of exercise. And we discussed the difference between making art, and experiencing the art of others. The group included painters, sculptors, print makers, photographers and sound artists.

Key interrelated themes that emerged included:

- Connecting with "something else"
- Connecting within yourself
- Altered states of consciousness
- New levels of understanding of the world
- Finding new meaning

Connecting With "Something Else": One of the things that struck me most forcibly while talking to these artists was their sense of the need to connect with something outside of themselves to facilitate their full creative potential. Several of them discussed the need to be "out of yourself" so as to let "something else" come in. These were difficult concepts for many of them to articulate, particularly those who did not have English as their first language, but it was a common thread. You have good days and bad days, they said, sometimes it happens, and you cannot always predict when they will be. Others spoke of it being something quite separate from technical ability, using the analogy of the musician who knows the piece and all its notes so well, that on some occasions they can "let go" and allow their "feeling and soul" to come through in the music they produce. Many artists attributed their best work to this ineffable "something else".

Connecting Within Yourself: Many of the artists stressed the fact that being a part of an artistic community is a brilliant way of connecting with others. But, in addition, and perhaps more importantly, many people talked of connecting within themselves. This is the sense that being involved in some artistic activity allows you to make new, valuable connections within and between your own mind and soul.

Altered States of Consciousness: Some artists talked directly of entering an altered state of consciousness when absorbed in their work, and of the sense that some sort of "primal consciousness" could then come through into their art. Many likened the mental state they entered when being creative to a meditative state. The need to concentrate fully on their work, and nothing else, was often stressed, and some used the concept of being "in the flow" to describe their mental state when at their most creative.

New Levels of Understanding: Art allowing us to see the world in different ways was another common theme. People were most likely to mention this when talking about enjoying the art of others, rather than their own creative practice, and the concept was linked to the next theme of finding new meaning.

Finding New Meaning: This very similar concept was mentioned often, people saying that either doing their own art work, or experiencing that of others both helped them make more meaning of the world and put their problems and worries into a better perspective.

Jaana Erkkila-Hill, had an additional idea: she thought that one of the most important results of a creative practice was in *"making loneliness more tolerable"*. This is an important idea, I think, particularly in times of increased isolation and loneliness caused, for example, by the COVID-19 pandemic. When you are creating something, you are not really on your own, she explained – you are, in some strange way, a part of the whole of creation.

Somewhat to my surprise, few if any of the artists I talked to raised the issue of their own art providing value to others. This contrasted with their deep appreciation of seeing, hearing or reading the art created by other people, and how much that helped them understand the world and find new meaning. Perhaps the quiet, retiring Finnish artists I talked to were just too modest to think or talk about the ways in which their art helped others.

What I Learnt from These Interviews

The take-home message for me was the similarity between what artists were saying about the ways in which art affected them and the stories that the doctors and healers had told me about healing. Both groups stressed connections and the ineffable. It was clear that there was a considerable spiritual element in their work.

I concluded that art might allow us to heal in the same way that healers can.

Art Can Change Places as Well as People

During my time in Finland, I also learnt a lot about the ability of art to change us through our experience of place and our physical surroundings. A particular example was when I joined Jaana's team on a visit to an open prison to install some art there.

The prison was in the middle of snowy "nowhere", somewhere in Lapland. The University took five of us there from Rovaniemi. We had brought about 15 artworks with us, all of them prints, some black and white, some colored.

Which artworks should go where? First, we needed to decide which ones might go in reception, described to us as the area in which children are allowed when visiting prisoner relatives. The prison governor contributed "That one is too scary for children", she said, pointing to one of Jaana's prints (which did not look at all scary to me), "and this one is no good either", she said, pointing to another. I found myself contributing to the conversation: "This one would work well here", I said, picking out a large black-and-white family scene print. There was nothing on the walls of this room, and we finally agreed on hanging three black-and-white prints, one of which was the one I had picked out. It was a changed room now, less bare and austere, a little friendlier, much more "human". But I struggled to understand what had happened and why.

Later, we went to a teaching/kitchen area. It was a moderate-sized room, with a few really tacky, awful seaside images on its main wall. It felt cold, unfriendly and "wrong" as we entered it. We had three large, lovely colored prints of an "egg" which I decided needed to go on the main wall. One of them had a little red at the top, the others did not. I "knew" that the red one needed to be in the middle of the row of three eggs, and that they needed to be on that wall, and I gently "insisted" on that. After some discussion (mostly in Finnish, which I do not understand!), my view was accepted, and the three eggs were hung on the wall in place of the gaudy trinkets. The change was quite remarkable. I was rather "blown away" by the experience and find my feelings hard to describe. The room had been transformed; it was now softer, kinder, more welcoming and warmer, where previously it had been cold and harsh. For me, in spite of my insistence about which goes where, it was not really about what was in the frames, it was not the individual pictures of the eggs somehow, it was the overall totality of the appearance of framed, elegant pictures on a clean wall that achieved the transformation.

I found two things about this change particularly confusing. Firstly, my own certainty about what should go where, even though the individual pictures turned out to be not quite the point for me, and secondly, the depth and profundity of the change in atmosphere within the room. "What the hell is all this about?", I wondered (and am still wondering).

Subsequently, I learnt about academic research on the concept of "atmospheres" in rooms, and the things that influence them, which seems relevant (17). But I still don't understand!

We can all experience this feeling of an atmosphere in a room; we often say that a meeting or a space has a good or a bad atmosphere, and we use phrases such as "You could cut the atmosphere with a knife". Performance artists depend on the creation of atmospheres, and actors can "feel" what is happening to the audience they are playing to. They talk of the "space between" and liminality. But what are these "atmospheres"? The study of this subject crosses disciplinary boundaries between science, philosophy, psychology, religion, spirituality and the arts, and challenges our very understanding of life. A simple, purely materialistic understanding of the world cannot explain these atmospheres

---

ART IN HEALTH CARE AND HOSPITALS

Art has been in use in health care facilities for centuries. For example, the Ancient Greeks adorned their healing sanctuaries with artworks. However, it would seem that the importance of art for health and healing has not been exploited a great deal in the West until relatively recently.

Google searches suggest that academic publications on the subject were few and far between before about 1980 but have increased exponentially since then.

Art for health includes practices such as:

- Art therapy and arts on prescription
- Art in hospitals to improve their atmosphere
- Art in medical education to aid understanding of illness and suffering
- Creative practices for health and well-being

Art as "Therapy"

Sometimes, a specific artistic intervention is used to help alleviate or "cure" a particular disease. For example:

- Music is widely used in the management of people with dementia
- Dance is often prescribed as a therapy for those with Parkinson's disease

The explanation for their efficacy may be fairly simple: uncovering old memories through music in dementia, and a form of physiotherapy for stiff muscles in Parkinson's disease perhaps? Of course, there may be a lot more to it than that.

But there are many other types of art therapy that are less easily "explained away". I have personal experience of one form of these, used for young people with mental health problems. I had the pleasure of working with Laura Blatherwick and her charity, the "Youth Arts Health Trust" (YAHT), which she set up in Exeter. I tried to help Laura evaluate the interventions, which generally involved weekly creative work with an art therapist – either visual art production or drama therapy – over a period of two to six months. We did some questionnaires with the first 30 clients, including "before-and-after" ratings of well-being, and my wife interviewed a few of them at the end of their therapy to try and get behind the numbers.

I was genuinely amazed by how good the results were. Many of the young people who came to Laura were quite disturbed and had experienced many bad things in their lives; they were referred by their doctors or schools, who were seeking help with their management. And nearly all of them improved (on our rating scales) with the art therapy intervention.

The following illustrative, anonymized case study was excerpted from a YAHT report. It is based on one of my wife, Liz Dieppe's, interviews.

Case Study

"Jenny", a 17-year-old lady, was referred by her GP, after she and her mum went in to discuss her low mood and anxiety. She was offered a series of drama therapy sessions with YAHT and chose the goals of wanting to reduce her self-harming and improve her depression. At first, Jenny used drawings of masks to explore the different ways she faces the world and what might lie underneath; this led to her feeling safe enough to talk about what had happened to her in the past. She was also able to use creative writing to help her find her voice and "listen to the younger parts of herself", which had been through painful experiences, building her self-compassion and strengthening her feelings of self-worth. During her time with us, Jenny also used the sand tray and objects to articulate and explore her emerging eating disorder and work on her preferred coping strategies. By the time she completed the sessions, she had significantly reduced her self-harming behavior, and had made progress toward being more independent and confident.

Below are her own words (J), in response to questions from the evaluator (E):

E: *Tell me about your experience of coming here.*

J: *I found it more useful than talking therapy, because you get the chance to talk, and then do something with it ... you make something, and, because you have been talking about it, it means more than if you just look at it. (My therapist) was really great, we get on really well, and I feel like she understands me really well and gives me lots of time to talk, but she also offered things back ... I did a couple of drama therapies, and I found them really, really helpful. And, at first, I was a bit shy, and I didn't think I would be able to do it, but actually, it was really useful, giving a different perspective.*

E: *Can you elaborate on that at all?*

J: *I wrote a letter to myself, like little me to big me. And then I read the letter as little me, to big me, my voice changed, and my demeanor changed, and everything, I thought I was just going to read the letter, and then I read it, and I felt "wow".*

E: *Would you recommend this intervention to anyone else?*

J: *I would say definitely go, I would say do it, because it is quite difficult to find people who are really responsive and not someone who will just sit there and make you feel like you could be talking to a wall. And I think it's the best therapy I have had, and other things I have had might have been leading up to this, but this art therapy has been the most effective for me. And I like to do drawings and take them home with me.*

E: *Ok, so you continued at home?*

J: *I was given a journal to do, and I brought it in to show. Everyone knows I come here, I'm really proud of it. Some of them do not know what art therapy is, they are sort of "Oh, so what does that mean?" and I say, well it's like you do a bit of talking then you draw what you are talking about or make stuff. And then they seem quite interested, and that it is like a good thing and yeah, so everyone seems to be quite supportive of it.*

I do not know why art therapy of this sort is so helpful to people like "Jenny", but I was struck by her comment that the art helped give her a different perspective on things. And it was clear that she got on really well with the therapist. My reading of the literature suggests that most investigators have concentrated on concepts within psychological and psychoanalytical thinking to try to explain how and why art therapy of this sort might help people like Jenny (18).

I wonder? Perhaps it is more about connecting again?

Art in Hospitals and Care Homes

When I started my career in medicine, hospitals in England were dour, functional buildings. Very little attention was paid to their appearance – either internal or external. Things have changed enormously since then; there have been massive developments in the aesthetics of hospitals and care homes. Modern hospitals in the West nearly always have art within them, as an intrinsic part of the fabric of the building, and many have artworks or "healing gardens" in their grounds. Art is now considered an important part of the many ways in which a hospital can be made to feel safer and friendlier for anxious patients and relatives. Artworks are also thought to help the staff who work within these buildings. Many hospitals have staff members whose sole responsibility is the management of their artworks. Their work is not just about pictures on walls, it is about color, sound and lighting, the use of music, performance and creative practices for staff and patients.

There is a huge range of different aspects of art within hospitals and care homes. Music, group singing, creative art classes, flower arranging and performance activities are a part of the routine in care homes, available to everyone there. In many cases, the staff join in and enjoy these events as much as the patients.

Similarly, in hospitals, there are often a range of activities going on. Music is often an important feature, provided by professionals perhaps or maybe made available through a piano in a corridor or room that anyone can use. Creativity classes, such as painting, may be available for long-stay patients and those in geriatric care, as well as in children's wards. A mass of other activities are often made available to sick children, such as performing clowns and creative games.

But perhaps the most constant, obvious sign of art in most hospitals is the visual art on the walls of the corridors and wards. There is absolutely nothing new about this. As the King's Fund report (19) says, "The practice of decorating hospitals with paintings, sculptures and murals has a long history. From the medieval period, with its religious and spiritually themed works, to the philanthropic endeavors of the artists of the eighteenth and nineteenth centuries". But that report goes on to lament that, for a period in the late nineteenth and early twentieth centuries, the use of art in hospitals seemed to die out. Its revival is sometimes ascribed to scientific studies suggesting that recovery might be improved in better environments.

Visual art in hospitals today is flourishing and has been the subject of an in-depth study by Judy Rollins (20).

Hospital design now takes into account issues of lighting, color and the use of visual art from the beginning in order to try to create a suitable environment to aid recovery from disease. And, just as we have evidence-based medicine (EBM), we now have evidence-based design (EBD) to help us build hospitals that can optimize the care of both patients and staff (21).

The evidence cited suggests that such design, which includes art as well as concerns with lighting and color, makes both patients and staff feel safer, and more comfortable.

How Might Art Promote Healing?

When I ask healers how and why healing "works", they often look at me quizzically and point out that this is an inappropriate question, as healing is experiential, and you just "know". Similarly, when I have asked some artists what art does and why it makes us feel good and the world a better place, they find the question baffling. It just does!

But those of a scientific or materialistic mind-set want to know about the evidence and the theories. In the case of nature and healing, I said that there were two main theories as to why nature might heal – the physical and the psychological. In the case of art, the two main ideas seem to be the psychological and the spiritual.

Psychological studies have shown that exposure to arts can ease anxiety, reduce stress and improve communication between people – both in ordinary life and in hospitals. And there are huge numbers of studies showing that doing something creative is good for your general health and well-being. Some of this work was quoted in the All-Party Parliamentary Report on Art and Health, published in the UK in 2019 (22). This government-backed initiative led to an influential report that left little doubt as to the psychological and physical benefits that art can have.

Research into the spiritual dimension of art is also extensive. For example, sociologist Robert Wuthnow writes that art is now in the spiritual vanguard of our time, pointing out that as societies become more secular, the search for meaning becomes the province of art instead of religion (23).

But what do we mean by spirituality? It has been called the recognition that there is something greater than yourself, something more to our being than our sensory experience alone. Art can certainly make us feel we are a part of "something greater" and can induce those intense moments of enchantment or a noetic, transformational experience.

Art is a universal language: we can tell our stories and understand those of others through art – it can connect us in a very profound way. And art can change us. I have mentioned the ways in which nature helped me on my healing journey. Art/creativity did too. While in Kuwait, I wrote a student booklet and a chapter for my textbook of rheumatology. When I returned, writing the textbook and the practice of writing "morning pages" (24) helped me on my way to recovery.

"Oh, Now I Understand!"

It was during my last school holiday before I started medical school. I went hitch-hiking around part of England, on my own, staying in youth hostels.

I found myself in Stratford-upon-Avon, Shakespeare's birthplace. At school I had not liked Shakespeare, but I thought I would try and see one of his plays in the theatre at Stratford, which had a great reputation. I was lucky; there was a single ticket available for that day's performance of "The Merchant of Venice". I took my seat, not expecting much. It took me a few minutes to tune into the Elizabethan English but, once there, I was totally entranced. Judy Dench was playing Portia, and her mercy speech ("The quality of mercy is not strained …") completely floored me. It was wonderful. And I began to understand so much in so many new ways: the anti-Semitic views of folks, both then and (sadly) now, the desire for revenge, and, of course, the need for and the quality of mercy. I was changed, and I have been going to Shakespeare's plays regularly ever since.

NATURE, ART AND HEALING ·

We are a part of nature; we are nature. And art is an essential part of our humanity and a critical part of the way in which we communicate feelings and experiences. Both art and nature shape who we are and can change us profoundly.

Nature and art change the feel and atmosphere of the places and spaces we spend time in. They can change a space that feels uncomfortable into one in which healing might take place. We need to learn to optimize that in our homes and our institutions, such as hospitals and prisons. We need to create what are called "Optimal Healing Environments"*.

*The term "optimal healing environment" describes a health care system designed to support the inherent healing capacity of patients and staff and involves relationships and behaviors as well as the physical environment. See: Sakallaris et al. (25).

But we are all different individuals, with varying likes and dislikes, allergies and foibles, and we are the products of our unique culture and upbringings. So, some want to roam in the woods, while others need to be at the seaside. Some of us love poetry, others cannot abide it but love fine art. Some of us need to be making things, painting or writing, whereas some of us want to be tending the land, sowing seeds and growing plants or vegetables. Others prefer to enjoy the art and natural produce brought to fruition by those who do.

Each of us, I think, needs to find what it is that we love most, and the experiences that are the ones most likely to provide us with a sense of connection. That feeling of being at one with something else. And then, if we nurture those opportunities, relax into them and allow the magic to occur, we will sometimes have a profound spiritual transformation.

Is that healing? Well, as we have seen already in this book, it depends on what we think healing is, which is a focus of the next and final section of this book.

REFERENCES

1. Curry P. *Enchantment – Wonder in Modern Life*. Edinburgh: Floris Books, 2019.
2. Foote F. *Medic Against Bomb: A Doctor's Poetry of War*. West Hartford CT USA: Grayson Books, 2014.
3. Ameli R, Skeath P, Abraham PA, et al. A nature-based health intervention at a military healthcare center: A randomized, controlled, cross-over study. *PeerJ* 2021; 9: e10519.
4. Ulrich RS. View through a window may influence recovery from surgery. *Science* 1984; 4647: 420–421.
5. Social prescribing – NHS England see: https://www.england.nhs.uk/personalised-care/social-prescribing
6. Shanahan DF et al. 2019. Nature-based interventions for improving health and wellbeing. *Sports (Basel)*: 2019; 10: 141.
7. Marselle M, Warber SL, Irvine KN. Growing resilience through interaction with nature: Can group walks in nature buffer the effects of stressful life events on mental health? *Int J Environ Res Public Health*; 2019; 19: 986.
8. Cooper Marcus C, Sachs NA. *Therapeutic Landscapes: An Evidence-Based Approach to Designing Healing Gardens and Restorative Outdoor Spaces*. Hoboken, NJ: John Wiley, 2014.
9. Hardman I. *The Natural Health Service*. London: Atlantic Books, 2021.
10. Williams F. 2017. *The Nature Fix: Why Nature makes us Happier, Healthier and More Creative*. New York: W W Norton and Company, 2017.
11. Wilson EO. *Biophilia*. Cambridge, MA: Boston: Harvard University Press, 1984.

12. Louv R. *Last Child in the Woods: Saving Our Children from Nature-Deficit Disorder*. Chapel Hill: Algonquin Books, 2005.

13. Batman GN, Hamilton JP, Daily GC. The impacts of nature experience on human cognitive function and mental health. *Ann NY Acad Sci* 2011;ISSN 0077-8923.

14. Kuo M. How might contact with nature promote human health? *Front. Psychol* 2015. http://dx.doi.org/10.3389/fpsyg.2015.01093

15. Kaplan R Kaplan S. *The Experience of Nature: A Psychological Perspective*. Cambridge: Cambridge University Press, 1989.

16. Kamitasis I, Francis AJP. Spirituality mediates the relationship between engagement with nature and psychological wellbeing. *J Env Psychology* 2013; 36: 136–143.

17. Bille M, Bjerregaard P, Sorensen TF. Staging atmospheres: Materiality, culture, and the texture of the in-between'. *Emot Space Soc* 2015; 15: 31–38.

18. Beans C. Searching for the Science behind art therapy. *PNAS* 2019; 116: 707–10.

19. *Art in hospitals*. A Report published by The King's Fund, London, 2016.

20. Rollins J *Purpose Built Art in Hospitals: Art with Intent*. Bingley, UK: Emerald Publishing Ltd., 2021.

21. Brambilla A, Rebecchi A, Capolongo S. Evidence Based Hospital Design. A literature review of the recent publications about the EBD impact of built environment on hospital occupants' and organizational outcomes. *Ann Ig* 2019; 31: 165–180.

22. All Party Parliamentary Report on Arts and Health, UK 2019 see: https://www.culturehealthandwellbeing.org.uk/appg-inquiry

23. Wuthnow R. *Creative Spirituality: The Way of the Artist*. University of California Press, 2003.

24. Cameron J. *The Artists Way: A Spiritual Path to Higher Creativity*. New York: Tarcherperigee, 1990.

25. Sakallaris BR, MacAllister L, Voss M, Smith K, Jonas WB. *Glob Adv Health Med* 2015; 4: 40–45.

Section Three

Integration

10

Doctors as Healers

One of my aims in writing this book is to warn modern medicine against what is known as "scientism" (1). Its use of science is fine, and quite different from "scientism". Science is a set of methods used to explore and help understand our world. Scientism is the claim that only science produces truth. Over the past 50 years, I feel I have seen medicine slipping toward scientism.

I have spent much of my working life using science to explore medicine in the hope of improving the understanding and treatment of disease. But I have also had a lifelong interest in the power of caring and healing. Toward the end of my career, I started to talk about these subjects in medical meetings. This felt a bit like "coming out". To admit that I believed in spirituality, in the paranormal and in healing seemed to lead to a mixture of shock and disapproval within my colleagues. Many accused me of being unscientific (believing that you could not both use science and believe in phenomena that science cannot explain).

But as I have given lectures about healing to audiences of doctors and nurses, something else has happened. Although the open questioning and comments have usually been skeptical at best and aggressively negative at worst, many delegates have sidled up to me afterwards to express their support (while making sure that their colleagues were not listening!). Doctors and nurses are constantly confronted with phenomena that do not make scientific sense and many experience spiritual moments of the sort that I have described throughout this book. And some of them are happy to work with the inexplicable within their practice.

One of the most wonderful and illuminating strands of the research I have done on healing has been in-depth interviews with doctors who are, like me, accepting of the concept of healing. These interviews have

DOI: 10.4324/9781003461814-13

provided me with as clear an insight into what healing is about as any of the other work I have done. Therefore it seems appropriate to begin Part 3 called "Integration" with a description of some of these interviews and what they taught me.

INTERVIEWING HEALTH CARE PROFESSIONALS ABOUT HEALING

I have spoken informally to dozens of medical colleagues about healing: doctors, nurses, clinical psychologists, physiotherapists and others. Many of them have agreed that amazing healing moments occur in their everyday clinical practice of Western biomedicine.

In addition, I have done several formal, in-depth, recorded and transcribed interviews with colleagues. Below, I present highly edited versions of six of these. I have structured each one around the three central themes within my interview schedule:

- What the word healing means
- How they try to facilitate healing
- An example of a healing event from their practice

These transcripts have been carefully anonymized, but I can say that five of the six participants were or had been General Practitioners in the UK's National Health Service and that their ages ranged from 48 to 80.

I have added a note about what struck me most forcibly about each doctor, based in part on the "field notes" I made immediately after each interview.

"James"

What does the word healing mean?
   I think that depends on the context. It is restorative, and about wholeness more than wellness; it is different from curing but can facilitate cures. Acceptance and serenity are important endpoints, I think. Healing is also relational, being about two-way interactions. People refer to the concept of energy as a sort of shorthand for this relational element, I think. However,

I struggle with this question, and, in a sense, the more I think about healing, the more I am uncertain about it. Something very important can go on during human interactions. That is the essence of it, but I am not sure what that is.

What techniques do you use to facilitate healing?

Well, I do not really see myself as a healer. I am a doctor, and that is how I introduce myself to the patients I see. But sometimes, I will work in a different way with a person, and that can probably be more about healing. I think there are some very important things that you can do with patients that might allow healing to occur. It is about presence, being with people on their journey and letting them know they are valued and being heard. I find that I often need to disengage my scientific, medical brain and just be with the other person, perhaps without words. And I will ask myself not to do or say anything stupid, and to be as attentive to the patient as I possibly can; I need to settle and be in the right place.

Unconditional acceptance and good intentions are important, but I don't think it is right to imagine that I know what the right outcome is, so I simply ask that the "right thing" will happen. I do not really know whom I am asking – I am not very religious – and I found a comment from a colleague helpful when he said that "religions are metaphors for the ineffable". I think it is the ineffable that I am working with and asking help from when I do the healing sorts of activity. Sometimes, I will do things that formal healers do, and that are somewhat illicit and subversive for a doctor. I will sit with people, hold their hands perhaps, and then put my hands near their heads and feel the energies, auras or chakras perhaps, and I may feel a point of resistance. Sometimes my hands feel warm. These are things I do not often share with my medical colleagues.

Can you describe someone who was healed?

I had one very profound experience a while back that I want to tell you about. I had been to see a friend in hospital, who was very ill, dying in fact, and afterwards I was just walking the corridors, thinking and wondering what to do next, when I saw another person walking nearby, who was in tears. And her pain suddenly hit me in a very visceral way; it was as if her pain had transferred itself to me. I have no idea what happened to her, we had no eye contact or conventional interaction of any sort. But that deep experience triggered a realization that there was more to this life than the science that I had been taught and work with.

The patient I will tell you about is a lady who died recently, just a few days after my healing interaction with her. She was someone who had been a healer herself and came into the hospice in the final stages of cancer, with a lot of pain. She asked me to do healing with her, to be a healing channel for her as she put it. So, I prepared myself as best I could and sat with her. I held her hand. And she seemed to enter some sort of altered state of consciousness. I felt a real connection to her and to something bigger, the ineffable perhaps. And I felt very calm. At one stage, she said that the pain was better. Time stood still. Later, she thanked me and said it had been healing and that things were OK for her now. She seemed more serene. And I felt healed too.

Notes about my interview with "James"

James struck me as a remarkably humble, honest and caring man, careful with his words and actions. But what hit home for me was his talk of *the ineffable*. Here was an experienced doctor saying quite clearly that there were metaphysical or spiritual aspects to healing which he could not hope to understand from a simple materialistic, scientific or medical perspective. Talk of these aspects of healing was fine with him. I was also greatly impressed by his description of what mattered most when interacting with patients (unconditional acceptance and good intentions) alongside his just being with people, and maybe feeling their energies, auras and chakras.

He seemed to be able to dance between his scientific biomedical world of symptoms and diagnoses, and the "ineffable" world of healing.

I also liked his use of the word "serenity", and his saying that what healing is about is context-dependent and relational. I also agree with him that healing is more about wholeness (which I think of as integrity of mind, body and soul) than wellness (in its narrow meaning of freedom from disease or symptoms).

Finally, I loved his last point: when in a healing relationship with his patient, he too felt healed. Healing of this profound sort can be a reciprocal process. I have experienced that: with the dying man described in Chapter 1, and when with my hostage friend, mentioned in Chapter 2.

"June"

What does the word healing mean to you?

We all have an innate ability to self-heal, and a lot of medicine is about ramping that up, facilitating people's need to heal themselves. That is not the same as curing; it is not necessarily about getting completely rid of some health problem, but more about suppressing it, making it alright, coping with it, being comfortable with who you are and not being an outsider because of your illness.

What techniques do you use to facilitate healing?

Things that facilitate that ramping-up of the self-healing process include connecting with another person in a real way. In the context of a doctor's surgery, that is helped by empathic listening and allowing someone to open up. Other important things include trust in the other, and ritual – rituals such as the use of the stethoscope are an important part of it, because they symbolize power, the power over illness. And metaphor is another thing; imagination and metaphor can help, and this is where hypnosis can come in. I use hypnosis alongside more conventional medical approaches.

Can you describe someone who was healed?

So, there was this chap with terrible psoriasis all over his body, nasty scaly lesions everywhere that really interfered with his life. And all the usual creams and potions had not really helped with it. So we discussed the idea of using hypnosis and he agreed. He was a great subject who went into deep trances. And the imagery I used with him took him to his perfect place, where he lay down and then a fleecy dressing gown descended onto his body and it was cooling and soothing. And after several sessions of this, he came into the surgery, took his top off and showed me his normal skin – and he skipped about in joy in front of me.

And there was another amazing one. There was this chap in his late 40s with a young family. He developed a rare and very malignant form of cancer of his gall bladder. It was biopsied and imaged and everything and pronounced inoperable and incurable and he was given about six months to live. And he came to me and asked me if there was anything we could do. So, we talked about hypnosis and he wanted to go for it. I asked him to visualize his tumor, which he saw as a big knobbly rock under his liver. Then I asked him what he thought might get rid of it, and he said "Pac-Men" – they could come through his body and eat it up. So, we agreed to work on that under hypnosis. So, in a trance, he went to his special place – which was a beach on his home island in another country – and we worked on the visualization of an army of Pac-Men in his body, going to eat up the tumor. We did this for a bit, and then he went back to his home overseas and drank tea made with some native leaves that his granny had told him could have healing properties. And he told me that he had a dream in which his granny asked him what the trouble was, so he told her about the tumor, and she put her hand in his abdomen and yanked it out. Anyway, he returned and went to hospital for another scan, and the tumor was gone. The doctors at the hospital would not believe it. He went to another specialist and he would not believe it either; he said they must have mislabeled the histology slide, as no one ever had that sort of tumor go away. I chased up the records and it was clear that it had been his histology slide OK, but they just could not accept it. He was fit and well for about eight years after that, and then the family went through a very traumatic period of problems and his tumor recurred and he was dead in three months.

I think that in each of these cases, the hypnosis, the rituals around it and my connection with the patients allowed their immune systems to suppress the disease.

Notes about my interview with "June"

"June" started off with the concept that all healing is really self-healing, and that the job of the doctor or the healer is to "ramp-up" the process that allows us to heal ourselves. This is a rather subversive concept for a doctor, as we are taught that it is our interventions and what we do to people that cures them; but June, of course, was clear that healing was not the same as curing.

Having said that, each of the two amazing exemplars of people she had seen who she described as having healed might be said to have been cured (if only temporarily) of their illness. Again, however, she pointed out that healing could result in a subsequent cure. I was interested to hear about the inability of the specialists to accept the disappearance of the cancer, since it sounded similar to the ways in which my colleagues had not been able to accept that an energy healer had got rid of "Joan's" arthritis, described in Chapter 1.

While putting the emphasis on connecting with people, as noted by many other health care professionals I have talked to, "June" also thought that ritual was important. She considered that what doctors do when consulting with patients, such as wearing a white coat or stethoscope (things that are disappearing from practice now) and wielding a pen to write a prescription on a special piece of paper that would allow a treatment to be prescribed, were all very important.

Finally, I really like "June's" description of an outcome of healing being about becoming "more comfortable with who you are". But, it has to be said that, in many ways, June was the most conventional of the medics whose interviews I report here.

"Frank"

What does the word healing mean to you?

I have a love/hate relationship with the word healing. Healing can occur in different contexts and can mean many different things. Sometimes, special healers can cause amazing things to happen, but I think that is rare, and we must not seek that in place of good conventional medicine. Our role as doctors is to do the best we can with scientific medicine first. A problem I have with healing is the consumerism aspect of it.

But I suppose I think it means restoration. Removal of blockages to living well. Flourishing is a way of looking at what healing is about.

But there is also some magic that can occur, a sort of spiritual thing that is beyond our understanding.

What techniques do you use to facilitate healing?

I am not a healer, but I do try to care for the whole person, which might be another way of looking at what healing is, I suppose. I use conventional Western medicine, but I also use manual therapy and acupuncture. I think touching people is very important, and I sometimes feel some sort of special connection with a patient when I am touching them or doing some sort of manual therapy. I try to work with their beliefs and expectations because that is an important part of the chances of their responding. But it is not just placebo; there is something else going on when we connect with another person.

Can you describe someone who was healed?

You know my mother is dying at the moment, and this conversation we are having about healing has helped me make more sense of that. I realize that there is no need to be scared of death, and that you can die healed, reconciled if you like. Reconciliation, another useful concept here, I think. Yes, this has been helpful.

I will tell you about one of our students who was having lots of troubles, many health problems, and she developed a bad knee. She asked me about it and I told her she should go to a knee doctor. And she said a "knee doctor", are there such things, people who just deal with knees? And I said yes, and she went to see this man who was indeed a knee doctor. And he looked at her knee and did the usual things. And then he asked her how the knee was affecting her life, and how she was in herself, and there was a sudden connection between them, and she came out saying that he was the most amazing doctor and her symptoms went away, she was healed.

Notes about my interview with "Frank"

This was an amazing interview; because "Frank" changed as it went on (we were talking together for about 90 minutes). To begin with, he was very biomedically oriented, saying that he used conventional biomedicine and was a bit skeptical about healing (while recognizing that strange things did sometimes happen), but, as time went on, his stance "softened" and he seemed more comfortable with healing and metaphysical/spiritual explanations of what might be going on between him and some of his patients. The "crunch" came when he told me that his mother was dying, when he said that he now realized that she might die healed, or "reconciled" as he put it. He became quite emotional and thanked me for the insights I had given him. I had not given him any insight, of course; he had found his own way to them as he talked to me.

By the time we parted, he was talking of "magic" and wondrous things happening during consultations. Like many other colleagues of mine, he put a lot of emphasis on the relationship between the patient and the professional. "Connecting" with the other was crucial for him, and many others I have spoken to.

"Archie"

What does the word healing mean to you?

For me, healing is largely about the outcomes for people, to some extent the process, certainly not the practices of healers; mainly about outcomes. At medical school, I became aware that there was a sort of chasm between medicine and healing. And then as, a general practitioner, I realized that the biomedical equipment that I had been given at medical school was just not enough; that medicine as she was taught and practiced was inadequate for helping lots of my patients.

But I hate the concept of calling yourself a healer, or of giving healing to another. That is not at all what it is about for me. You cannot "give" healing. The healing outcome is about a greater abundance of life for people and increased "worthship" – not worship but "worthship", by which I mean the sense of self-worth that a person has. And it is not just about the outcome for an individual; healing is somehow not an individualistic thing – it involves exchanges, mostly exchanges between different people. Healing must always involve other people; after all, if one person is changed, then others around them must benefit from that change, in addition to the individuals themselves. But it can be other sorts of exchange, as in nature, for example.

Metaphor is helpful when trying to talk about healing. I like the metaphor of the butterfly and the chrysalis. Many of us are trapped in the chrysalis and need to be helped to escape and become the butterfly that we are meant to be. We need to be released from fear, from doubt, and to be helped to fly, even if only for a short time. We all have beautiful souls, but they are often trapped somewhere, and we need to help them escape into the open. And the jigsaw is another metaphor I use for healing; it is about becoming more whole. I like the word "completeness". And it is about transcending imperfections, as happens when you do a jigsaw. But it is not about being perfect; we cannot be perfect.

Another aspect of healing is about finding meaning.

What techniques do you use to facilitate healing?

There are multitudes of different ways of creating the conditions that can lead to good healing outcomes. Loving, caring, laughter, tears, friendship and many others. And healing is a journey, a journey toward improvement and enrichment. And it can be triggered by things, as well as people. Some people find that being in natural environments, or with flowers, or listening to the birds is what brings them enrichment and peace, and that is a form of healing.

As you know, I found homeopathy a very useful adjunct to biomedicine. I am disappointed that the scientific community will not take it more seriously. The dismissal of homeopathy is something I feel bad about – I think it is inappropriate. Homeopathic consultations and treatments are a catalyst for change, for healing. I also found that homeopathy helped me become increasingly intuitive about people's real problems, and what they needed help with. And I think that made me a better doctor since it allowed me to work better with my patients, and to create circumstances that were conducive to their healing. Healing involves a sudden awareness of an aspect of the other person, of their hurt or pain, or some problem or blockage that they have, a sudden sense of knowing. I think it is an aspect of empathy. It requires attentiveness to the other person. If you give the other person your full undivided attention, which gets you/your ego out of the way, and allows intuitive understanding, that also facilitates healing, I think.

Can you describe someone who was healed?

There was this lady whose life was transformed when I suggested she take a homeopathic dose of aluminum. She had severe peripheral vascular disease. After she got better, she asked "Was that aluminum you gave me?", and I said "Yes, it was a homeopathic dose of aluminum"; and she then said that she had worked in a factory in the war and had been exposed to a lot of aluminum. That was amazing and made it real for me.

And there was this lady who came to see me with food intolerance, but I intuited that her problems were much deeper than that, and homeopathy helped her, and I sort of became a "spiritual Sherpa" for her and others. Things went in a different direction from what either I or those patients expected.

Notes about my interview with "Archie"

Archie was a humble and caring general practitioner, who came to realize that biomedicine was often not enough for him to help his patients. He learnt and applied other approaches, ones that are largely rejected by mainstream medicine, including homeopathy.

Some of my medical colleagues talk more about process than outcome when discussing healing, but, for "Archie", it was all about outcomes – about people feeling better. I liked his emphasis on ideas like "worthship" and "finding meaning" when discussing the sorts of outcomes that come with healing. And he, like others, put a lot of emphasis on inter-personal exchanges being critical for the facilitation of healing.

How wonderful, it seemed to me, was his response when I asked him what things he did to facilitate healing. It could result from all sorts of things, he told me, including: "Loving, caring, laughter, tears, friendship". I thought that was beautiful. In addition, I liked his willingness to use intuition when with patients. It reminded me of the times I have had sudden moments of intuition with patients, as with the curate described in Chapter 1.

"Lucy"

What does the word healing mean to you?

I think healing means working toward wholeness – not just wholeness of the body or mind, but wholeness in the sense of knowing who you are. It is easier to say what healing is not than what it is: it's not about being rid of symptoms or disability, it is more than that. In a way, it is about consciousness – it is a deep knowing, akin to spirituality. I also think that healing encompasses aspects of the world that are outside the normal boundaries of our perceptions; there is a wider reality. One of the problems with talking about healing is language; it seems to involve energies and aspects of the world that we cannot detect with our senses, so we use images, metaphors and words to try to describe feelings that in a way make no sense to us. And it is culturally conditioned, so, for example, you find that, in the New Age discourse in this country, there is talk of angels, because of our Christian culture, whereas, in other parts of the world, the same phenomena might be attributed to spirits.

What techniques do you use to facilitate healing?

I am loath to describe myself as a healer because that can imply that I can get rid of diseases, or symptoms, and that is not really what I do. I listen, I talk and I try to help people reprogram their minds by addressing some of their underlying beliefs and looking for inconsistencies and conflicts. I also use hypnosis, not in the sense of formal induction of a trance state, but in the sense of allowing people to use images and access things when in an altered state of consciousness. And when I am with people, doing this, something can happen. I don't really know what it is, but I feel change through connection with the other person. It is difficult to put into words, but we – the client and myself – seem to have accessed something else. Maybe geniuses, like Mozart, were able to access this something else, and that is why they could achieve such wonderful things. Sometimes, this connection is so profound that I almost seem to be in the other person's brain and I know what is going on and what their problems are. And something comes through. The ritual surrounding a consultation is important, but the key to it is the rapport between you and the other person, and those moments when "something else" happens, that allows healing.

Can you describe someone who was healed?

So, there was this lady who developed a cancer that needed surgical removal. But she was terrified of the surgery and had cancelled the operation at the last minute on three occasions. So, I was asked to see if I could help her overcome her fear of the operation. We discussed it and she told me that she knew – she just knew that she was going to die on the operating table. So, we talked a bit, and I found out that she had been brought up in a devout Christian culture in the West Indies. I suggested to her that she imagined herself back in Church as a child, and in a sort of hypnotic state – an altered state of consciousness. I asked her to make that experience really big in her mind, to be there and to think about what the Church would have her do. I wanted her to recreate her beliefs then. And she did, and she said that the Church would want her to put her faith in God, and that was what she should do. So, she had the operation and the cancer was cured.

And I want to tell you about another person, whom I have written about. This was a lady whose 8-month-old child had died of meningitis, leaving her devastated. She was in a terrible state and was considered suicidal when I was asked to see her. When I was with her, she was crying most of the time. She told me of her loss, looked at me and asked, "Can you understand that?" I told her no, I could not, but that I had worked with other people who had lost children, particularly in other countries where things were dealt with in different ways. I told her about my experience of Buddhist rituals in which people were encouraged to let the souls of their dead relatives go. She listened, and, a little later, she asked me, "Do you think you could help me by doing such a ritual for my child?" Well, we discussed that further, and with her bereavement counselor and we agreed that we would undertake such a ritual for her. She came with her sister, and we all enacted a Buddhist-style ritual to allow us to let the soul of her dead child go and rest. It seemed to help and, a few weeks later, she asked if we could do it again for the whole family. We did; this time, her whole family came and shared in this experience with her. And that seemed to lift her out of her misery and allow her to start the healing process.

Notes about my interview with "Lucy"

I did this interview fairly early in my exploration of healing, and felt I had learnt a lot from "Lucy". She, like most of the other health care professionals I talked to in depth, was humble and would not describe herself as a healer. I loved her description of the healed state as knowing who you are and "deep knowing". And she was not afraid to use concepts like energy and was comfortable with other metaphysical concepts to help her explain what might be going on. And she said, she *listens*.

What struck me most forcibly when talking with her was her description of the moments of real, deep connection between her and a patient. This was because I too had occasionally felt that something important, massive and deeply meaningful was happening, and I seemed to connect with some of my patients in a special way. For me they were rare, wonderful, beautiful, but inexplicable moments. It helped me to hear Lucy talk freely about having had the same types of experience. She talked of "accessing something else" and suggested that such connections could be the basis of creativity by geniuses like Mozart. That concept affected me deeply and has stayed with me.

"Judith"

What does the word healing mean to you?

Wholeness in place of fragmentation, I think.

Let me explain. I saw this medical colleague recently who was complaining of a problem in her foot. We talked for a while; I listened. And it became apparent that her foot was somehow not a part of her anymore, but, as we worked together, she was able to reintegrate the foot into the totality of who she was, and she became whole again, and the foot stopped being a problem.

So that was a sort of healing, which is quite different from curing a disease. As a doctor, I can sometimes help some people toward a cure for a particular disease, but healing is more about their integrity as a whole person.

What techniques do you use to facilitate healing?

Listening, mostly. As you know, I also use homeopathy. I have been practicing that, alongside my conventional medical work, for years now and it has taught me so much about listening. The homeopathic consultation methods show you how to go deeper and deeper into who a person is and what their innermost contradictions are, and then somehow get to a point of connection with them, with another, or with something else, that allows them to move on. My family teases me that my mantra in my practice is like that of Olivia Newton-John's song – "Tell me more, tell me more, tell me more".

Intuition is important.

And so is love.

I think there are many different roads to healing, but this is the one I use. I am happy that others use different approaches and modalities, and I suspect that the results are similar. I listen for the inner contradictions that people find as they talk about themselves and help them recognize those contradictions, and that helps them, and me, intuit what needs to change and how they can go forward.

This is so different from the standard medical model that we were brought up in and then formally taught in medical school. The usual position in consultations is that of the macho, powerful doctor meeting the vulnerable, nervous patient. As a healer, I think you need to turn this dynamic completely on its head. You, the healer, need to be the vulnerable one, and the patient needs to be able to be assertive.

Can you describe someone who was healed?

I don't know; I am not sure that I can.

The problem is that we do not see the long-term outcomes and effects of what we do in medicine; I am not sure that we ever know what happens afterwards, and I am not sure that I can easily describe what a healing outcome is anyway. I think it varies with different people and their varying problems.

What I can tell you about is what I call healing moments – those events during a medical consultation in which you feel and know that change is happening. Those are wonderful; they are sort of orgasmic, "bingo!" moments of shared joy and understanding. There is a moment of real connection between you and the other person – but, in addition, you feel that you are connecting with something bigger, some awesome "other" and that this connection allows you both to move forward. Those healing moments heal me, as well as changing the client, I think; although, as I said, it is hard to know about their longer-term changes.

Notes about my interview with "Judith"

"Judith" made some very important points about healing, some of which had not featured in my other interviews. Her emphasis on listening in a way that allows real meaningful connections to be made, so that the client can see their own ways forward, was striking. My own experiences of sitting in with homeopathic practitioners would support her saying that their way of delving into a client's problems is very special and hugely important, as is intuition. I was struck by the way in which she, a classically trained doctor, was quite at home with trusting moments of intuition that came to her about her clients (patients); and the eclectic way in which she was happy to mix conventional biomedical approaches with her homeopathy. I believe that Judith is spot on with her diagnosis of one of the main problems of Western biomedicine: the fact that the doctor is in a position of power, and the patients feel vulnerable.

The other key point I take away from what Judith told me, that I am rather surprised not to have heard from others, is that we never really know if someone has been healed. We do not see the long-term consequences of how we may have affected a person's life and have no idea what might have been different if the "healing" had not taken place.

My Conclusions from These Interviews

These interviews were carried out at irregular intervals over a period of years when I was pursuing my interest in healing while at the University of Exeter. So, they have informed my views and contributed to the concepts of healing that I provide in the last chapter of this book.

These stories seem to me to describe the very essence of healing.

I was struck by the fact that the patient encounters which these medical colleagues of mine described seemed very similar to some of my own. And, like me, they were happy to accept metaphysical explanations for some of their experiences and talk openly about them (some admitted that they did not normally share such ideas with others in the medical profession, for fear of ridicule or worse!). I feel very grateful for their generosity and privileged to have heard their stories.

The main message that seemed to emerge was that healing is facilitated by *connecting* with the patient in some special indescribable way. My colleagues, like myself, shied away from the concept that they are themselves healers, or practice healing; rather, they presented themselves as "witnesses" of healing. But they accepted the fact that the special connections they made with their patients were critical.

REFERENCE

1. Stenmark M. *2020 Scientism: Science, Ethics and Religion*. London and New York: Routledge.

11

Modern Medicine and Healing

The interviews described in the last chapter taught me that doctors could be healers. Conversations with many other health care professionals, including nurses and physiotherapists, have further convinced me that healing takes place within medicine. But healing is not recognized or accepted by medical science or by the medical establishment.

This conundrum needs unpacking. What is going on within modern Western biomedicine? Why will it not embrace healing?

MODERN BIOMEDICINE AND HEALING

I should know quite a lot about those questions. I qualified as a doctor in London in 1970 and did clinical work within the UK's National Health Service until 2015. I have visited modern hospitals and clinics in numerous different countries. I have been a Dean of a medical school and taught generations of medical students how to practice medicine. Throughout my career, I have also undertaken a lot of biomedical research – participating in the global endeavor to improve diagnosis and treatment of disease, using modern science. Biomedicine and its science are a major part of my identity. I do not regret that. Medicine does wonders for us and has improved our longevity and health to an incredible extent. But now I am interested in healing, and I find that many of my colleagues think I must be slightly "mentally deranged" to be working in this field.

The basic problem is that medicine is taught and practiced within an entirely mechanistic paradigm, based solely on materialistic science. The body and mind are seen as machines. Machines that can go wrong. And

 DOI: 10.4324/9781003461814-14

when they go wrong, medical science believes it can find out why and put things right. In other words, medicine is about the diagnosis of disease, and prescribing possible cures.

Healing Is Different from Curing

Healing, with its basis in spirituality, is not compatible with the biomedical approach. Healing is quite different from curing. One of the people who taught me this was Sister Delia.

Sister Delia was an Irish Catholic nun in her 70s, whom I met in a hospital in Lourdes, where she was one of the *"malades"*, on bed rest between visits to the various healing sites and rituals available. She told me her amazing story while the team I was with filmed and audio-recorded my interview with her.

She had developed severe abdominal pain and vaginal bleeding soon after she first went to her convent in Ireland, at the age of 17, so the nuns assumed that she was pregnant! She was taken to hospital, where it was found that she had polycystic ovaries, which were removed, (she was not pregnant). No advice, aftercare or hormone replacement had ever been offered to her, so, not surprisingly, she developed severe osteoporosis* later in life, with fractures occurring in her spine, causing a lot of pain. "No one seems to be able to offer me much help for the pain", she told me. We talked quite a bit about her pain and her hopes for improvement in Lourdes, what doctors could do to help her with the pain and suchlike, after which I started to wrap up the conversation. I had been speaking to her as a doctor with an interest in musculoskeletal pain (that was how I had introduced myself to her).

Osteoporosis is thinning of the bones; it is age-related and particularly common in post-menopausal women (estrogen protects against it, so removal of the ovaries causes premature bone loss). It can lead to painful fractures in the spinal vertebrae.

However, just as I was trying to bring the conversation to a close, Sister Delia looked at me and said, "We have talked about my physical pain, but you do know that there is another sort of pain troubling me, don't you?" "Tell me more", I prompted. "There is spiritual pain as well as physical pain", she said, and promptly burst into tears. She then told me that one of her biggest problems was grief at the loss of members of her family, and the fact that she had not had the chance to say what she wanted to them before they died. She was also fearful about her own death, a feeling which she, as a nun, felt guilty about. I encouraged her to talk about these issues some more, which she did, tearfully and very frankly. As we talked softly together, my hand on her arm, the room disappeared; we were just together, as one. After a while, she told me that she had not had the chance to explain any of this to anyone before, ever; and that talking about it was healing. *"These things – my spiritual pains – need healing"*, she said, *"which is why I am here; doctors cannot help with that"*.

What Sister Delia was pointing out was that the material body is not all there is to being human; we have a spiritual dimension as well. She was (correctly, I think) saying that medicine only deals with the physical issues (the mind/body rather than the mind/body/spirit). In addition, she noted that she had found our conversation healing. And so had I, an example of what Sara Warber and I have called "reciprocal healing" (Chapter 7). I was deeply moved and affected by our conversation, during which I had become totally a part of our union, forgetting about the camera and recorders in the background, and the time or place. We were connected. Afterwards, I felt a mixture of immense sadness for her and her story, but I also felt "cleansed" (I cannot find a better word for the strange feeling of peace, calm and serenity that was within me).

I did not cure Sister Delia, but I may have helped her heal. Healing through a connection of this sort was emphasized by my medical colleagues, as described in Chapter 10.

So, healing can be different from curing (which is ridding the body of disease). We all need both healing and curing for different problems we experience.

The Success of Biomedicine

Scientific biomedicine now dominates health care in the Western world. Only those of us who are trained in scientific biomedicine are sanctioned to administer health care.

And this form of health care has been staggeringly successful.

Not a lot needs to be said about this success – it is self-evident to all of us. I know no one who has not benefitted from biomedicine. Our ability to deal with acute medical crises is particularly remarkable. We rescue people from the consequences of serious trauma and successfully treat life-threatening acute infections like meningitis. The list could go on. Similarly, modern surgery does wonders for many of us, repairing troublesome hernias, giving us new hips, removing our cataracts and opening up our narrowed coronary arteries. Deaths as a result of childbirth or in infancy are uncommon, and many of the ailments we acquire can be cured. We are living much longer, healthier lives than our predecessors.

In my own practice of rheumatology, I saw a huge number of advances over the 45 years that I worked in the field. When I started, we had hardly any effective interventions to offer people with common, painful, disabling disorders such as osteoarthritis and rheumatoid disease. Safe and effective hip joint replacement was only just becoming possible, and symptom control was generally poor. Now we can effectively replace most damaged joints and we have a large arsenal of amazing drugs for both disease and symptom control. Chronic musculoskeletal pain remains a difficult problem, but we see far fewer people with the terrible deformities and disabilities caused by arthritis that I witnessed early on in my career.

The recent rapid development of fairly safe, effective vaccines for COVID-19 is another recent example of what biomedicine can do for us.

Problems Arising from the Success of Biomedicine

Medicine also has increasing numbers of major problems, stemming in part from its success. A number of recent books have argued that it is now losing its way (1, 2, 3).

Problems stemming directly from its success include the following.

Hubris

There is a huge amount of hubris and arrogance within the medical profession today. The fact that we are so good at understanding and treating so many ailments has led us to believe that our science and practice can do anything. We are so pleased with our ways of doing things and our achievements that we ignore all other ways of thinking about health. Indeed, we tend to dismiss "alternatives" as nonsense, simply because our science cannot explain them. We believe that if we just put a bit more scientific effort into things, we will completely understand how our bodies work and have control over all diseases. We are encouraged in this by the general public, who have been led to believe the same story. Some medical scientists believe that they will soon understand big problems, like ageing and consciousness, therefore being able to prevent age-related disorders and have control over mental health issues.

I don't think so.

Pressure to Conform and "Scientism"

Accompanying the arrogance of my profession, there is a huge pressure to conform to its way of doing things. Conformity has become a part of its culture. When I started out, there were "mavericks" within our ranks: doctors who did things differently, who used strange "alternative" approaches and did not conform to the "proper" way of doing things. They were tolerated. Not anymore. Now, there is massive pressure to conform to the accepted "scientifically proven" ways of doing things and, in many cases, legislation means that we *have* to conform. There is no room for dissent. It seems to me that medicine is now suffering from what is called "scientism" – absolute belief in the power and truth of materialistic science as the only way of finding truth.

Longevity and Chronic Disease

Because modern medicine and public health have been so successful, we are living a lot longer than we used to. So, many of us (including myself!) are suffering from age-related disorders and chronic disease. Many of our systems are not "designed" to last for much longer than the apocryphal "three score years and ten". There was no evolutionary pressure to get rid of age-related diseases that come on after our reproductive years are over. So, problems like osteoarthritis, dementia, and age-related loss of sight and hearing are increasingly common. In addition, we acquire minor problems with other parts of our bodies as life goes on, which lead to the demand for more medical help from us older folk. Chronic health problems, particularly among older people, are threatening to overwhelm medical services in many parts of the world.

Death and Dying

We can now do a lot to keep people alive, and death is sometimes seen as a failure by medical professionals. A common refrain from patients – or, more often, their relatives – is "You will do everything you can, won't you doctor?" So we do, at tremendous cost – both emotional and financial. We do have many wonderful hospices in which people can die in dignity when the time is right. But, in general, as Atul Gawande (4) and many others have pointed out, our management of mortality is failing.

I was discussing this problem with some medical colleagues in the USA some years ago. One of them said, "Yes, Paul, you see, deep down, all Americans now think that death is optional".

Oh dear!

Some of Medicine's Other Problems

There are, sadly, several other problems inherent in the way biomedicine has taken control over our health care in the last 100 years or so.

The Medicalization of Emotions and Behaviors

In previous times, as I understand it, people who behaved oddly or had horrible outbursts of emotion were tolerated and looked after by the community. In England, we talk of places having their "village idiot", or of a person being a "melancholic". Now we attach formal medical diagnoses to these people, such as schizophrenia or depression, and then fill them with medications to make them "more normal".

This trend has been accelerating of late, with the famous DMS (Diagnostic and Statistical Manual of Mental Disorders) expanding almost exponentially, as the pharmaceutical industry finds more drugs that need a disease target.

My own problems after being a hostage could have been in this category. I only managed to avoid being given a label of a mental disorder (such as PTSD) and plied with medication by not going to my colleagues for help. I found healing instead.

The Tyranny of Diagnosis and Guidelines

One of the alternative practitioners with whom I have discussed medicine said, "If you go to a doctor with an illness, you come out with a diagnosis and not much else".

There is a terrible singularity to a diagnosis. It seems to offer a simple explanation, a single answer to a problem. But illness and disease are complex. Not just complicated, but genuinely complex; by which, I mean that there are many different factors involved, and they interact with each other in unpredictable ways. Doctors like myself have been taught to look for *the* diagnosis and *the* cause of the problem. And, as potential patients, we ask ourselves, "I wonder why I am feeling ill. Perhaps I have got something wrong, like cancer. Perhaps it is because I have been eating the wrong things". We then go to our doctor, who does some tests to see what disease we might have. But illness is often more about several socioeconomic and environmental factors interacting with other contextual issues and our "constitution", rather than a single factor, or one disease. This diagnostic oversimplification of our health issues really troubles me.

Furthermore, as our approach has it, if we have the diagnosis, we can then intervene with *the* treatment. That treatment, often a drug, must be given according to guidelines dictated to us from above, and based on randomized controlled trials (RCTs). I have already pointed out the limitations of RCTs: they are good for relatively simple, acute issues, and things like vaccines, but not for much else. But every intervention has to be backed by RCT-based evidence these days, so that the guidelines can be written. Doctors have to abide by those guidelines. And *the* treatment is thought to work for everyone with *the* diagnosis. This leads to silly management, as in the case of Gladys.

Gladys

Older people often have several different health issues, and more than one diagnosis. This can lead to the guideline for one disorder contradicting that of another. My patient Gladys found herself caught in this dilemma. She was in her late 80s when I saw her. She had loads of medical problems, including osteoarthritis (which was why she found her way to me), high blood pressure and asthma, as well as a number of other ailments. She told me that her main problem was that she could not get up and down her stairs at home because of the painful arthritis. The other issues did not bother her, but the doctors said she *had* to take tablets for them. The doctors had also told her that they could not give her any treatment for the arthritis because it would interfere with the other treatments that she *must* take. They had also explained that they were having difficulty managing her various ailments because the guideline on what to do for one of them contradicted the guideline for another, as well as precluding the use of any effective pain medication. And each time Gladys went to the pharmacy to ask for something for pain, she was told that she was not allowed anything because of the other medicines she was taking.

We stopped a lot of her medications (she did not seem to need them), and put a stair lift in her home. She was then able to take painkillers if she needed them, as well as get up and down the stairs.

Such stories are common in medicine now. All too often, we hear of the doctor in their surgery, surrounded by her symbols of power, such as the stethoscope, staring at the computer screen and consulting the latest evidence-based guidelines, instead of connecting with the patient and their problems.

I fear this is all getting worse, not better, as, in part as a result of the COVID-19 pandemic, we are moving away from personal meetings with our doctors to electronic consultations.

The Influence of the Pharmaceutical and Other Industries

Pharmaceutical and medical device companies now control much of health (disease) care, as well as the research agenda. They "buy" opinion leaders in medicine to help them promote their products and have insinuated themselves into the highest levels of decision making. We keep hearing of scandals, such as the recent promotion of addictive opioids by a company that concealed the dangers of their drugs, resulting in the unnecessary loss of many lives (5). But the industry in general does not change its ways. Much of the research being funded by rich countries still seems to be more in the interests of industry than of our patients.

I have been personally threatened by a drug company when I was about to publish data that was not in their best interest. And my colleagues shunned me for a while when I gave a lecture in which I suggested that the use of a new class of drugs being heavily promoted for arthritis might not be a good idea. They threw me out of one of the International Societies I belonged to, only welcoming me back (without apology) when I was proved right about those drugs a few years later (after a number of people had died from their side effects).

Money and Bureaucracy

In the wonderful play, "The Doctor's Dilemma", written by George Bernard Shaw in 1906 (before the introduction of the NHS to the UK, with its free access to health care), one of the players comments that it is an odd world that pays one man to cut off the leg of another, and is then surprised to see lots of people hopping about on one leg. His point, of course, was that if we pay doctors to do interventions, they will do them more often than is necessary.

Doctors making money out of other people's health problems does not seem appropriate to me, and that is one of the reasons that I never did any private practice.

These days, lawyers can also make a lot of money out of medicine, by encouraging patients, who think they have been mistreated, to sue their doctors. This means that doctors are constantly looking at their computers, to be sure that they are following recommended guidelines. They are also practicing "defensive medicine" which involves activities such as doing too many (expensive) investigations and prescribing unnecessary drugs.

Bureaucracy is another problem. The fact that we have commercialized health care and allowed bureaucrats to manage it is, in my view, a big mistake. When I started out as a doctor in the UK's National Health System, in 1970, the hospitals and general practices were run by doctors and nurses, and we were free to do what we thought was right for our patients. We did not know the financial costs of anything we were doing; our interest was solely in human costs. For example, at Barts in London, where I worked for many years, we used to arrange social admissions over Christmas – patients of ours whom we knew to be lonely and alone were given a bed for a few days, fed well and entertained by the staff. These days, such behavior would be thought of by the army of managers who control the system as nothing short of a criminally wasteful use of resources.

I first knew the writing was on the wall for old-style medical care in the NHS when I was doing a clinic in Bristol one afternoon, around 1988. A recently appointed young manager, smartly dressed and with clipboard in hand, came into my room after I had finished seeing one of my patients. She told me I had spent far too long with the last person, resulting in unacceptably long waits for those whom I still had to see. Her interest was not in the needs of the patients, it was in terms of efficiency and waiting time targets.

All these problems and issues have contributed to making modern medicine totally unaffordable for most citizens of our world. How ridiculous is that?

But I think the greatest problem we have is the lack of emphasis on caring, compassion and humanity in health care. They are talked about, and exist of course, but health care professionals today spend so much of their time filling in forms and looking over their backs to make sure that they are not making a mistake that they have too little time for being human.

So biomedicine does need healing.

Critics of Modern Medicine

I am not the first person to criticize aspects of modern medicine, and I will surely not be the last. In addition to the recent books cited earlier in this chapter, there have been previous serious critiques.

One of the most influential books to condemn medicine was that of social scientist Ivan Illich, whose book – Medical Nemesis (6) – opens with the famous statement, *"The medical establishment has become a major threat to health"*.

Illich was particularly critical of the way in which medicine as an industry creates disease (iatrogenesis). For example, it makes us all believe we are ill (through the "medicalization" of normal emotions and behaviors, for example), and directly makes us ill through the overuse of drugs with significant adverse effects. Another important book is that by James Le Fanu (7), who argues that scientific medicine has already won most of the winnable battles, and its rising costs for minimal gain are now counterproductive. Like Illich, he laments the hubris of the medical profession.

These and many other critics make important points about the limitations and faults of modern medicine.

But We Must Not "Throw the Baby Out with the Bathwater"

When I have told colleagues I am exploring the nature of healing as I am disillusioned with some aspects of modern medicine, in particular its inability to consider anything that does not accord with its scientific view of the world, they sometimes accuse me of being unscientific and of rejecting modern medicine. That is not the case; we need modern medicine and its science, but we need other approaches as well. I am arguing for more pluralism in our approach to health and health care, and the need to consider alternative views of the world. This is absolutely not the same as suggesting that people can pick and choose any "alternative" treatment they like. But to reject the wisdom and understanding of all other cultures and approaches – both ancient and modern – simply because their ideas do not fit in with our science, is folly.

We should not think of these things as *either/or*, either scientific medicine or something else, but as *both/and*. Medicine and health care should be about humanity, caring for each other, and helping us all to flourish together; it should not be about money. If making money continues to be a key determinant of health care delivery, I fear for our future.

Furthermore, despite the skepticism of most of medicine's leaders, who cannot believe in something so unscientific as healing or see its benefits, I believe that much healing can and sometimes does take place in modern medical practice.

Healing Within Biomedical Practice

To return to this more positive narrative, in spite of all the problems outlined above, there is a lot of wonderful compassionate care in modern biomedical practice (as shown in Chapter 10), that could serve as a model for the next generations of medical professionals.

Changes in the physical spaces in which we carry out our work are helping hospitals and clinics to become more like healing spaces than they used to be. But it is the words and behaviors of the people who work in our health care establishments that are the most important components of healing within medicine – the interactions between the staff and their patients.

Many of us are drawn to the medical profession, at least in part, because of its caring ethos. All of my preceding criticisms of modern medicine are countered by my respect and admiration for the huge numbers of caring medical colleagues I know. In addition, many health care professionals I have interacted with, because of problems that I or my loved ones have had, have been wonderfully compassionate and humane. And my research, documented in previous chapters, has shown me that really caring about someone else is an important starting point for the facilitation of healing.

I am not just talking about doctors, nurses and other professionals with qualifications in the health care business. In 1996, the general practitioner Julian Tudor Hart and I wrote an article about caring in *The Lancet* (8). We pointed out that patients in hospitals often relate well with their ward cleaners and other non-professional workers, who will smile and share a joke with them, and perform other small caring activities. We argued that these simple caring acts are vitally important.

Having said that, I think it is the professionals who get the opportunity to play the most important healing roles.

Nurses as Carers and Healers

In the current model of medical care, the doctors make decisions about what treatment patients should have, and the nurses then administer the treatment and care for the patient. Since the time of Florence Nightingale, it has been the nurses, not the doctors, who have been the key front line "carers" in health care.

Therefore, it comes as no surprise to find that whereas relatively little is written about caring in medical books and journals, there is plenty about it in the nursing literature. Nurses like Jan Watson, who has explored caring extensively, have made a big impact on the field. She and others emphasize the formation of "healing relationships" through caring (9).

In the USA and elsewhere, nurses' care of their patients may extend to the overt use of healing techniques, such as Reiki, healing touch and therapeutic touch. These forms of therapy are about the employment of the intentional influence of one person on another without known physical means of intervention (10). In other words, they are like the energy healing described earlier.

People who have an illness treated in a hospital or who witness the treatment of a relative will often comment on the caring they received from the nurses and the importance of some small things that a nurse did, such as making sure that you could reach your drink, or that the pillows of the bed were right for you. I think nurses often understand the importance of little things done with compassion better than doctors. Compassion and caring are not always seen as central to the work of doctors and are rarely a major part of their medical education and training. But many doctors are also healers, as outlined in Chapter 10 and below.

HOW CAN HEALTH CARE PROFESSIONALS FACILITATE HEALING?

I think my research, such as that discussed in Chapter 10, has largely answered this question. But I have also looked at the literature and found that other academics have interviewed doctors who are thought to be healers by colleagues and patients and written academic papers or books about that work.

For example, John Scott and colleagues (11) interviewed physicians thought to be good healers. They concluded that the key features of a healing relationship between the doctor and patient were:

- Valuing the patient and creating a non-judgmental emotional bond
- Appreciating power and consciously managing clinician power in ways that would most benefit the patient
- "Abiding": just being there for people and displaying a commitment to caring for them over time.

Similarly, Larry Churchill and David Schenck (12) reported their findings from interviews with 50 doctors who were identified by their peers as healers. The analysis of these interviews led to them describing eight key skills:

1. Do the little things
2. Take time
3. Be open and listen
4. Find something to like, to love
5. Remove barriers
6. Let the patient explain
7. Share authority
8. Be committed

Doing the Little Things

This wonderful phrase encompasses much of what I observed Wykeham doing over 50 years ago, as well as what I saw when I have sat in with homeopathy practitioners and healers as they interacted with their clients. It is about responding to the prompts and body language that come from the patient and being fully with them during a consultation. Things such as standing up to greet them, smiling, taking an interest in their lives as well as their diseases, a reassuring touch if and as appropriate, laughing and even crying with them as confidences are revealed. Being real. Being another vulnerable human, like the patient.

Then, in 2014, Thomas Egnew, who has also carried out extensive qualitative research on healing (which he describes as "transcending suffering"), published what he calls his "seven skills to promote mastery of the art of medicine" (13).

They are:

1. Take a moment to focus before entering the consulting room
2. Establish a connection with the patient by developing rapport and agreeing on the agenda
3. Assess the patient's response to illness and suffering
4. Communicate to foster healing
5. Use the power of touch
6. Laugh a little
7. Show some empathy

Finally, in our more recent article about caring, published in the *British Medical Journal*, Drs Ian Fussell, Sara Warber and I came to similar conclusions (14).

These publications all report similar suggestions of the key skills needed by health care workers to help their patients heal. Three central themes emerge: the importance of being in the right frame of mind before we see our patients (what I shall call "centering", in accord with the healers), listening properly (to which I would add "validating the patient's understandings"), and "doing the little things", many of which accord with the skills demonstrated by nurses and by doctors like Wykeham Balme (Chapter 1).

Centering

Soon after I moved to the University of Exeter in 2009, as described in earlier chapters, I started working with Sarah Goldingay and her colleagues in the Department of Drama. One of the issues we wanted to explore together was the teaching of communication skills to medical students – Sarah thought that drama workshops might help, and wanted to show me how such teaching sessions might work.

So, one day, three of us met in a large studio room in the Drama Department – a professor of drama, Sarah and myself. On entering the room, the other two said they needed to prepare the room and themselves and started to move furniture about. I took the opportunity to get my laptop out to check my emails. While I was doing that, they started doing a lot of strange breathing and moving exercises, using the whole space. After a while, they pronounced themselves ready. "What were you doing?", I asked. "Just preparing ourselves … what do you do before you see a patient?", came the response.

It was a pivotal moment for me. What do I do before seeing a patient? Well, finish my sandwich, check my phone, look at the notes perhaps but I never prepared myself, I never centered myself. And how obvious that I should, that I needed to be in the right frame of mind to communicate well with someone seeking my help.

That meeting changed me and changed my practice as a doctor.

We should all take time to prepare ourselves before seeing patients.

Listening

I used to teach medical students that listening was the most important skill they needed to acquire to be a good doctor, and that it was one of the most difficult skills to master.

I have listened to (or maybe just heard) countless presentations on "the art of medicine", many of which have mentioned the importance of what is usually called "active non-judgmental listening". But one in particular sticks in my mind. The speaker told us that, in ancient China, much was known about listening and healing, and showed a slide of the symbol as shown in Figure 11.1. A Chinese colleague has since confirmed that the symbols say what we thought they say, and that the script is indeed an ancient type of Chinese lettering. The Chinese, she explained, understood

FIGURE 11.1
An ancient Chinese symbol to represent how you should listen to others: with your ears, your eyes, your undivided attention and your HEART.

that you needed to listen to others not just with your ears, but also with your eyes, with undivided attention, *and with your heart*, as shown in Figure 11.1.

Validating with Compassion (Instead of Empathy)

There is much discussion in the medical literature about the importance of empathy in relation to listening to patients, and it is in one of the lists of healing skills quoted above. But, as stated previously, I disagree. Being too empathic with your patient's problems can lead to all sorts of trouble because you take their emotional pain into yourself, and you reflect their pain back to them. We need compassion, not empathy. And with compassion can come the all-important skill of listening well and validating the position of the patient – being sure they know you have understood them, as discussed in Chapter 6.

As G. K. Chesterton, the English writer and philosopher, once said, *"There's a lot of difference between hearing and listening"*.

Listening allows us to make connections and form potentially "healing relationships".

One of those homeopathy practitioners talked of the need to "dance with the other": the idea that you need to be fully engaged with the other person and willing to be totally responsive to their needs, ideas, words and body language. Smiling, touching, laughing and crying are all little things that may be appropriate when you are truly aligned with the other person.

CHANGING BIOMEDICINE

I think we need to ensure that all modern health care is based firmly within the ethos of compassionate caring for others, allowing the art of healing to be integrated with the science of curing.

Clearly, that will require some changes in values, attitudes, education and practices.

Values and Attitudes

A value can be defined as a belief that motivates someone to act in one way or another. One of the core values of medical professionals is that materialistic science is the framework (or paradigm) within which all clinical decisions should be made. With that come concepts of certainty and an absolutist notion of right and wrong. But the world does not work like that, and nor should medicine. The complexity of living things, with their connectedness to each other, and their multifaceted environments, ensure that. And we must realize that uncertainty is a key feature of medical practice; strange things that defy scientific explanation are commonplace (if you can see them). Scientific certainty and right/wrong dualism inevitably lead to attitudes that make it hard for the professional to accept the experiences of a bewildered, spiritual person who is consulting with them. We need to be more accepting of different ways of understanding the people who come to us as patients with the hope and faith that they will leave the encounter with us in better health.

Education

Although it would be inappropriate to place all of the blame for biomedicine's problems on education, it clearly has a major role. I think it starts with the selection of doctors and other health care professionals – we predominantly choose people interested in science and those good at passing exams, some of whom are "neurodiverse" (showing some autistic traits) and therefore ill-equipped to extend true compassion to others.

There are many dedicated teachers who teach their students in humane ways and instill the best values and practice. But science is the major scaffolding on which we build our medical education and understanding.

Alternatives to biomedical science get little teaching time, and even when things like CAM and healing are put into the timetable, the fact that many of the students' mentors dismiss it as "nonsense" or worse undermines such initiatives. Obviously, I think the curriculum and the attitudes need to be broadened; teaching needs to be open to all options for health care. We need to teach about the shortcomings of modern biomedicine and about other ways of thinking about health and illness.

Practice

Modern practitioners know that they need to listen to their patients and respect their needs, but such practices tend to play second fiddle to the drive to make a diagnosis and find a suitable intervention. Most of us do not prepare ourselves properly for our clinical encounters, and, although we may do a good job, we stick to what we know – we rarely "dance with the other" and we find it hard to find room (and time) within our science for the "ineffable", as documented in my conversation with Sara Warber in Chapter 7.

In addition, I think we need more doctors who can treat the whole patient. Most of us have become "super specialists", taking an interest in one system alone, and sometimes only a limited number of disorders of that system. For example, my expertise was in rheumatology in general and osteoarthritis in particular; I was not in a good position to understand the whole person and all their ailments, and I had little time to really understand their lives, their social circumstances and their wider needs, all of which were likely to be impacting on their problems.

What Alternatives Do We Have?

There are many alternatives and adjuncts to Western biomedicine. Some Eastern countries have their own form of medicine. For example India has its Ayurvedic system and China, Tibet and other countries have their own traditional medical systems working alongside biomedicine.

In the West, we have what are called complementary and alternative medicine (CAM) practices, such as homeopathy, acupuncture, herbalism and many more. I have already pointed out that I think many CAM practitioners are healers (see, for example, homeopathy in Chapter 5). But CAM, like biomedicine, has its own problems. The sector is bedeviled by large numbers of well-meaning people pushing a single, favorite intervention of theirs and making serious claims for its efficacy for all sorts of different ailments, without justification.

Many other approaches have been developed to try to get round the problems inherent in both biomedicine and CAM.

Holistic or Integrated Health Care

Integration of biomedicine with alternatives seems an obvious route to go down, and it is one that has received limited acceptance within Western medicine. We have some units based in hospitals and universities that promote and practice what is called holistic or integrated health care, combining many different approaches, including dietary and nature-based perspectives, to mainstream medical ones. But if you look up most of the treatments used by CAM practitioners in conventional medical texts – or the internet – you will see that most are still described as "pseudoscience", "unproven" or worse.

The Biopsychosocial-Spiritual Model of Health

The biopsychosocial model of health and illness was developed by American psychiatrist George Engel. He was disillusioned by the pure biomedical model. He emphasized our interactions with the environment and related social factors, as well as psychological issues, in the development of disease (15).

It is often described using a diagram of the sort shown in Figure 11.2.

Subsequently, others have suggested that we need to add a spiritual dimension to the model (16).

The valuable contribution by Saad and colleagues (16) points out that we need a complete paradigm shift in biomedical thinking if we are to fully incorporate the spiritual dimension into a biopsychosocial-spiritual model of health and illness. It requires us to accept fully the true meaning of our being spiritual beings, not machines. That is a big step for medicine.

Functional Medicine

Functional medicine emphasizes the need to find the "root causes" of disease. It considers the interactions between the individual and their environment, as well as gastrointestinal, endocrine and immune systems.

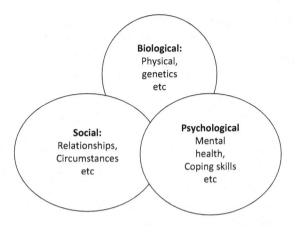

FIGURE 11.2
A diagrammatic representation of the biopsychosocial model of disease.

Practitioners develop individualized treatment plans based on the notion of there being a matrix of antecedents, triggers and mediators of disease and illness. Although popular with many general practitioners, this system is largely condemned as unscientific by the medical establishment.

Salutogenesis

Salutogenesis means the generation of health. This concept was introduced by Aaron Antonovsky, a social scientist who was intrigued by the fact that many holocaust survivors thrived and remained in good health afterwards (17).

Antonovsky believed that we need a combination of comprehensibility, manageability and meaningfulness in our lives to cope with health issues and maintain good health throughout our lives. From this, he developed the concept of a sense of coherence, and many measures have been introduced to try to assess this in people.

Salutogenesis has been of interest to many doctors and academics, in particular in public health, but has not gained much traction within mainstream medical thinking.

I like the concept and believe it should be taught in medical schools.

Slow Medicine

One rather different form of medical practice, that has gained ground of late and can incorporate the centrality of caring compassion and healing, is "slow medicine". The idea was developed in Italy in the 1980s and 1990s, in response to the slow food movement. As with slow food, it is not really about being slow, it is more about being thoughtful and respectful, and it is about the natural world and about process. It says we should not over-diagnose or over-treat our patients.

Our current "fast medicine" is all about the rush of both patients and health care professionals to find a cause for any ailment, to label and diagnose it, and to reach for some remedy to "fix" it. With fast medicine, we do far too many unnecessary tests – often defensively ("just to make sure") and go for often useless "routine check-ups". If you do a lot of tests, about one in 12 will come back abnormal by chance, leading to masses of unnecessary, dangerous interventions.

We do not pause to think and to let nature take its course often enough. Time, rest, a change of routine and common sense lead to the resolution of many illnesses, without any tests or medicines being necessary. Our forebears knew that better than we do.

When discussing how sick people were looked after in Lourdes (Chapter 6), I mentioned that I thought it was a "low-tech, high-touch" approach. In many ways the medicine that goes on in Lourdes could be described as slow medicine.

Victoria Sweet, whose book on slow medicine is one I think every medical practitioner should read, says that "fast medicine" is medicine without a soul (18). I agree.

Slow medicine, like salutogenesis, is an approach that I like and think should be taught in medical schools and accepted by the profession.

"Humanizing" Medicine

There are a number of other movements within medicine that attempt to deal with its apparent lack of humanity. "Medical humanities" are taught in most medical schools, and initiatives such as "narrative-based medicine" (which puts emphasis on the story of the patient), and person-centered care are gaining ground. Person-centered care is a concept that sees people using health services as equal partners in the planning of their care. These and many other approaches try to ensure that patients are empowered and that the professionals are caring and compassionate.

Hospices and End-of-Life Care

In my experience, the area of medical care that is most likely to embrace healing practices is end-of-life care. Hospices often have healers on their staff, as well as using a wide variety of alternative approaches. While applauding this, it does seem to me a bit as if the medical profession can only think outside of its constrained scientific box when all of its usual approaches have failed.

Conclusions about Healing and Biomedicine

A lot of healing clearly takes place in hospitals, as well as in hospices, general practices and other health care facilities. It may be facilitated more by nurses than doctors, and a lot of it clearly goes on "below the radar" of the individual doing it (in other words, without the individual's conscious attempt or realization of what they are doing). Indeed, in retrospect, I think that some of the encounters I had with my patients, long before I knew anything about healing, were of that nature.

I have come to believe that healing may even be biomedicine's "dirty little secret". A lot of it goes on in all walks of medical practice, but hardly anyone likes to talk about it or admit to it. We say that we have to "distance ourselves" from our patients and not become too involved emotionally, to protect ourselves. But many doctors and nurses have learnt, like healers, that you can allow yourself to make meaningful connections with your patients (or clients) without putting yourself at risk. And most of us have experienced those wonderful moments of connection with another: the formation of a compassionate healing relationship.

But We Do Need a Paradigm Shift

In spite of all the healing and other good things going on within it, modern medicine is in deep trouble. It has become a business based on a single, flawed belief system. Although of great value, it is becoming too cumbersome and expensive to be available to most people. It has lost its soul. It MUST change. Medicine needs to be honest about its shortcomings and about what it can and cannot do. It needs to accept that other ways of doing things, even if they seem "unscientific", might be of value. Above all else, it needs to remember that humans are spiritual beings. Spiritual beings who are all different, and whose interactions and connections with their environment and with other living things around them dictate their health and ability to flourish.

Had I Known Then What I Know Now

So what can I (or you) do? Perhaps get to a position of leadership or power within the current system and try to change it from within? But very few of us are capable of that. My mentor Wykeham told me, just before he died, that he thought I would get to the top in medicine, but, by the time I got there, I would be too tired and brainwashed to be able to alter anything for the better. As ever, I think he was right. I would probably have got to a powerful position in medicine if I had not been taken hostage in 1990. But, even by then, I was already heavily brainwashed into the restricted view of the world presented by biomedicine.

So what can I (we) do? My only answer is to summarize what I would have done then (when teaching and practicing medicine), if I had known what I know now about healing.

My Clinical Practice

I would have followed my simple rules outlined above – centering myself before each consultation, listening with compassion and doing the little things. I would have tried to put the patient first at all times and let them be in charge and have the power within the exchange. I would have tried to suppress my own ego and status. Hopefully I would have "connected", in a spiritual sense, with far more of my patients than I did, by my loving intentionality.

My Teaching

I would have taught medical students and doctors about spirituality and healing, and emphasized the shortcomings of modern medicine as well as its triumphs. I would have tried to instill the value and practice of compassion as primary in health care interactions.

My Research

I would have done patient-centered research, not biomedical research. I would have focused on the ideas and needs of people with the condition I was interested in (osteoarthritis), instead of the biological mechanisms and pathways being investigated by most of us.

And I think, if I had done all that, I would have enjoyed it even more than I did.

REFERENCES

1. Swayne J. *Remodelling Medicine.* Glasgow: Saltire Books, 2012.
2. Mueshsam P. *Beyond Medicine.* Novato California: New World Library, 2021.
3. Haslam S. *Side Effects: How Our Healthcare Lost Its Way and How to Fix It.* Atlantic Books, London 2022.
4. Gawande A. *Being Mortal: Wellcome Collection.* London: *Profile Books,* 2014.
5. Keefe PR. *Empire of Pain: The Secret History of the Sackler Dynasty.* New York: Doubleday, 2021.
6. Illich I. *Medical Nemesis: The Expropriation of Health.* New York: Random House, 1975.
7. Le Fanu J. *The Rise and Fall of Modern Medicine.* London: Abacus Publishers, 1999.
8. Tudor Hart J and Dieppe P. Caring effects. *Lancet* 1996: 347: 1606–1608.
9. Watson J. The theory of human caring: Retrospective and prospective. *Nurs Sci Q* 1997; 10: 49–52.
10. Zahourek RP. Intentionality in transpersonal healing. *Complement Health Pract Rev* 1998; 4: 11–27.
11. Scott J et al. Understanding healing relationships in primary care. *Ann Fam Med* 2008; 6: 315–22.
12. Churchill S, Schenck D. Healing skills for medical practice. *Ann Intern Med* 2008; 149: 720–724.
13. Egnew T. The art of medicine: Seven skills that promote mastery. *Fam Pract Manag* 2014; 14: 25–30.
14. Dieppe P, Fussell I, Warber SL. The power of caring in clinical encounters. *BMJ* 2020; 371: m4100.
15. Engel G. The need for a new medical model: A challenge for biomedicine. *Science* 1997; 196: 129–136.
16. Saad M, de Medeiros R, Mosini A. Are we ready for a true biopsychosocial-spiritual model? The many meanings of "Spiritual". *Medicines (Basel)* 2017; 31(4): 79.
17. Antonovsky A. *Unravelling the Mystery of Health.* San Francisco: Jossey-Bass Inc, 1987.
18. Sweet V. *Slow Medicine: The Way to Healing.* New York: Riverhead Books, 2017.

12

Toward an Understanding of Healing

Practicing medicine was rewarding for me. But I became increasingly aware of the fact that medicine was losing its way by ignoring the whole person, spirituality and the soul. So, I turned my attention to healers and healing. That change was also driven by curiosity and my need to understand my own spiritual experiences and encounters with healing.

As mentioned in Chapter 4, I had some funding from the UK's National Institute for Health Research (NIHR), that allowed me to get started. Then, I was invited to apply for a fellowship by the Institute for Integrative Health in Baltimore (now the Nova Institute for Health of People, Places, and the Planet). I sent in an application with the title "Toward an Understanding of Healing" – the title of this chapter. It was accepted, helping me further my research into the subject, as documented in this book.

SO, WHAT IS HEALING?

As stated in Chapter 11, during my journey, I have learnt that healing is very different from curing. Sister Delia taught me that, as have numerous healers and health care professionals I have interviewed.

I now agree with Dr Rachel Naomi Remen, who observed,

"We thought we could cure everything, but it turns out we can only cure a small amount of human suffering. The rest needs to be healed" (1).

DOI: 10.4324/9781003461814-15

Academics who are interested in healing often struggle with the lack of a clear definition, suggesting that it makes it difficult to study or understand the subject. This issue is well summarized in a special edition of the scientific journal *"Explore"*, devoted to the subject (2).

The most commonly used words to describe healing are "wholeness" and "transformational change".

For example, based on a rigorous concept analysis of the subject, Firth and colleagues came up with the following operational definition:

> *"Healing is a holistic, transformative process of repair and recovery in mind, body and spirit, resulting in positive change, finding meaning and movement towards self-realization of wholeness, regardless of the presence or absence of disease"* (3).

Others take a different view. For example, sociologist Arthur Frank*, commenting on Naomi Remen's quote (above), says that he regards healing as "attending to the rest" after medicine has done its best (4).

I really like the idea of healing being about *"the rest"* as it implies that it is complementary to biomedical approaches to health, which is where I believe it should sit. That is a central thesis of this book: we need curing and healing specialists working together. Or we need those who know how to cure to be healers as well.

These attempts to describe healing are all just words, whereas healing is actually about feelings, emotions and experiences. Like love. You know when you are in love – you can feel/experience it – but it is hard to describe. And there are different types of love: your love for your children is different from your love for your football team, for example. I think healing is similar: it includes many different types of events, some relatively commonplace, others profound, spiritual transformational changes.

From my own experience, I would say it is much easier to describe what it is like to need healing than to be healed. I know what it is like to feel fragmented, disconnected and separated from aspects of myself – the state I described earlier as soul separation (Chapter 2). And I understand that transformational changes lead to a return of wholeness – which I would call a state of integrity of mind/body/spirit.

So, for me, healing is transformational change, leading to a return to wholeness.

But, for others, it may be something different.

Some of the Components of Transformational Healing Change

Another way of approaching this is to look at some of the components of the transformational changes for the better that are at the heart of healing. They include:

1. The actions that facilitate healing change
2. The process of change
3. The outcomes experienced

The "Action": How Do You Facilitate Healing?

As detailed in previous chapters, this is a subject I have tried to explore with many of the doctors and healers I have interviewed and worked with – "What do you 'do' to facilitate a healing response?", I asked them. I gradually came to understand that this was the wrong question!

I now think, as it says in the song written by Melvin Oliver and James Young, and made popular by Ella Fitzgerald:

"T'ain't What You Do – It's the Way That You Do It"

I believe this is an important insight. There are many, many different things that healers do: a lot of varying practices and belief systems. But there seems to be one factor that is common to them all: whatever you do must be done with good intentions – and with love and compassion. As I concluded previously (Chapter 4), being a healer seems to be about:

- Focused attention with good intentions
- Being there for another: subjugating your ego and concentrating on love and compassion.

Arguably, healing is about "intentionality", as suggested by Rothlyn Zahourek (5).

The Process: What Happens When You Are Healing?

As to what is happening as your healing progresses – well, that too is difficult. Research with members of the public, complemented by the views expressed to me by healers, suggests that there are three interrelated ways of looking at this.

Energy is Being Channeled from Outside and/or Balanced Within You

This energy or force is ill-defined; some think of it as God, others as the essence of the Universe; Americans sometimes call it the "biofield". Many say they just don't know what it is, but it is clearly there to be felt. I would echo that: I too have felt it, as explained in many places in this book, but have no idea what "*it*" is.

Connection with Other Living Things Is the Key to Healing Processes

Again, the exact nature of this connectivity is unclear to me, but, as with energy, it is something I have *felt*. For example, I felt my connection with Sister Delia during the conversation reported in Chapter 11. In addition, when I healed a horse (Chapter 4), I was totally connected to that animal; the horse and I were as one. This is another difficult thing to describe in words or to understand if you have not experienced it. All I can say is that when you are connected you do not really know where "you" end and the "other" begins. If consciousness is the essence of the Universe, as the "panpsychists" say (see below), then perhaps we are linking with another *via* that universality.

Healing Comes from Within; All Healing Is Self-healing

The idea that you can heal yourself is popular, partly because it appeals to the self-centered nature of current society, and it plays into the hands of those who want to sell us quick fixes. In addition, it is reassuring – "I will be able to find a way to heal this problem I have". My own experiences suggest that healing involves connections with somebody or something else, the "ineffable" in some cases, rather than it being all from within. But that connection may be with an animal, a tree, a view, a painting or a piece of music rather than another human being.

Many members of the public present a view of healing that involves a combination of each of these three concepts: that some external force (energy) is channeled to you by connection with another, and this promotes self-healing.

I like that.

The Outcome: What Does It Mean to Be Healed?

The word healing is derived from the old English "*haelan*", which means "whole", so a return to wholeness as stated above. But humans are not beings that get stuck in a certain "state"; we are dynamic organisms interacting with others and our environment and changing all the time. So, "wholeness" as a static concept cannot be the whole answer. Maybe wholeness as the integrity of mind/body/soul is the outcome. And that allows you to flourish.

Healing from the Inside and the Outside

Another way of approaching this, as suggested to me by a colleague, would be to think of it as what is apparent from the outside, or the inside. What we see going on in others and what our investigations tell us *versus* what we ourselves experience and understand within us. And healing from the inside is bound to depend on the individual and their background, culture, context and so forth.

Perhaps one way of looking at healing, then, is finding meaning in the face of adversity, whereas another might be moving from fragmentation to integrity and flourishing.

A Different Approach from Ancient Greece: "*Eudaemonia*"

The concept of "*eudaemonia*" or "flourishing", is generally attributed to Aristotle, and the wisdom of the ancient Greek philosophers (6, 7).

The word *eudaemonia* is derived from "*eu*" – meaning good or well – and "*daemon*", which means spirit. Aristotle said that well-being is not so much an outcome or state as a process of fulfilling or realizing one's "*daemon*" or true nature. The concept is linked to virtue ethics and the need to realize our virtuous potentials to the benefits of others as well as ourselves. We can only "flourish", said the Greek scholars (including Plato and Socrates, as well as Aristotle), if we pursue our full potential through virtuous behavior. They recognized that we all have different abilities, and therefore different contributions to make to society.

Eudaemonic behaviors (8) have been said to include:

- Volunteering one's time
- Giving money to someone in need
- Writing out one's future goals
- Expressing gratitude for another's actions, either written or verbally
- Carefully listening to another's point of view
- Confiding in someone about something that is of personal importance, and
- Persevering at valued goals in spite of obstacles.

Plato, Aristotle and others thought that you could flourish even if you were sick or disabled. But I think I was only able to return to a state of flourishing once I had healed from the trauma of being a hostage in Kuwait/Iraq.

Some of the patients I saw as a doctor seemed to flourish in spite of disease – people like "Bert" the bricklayer.

"Bert" the Bricklayer

Bert first came to see me when he was in his mid-40s. It was clear that he had developed rheumatoid arthritis, a severe form of inflammatory joint disease that, in those days (the 1980s), was quite likely to lead to joint deformities and disability, as well as a lot of pain, stiffness and fatigue. I did what I could to control the disease and reduce his symptoms, without a lot of success. He admitted to a lot of continuing pain. I remember telling him about "joint protection" (not putting too much stress on the joints, as that might increase the amount of damage they sustained), and him smiling at me in response. I advised him to give up his work as a bricklayer, and he told me he liked the job and wanted to go on doing it. His arthritis got worse, but he went on working and, whenever I saw him, he was smiling and seemed quite content, in spite of the pain and increasing disability. He started doing voluntary work with arthritis charities and helping others with these diseases in a number of different ways, while continuing to lay bricks for a living. He was a source of joy and encouragement to countless others, including me.

On the last occasion I saw him in my clinic, soon after I got back to work after my prolonged absence when a hostage, he hobbled into the clinic on his grossly deformed feet and ankles, smiled at me, and said how nice it was to see me back. He told me that he had not bothered to come to clinics whilst I was away as he did not need any help from us doctors anymore; he was doing just fine. He then delved into a bag he had with him, laughing to himself, and asked me to look inside. I saw a brick and a bricklayer's trowel. "See how well they fit in my hands, Doc", he said, showing me his horribly deformed hands, which lacked any movement in the fingers. So I put the brick in one hand and the trowel in the other – they fitted perfectly, and when I gently turned his hands over, they stayed put! I got some pictures taken that I subsequently showed at arthritis meetings and published in books (with Bert's permission!).

Bert had flourished in spite of bad arthritis and had done much to help others, while continuing with the job he knew and loved.

Is that a form of healing? I think it is.

Wouldn't it be wonderful if we could all be like Bert and, in spite of what life throws at us, flourish for the benefit of other individuals, as well as our communities and ourselves? Perhaps medicine should spend more time trying to help people flourish, rather than trying to eradicate disease and illness?

What One Word Would You Use to Describe Healing?

A research technique I have used to try and get a handle on people's idea of the essence of healing is to ask them to provide the single word that they think is most important in relation to healing. I asked many people that question at several different medical meetings I attended, when presenting some of our research on healing or showing our exhibition. Participants did it totally anonymously; all they had to do was pick a card, write one word on it and pin it to the board, or put it in a pile of "returns". We did not talk to them or find out who they were.

The results are shown in the word cloud (Figure 12.1).

I was quite surprised to see that these health care professionals used the word "love" more often than any other word. Nature, compassion, authenticity and acceptance were also right up there, alongside birds, balance,

FIGURE 12.1

The words by health care professionals asked (anonymously) to write down the one word they thought most important to healing.

peace and children. Most of the commonly used words make complete sense to me, but why so many "birds", I wonder?

One of my favorite books on healing is called "Healers on Healing" (9). It contains essays by 39 different healers, some of them health care professionals, others not, each of whom was asked to write an essay about the nature of healing in order to help find the "golden thread". What that meant is that they were hoping to find commonalities and general principles within the phenomenology of healing.

In this book some authors write about the process of one person healing another, others about the healed state. Within the various "definitions" of healing offered by the authors, the words used most often are:

- Love
- Wholeness
- Relationships
- Trust
- Truth/honesty
- Harmony

So, not only is healing like love in many ways, it seems that many people think that love is the key to healing.

SO, WHAT IS HEALING?

In spite of all this, and my studying the subject for over 15 years, I don't know what healing is and I don't think anyone else does either. It cannot be pinned down or defined as if it was a thing. It is experiential. And there is a huge diversity of experiences and phenomena that we call healing. It is a very individual, context-dependent experience.

I also like the idea of our thinking of it as healing from the outside (what we hear/see happening to others) or the inside (what we ourselves feel and understand).

However, my scientific background and culture make me want to find some sort of way of putting the key elements that have emerged into a pattern. As outlined in this chapter, my research has led to a number of concepts and words emerging as being central to the issue – those are all in capitals in the schema (Figure 12.2).

LOVING CONNECTIONS

Can lead to

TRANSFORMATIONAL CHANGE for the better

Which can result in

Peaceful INTEGRITY of mind/body/spirit

Allowing

The individual sand communities to FLOURISH

FIGURE 12.2
My schema of healing.

A Schema of Healing

It starts with some form of connection between an individual and something or somebody else within the infinite Universe, facilitated by LOVE.

So healing, perhaps, is ***love in action.***

Can Healing Be Harmful?

Modern medicine is often harmful, as discussed in Chapter 11. So, what about healing? Has that got "side effects" too? Can it harm you? I think the general answer to that is no. However, there are obvious potential problems, such as high expectations not being realized, or the sense of "being taken for a ride" after paying a practitioner and not receiving any apparent benefit. Another issue is what Dr Patricia Muehsam calls "sponge healers" (10). These are caring individuals who have their own problems and get emotionally involved with their clients and sap the energy from them, leaving them feeling drained.

I have been told that the insurance premiums for healers in the UK are very low, as claims against them are hardly ever made. The same is not true for doctors.

The Search for Health, Happiness, Well-Being and Healing

Everyone wants to feel happy and well. No-one wants to be ill or to suffer. And in our modern, individualistic world, we think of these things as being all about ourselves, rather than a collective issue, as with *eudaemonia*.

We seek personal *happiness* (11), which is a feeling of joy or contentment. But we know that this can only be a transient mental state and that life brings us periods of sadness. We all have our ups and downs.

We look for improved personal health and well-being. But there is no general agreement on what those words mean. Health is often defined negatively (as the absence of disease). Well-being is generally thought to involve four main components (12):

- Mental: absence of distressing thoughts and feelings
- Physical: movement and senses functioning well
- Socio-economic: enough relationships with others to have good "social capital" and sufficient money/possessions to be able to manage in your society
- Spiritual: contentment with your understanding of life and its meaning

We are bombarded with advice as to how to be healthy and happy and improve our well-being. We are told about diets, supplements, exercise, meditation and a host of other specific practices that we should follow to keep us fit and well. Furthermore, we are told that each of the activities, interventions or practices that we are told *must* be undertaken (at a price of course!) will help every one of us. One size fits all, it seems; as long as you pay for it!

But, even in the West, it was not always like that. Some of our predecessors were mindful of the community at large, as much as the individual.

Back to Ancient Greece – "Each According to Their Constitution"

We are all different. One of the things that annoys me most about the health and well-being business is the way that so many scientists, authors, commentators and others offer people a recipe for their well-being or healing – a set of simple rules or a particular activity that will allow everyone to heal. That must be nonsense. And I think it exploits vulnerable people. One answer cannot be right for each and every individual.

The renowned Graeco-Roman physician Galen and others of his time recognized that we all respond differently to health and well-being interventions. Galen thought that we should listen to our bodies, to find out what interventions for health would suit us best – that might be more exercise for some, a change in diet for others and so forth – all according to their individual constitutions. These days we want to put everyone's health problems into a box marked "diagnosis" and we have a "one-size-fits-all" approach to the intervention that is best for that diagnostic label – irrespective of the individual's "constitution". Some CAM practices, such as homeopathy, also emphasize the constitution (13).

I think each individual needs to find our own pathways to healing, and see what sorts of change will allow us, as an individual, to heal, as well as which types of healer or intervention are likely to suit us best. How do we do that? Well "listen to your body", trust your intuition, and be open to synchronicity (the unexpected occurrence of an event with meaning for your predicament) and to spiritual experiences. Look for the ways you may be constraining yourself, let go and be open to new ideas and experiences.

What Explanations Might There Be for Healing Transformations?

I have already mentioned that I have found many of my experiences in relation to healing difficult to cope with. This was because they did not fit into my understanding of the world, which, as with most people, had been largely dependent on a belief in materialist science. My healing encounters were a source of cognitive dissonance and therefore anxiety. In spite of an increasing awareness of my spirituality and of there being more to this world than the physical, I have continued to struggle with these issues. So, I have looked for some different frameworks and ways of thinking about things to help me out.

I was helped out by a neuroscientist.

A Neuroscientist Talks about Consciousness

I went to listen to a talk about consciousness; what has been called the "hard problem" of science. The speaker was a well-known neuroscientist. Quite early on in his talk, he challenged his audience, "What makes you think that the brain produces consciousness?", he asked us. "Good question" I thought, as I listened intently for his answer. He went on to explain that, as far as he knew, there was absolutely no evidence that the firing of our neurons could result in feelings in the way we experience them, and that there was quite a lot of evidence against that hypothesis. And he reminded us that the idea that the brain is the generator of consciousness is quite a new one and that most ancient and Indigenous peoples have never believed it.

He concluded by saying that he thought that the brain was the receiver of consciousness rather than its generator. Consciousness was "out there" in some unfathomable way.

That amazed me at the time (many years ago). It amazed me then because although I had not come across the idea before, I immediately "knew" that he was right. Now, I have read and heard a lot more about the concept that consciousness is a general property of the Universe, and not a product of our brain. But when I first got to understand *and believe* such ideas and their implications – well that, for me, was "mind-blowing". I knew in that moment that we are all a part of something much, much bigger and more profound than our bodies and the material world around us.

The belief that there is something beyond us is often deemed "spirituality", and I felt compelled to explore that issue, and to pursue it further through healing. I had apparently been healed when a boy, and the research into placebos that I was doing at the time was pointing to there being something more profound going on than was explicable by materialistic science – something called healing.

That lecture was a turning point, leading to my increasing rejection of simple conventional science as the only way and to understanding that healing research had chosen me rather than the other way around. And it led to the need for me to understand more about my own spirituality.

Spirituality

Spirituality can be thought of as the recognition that there is something greater than ourselves in this Universe – that there is something more to being human than our bodies and sensory experiences alone. Spirituality used to be equated with religion but, in recent years, we have developed non-religious ways of thinking about it. For example, David Elkins and colleagues (14) discuss "humanistic spirituality" and define it as "a universal human phenomenon, an inner experience that can only be defined in a phenomenological way".

As discussed by William James (15) and others, one of the most common spiritual experiences that many of us have are those "noetic" moments, of the sort I have had. These are the transient, wonderful incidents in which we just "know" that we are a part of something much bigger: what Steve Taylor (16) has called "spontaneous awakening experiences", these phenomena have also been called "mystical transformational experiences" and "sudden spiritual transformations" among other terms.

Research by Taylor and others (16) clearly shows that many of us have such experiences, whose properties include:

- Transiency – they do not last long
- Passivity – the feeling that they come, unbidden, from somewhere else
- Noetic – the sense of truth, knowledge and importance
- Ineffable – they defy expression or explanation

I agree. I have had such experiences. In my youth, I rejected them as probably being some sort of hallucination or hormonal disturbance of the brain, because my culture and education had "brainwashed" me into thinking in such ways. But I do not think that now.

And such experiences appear to be a feature of many healing transformations; particularly, those magical moments of "connection" to another, that occur between healer and "healee". For example, the connections I have made with people like Sister Delia and others are truly magical, spiritual moments.

But such experiences are not explicable in conventional terms, and are dismissed by most mainstream scientists. They are "inexplicable" and thought impossible by those who believe in materialism alone.

"Inexplicable Phenomena"

Healing and noetic experiences are not the only inexplicable phenomena that are everyday occurrences in our world.

Near-death and shared-death experiences, mentioned previously, are some of the most striking. Those who have "died" and then returned to this earth, such as neurosurgeon Eben Alexander (17, 18), describe another dimension beyond the grave, and the descriptions are often strikingly similar across varying cultures and educational status of the individuals who have them. Many of those who have been "there", including Alexander, go on to try to help the rest of us understand that our physical lives are just one part of our being.

I believe I got a brief glimpse of that dimension when on the tarmac at Kuwait airport, about to be shot dead (Chapter 2).

Other so-called "paranormal phenomena", such as telepathy, are also inexplicable, although clearly commonplace and real. There are many of them that have been studied in depth by scientists like Dean Radin (19) and Rupert Sheldrake (20), who have statistically "proved", beyond any reasonable doubt, that they exist.

And yet the doubt persists, and people like Radin and Sheldrake get pilloried by some mainstream scientists.

These "inexplicable" phenomena, including some healing events, are a major part of our experiential lives. As Dr Patricia Muehsam (10) says:

"Miracles are indeed the natural order of things when we get out of the way"

They challenge our materialistic ontology. It may well be that we cannot understand such things with the tools we have to explore our world. We can use statistical techniques to "prove" that phenomena like telepathic communication do exist (21), but maybe we do not have the brains or the techniques to understand how or why.

And perhaps we cannot understand our conscious experiences (or *"qualia"*). But that, of course, does not stop us trying.

Different Explanations of "Qualia"

As far as I can see, we have three different ways of trying to explain our subjective experience of the world:

1. The dominant medical scientific proposition is that qualia, emotional experiences, consciousness and the rest are all products of our individual brains. We are all isolated "pieces of meat" which, in some indefinable way, generate feelings. This is the view that has been promoted by famous scientists and philosophers such as Francis Crick and Daniel Dennett. They imply that free will is an illusion. But such views are now disowned by large numbers of scientists and philosophers. And yet it is the view that Western biomedicine (and a lot of the public) clings to.

2. An alternative view, held by a large proportion of humanity, is that there is a supreme being, a creator of our world, who is responsible for our nature. This, of course, is the basis of most religious understandings of the Universe. Many scientists and health care

professionals believe in their God, as well as the simple scientific view that our brain produces all our feelings: these two views are clearly not incompatible.

3. A third view is that there is something else that is fundamental to the Universe, to which we are all potentially connected. Again, this view is not incompatible with religion. But many current scientists and philosophers have suggested that the fundamental essence of things is not a supreme being, but is something like consciousness, information or love (22, 23).

As my neuroscientist lecturer reminded us, many ancient civilizations held similar views. A more recent example is the *"Unus Mundus"* (one world) concept put forward by psychoanalyst Carl Jung and quantum physicist Wolfgang Pauli. This idea, which can be traced back to Plato, has now been developed into what is called "dual aspect monism" (24) or "double aspect theory" – distancing itself from the dualism (mind and body are separate) attributed to Descartes.

The idea that consciousness resides in everything, all living things, and maybe in all inanimate things as well, is a very old one, now described as "panpsychism". If correct, then we are all interconnected with each other and with everything else we experience. That could make sense of phenomena such as telepathy, synchronicity and intuition, as well as healing, including the "inexplicable" miraculous cures resulting from healing, as well as distant healing.

CONCLUSIONS

There is no way that I or anyone else can explain or understand healing. As stated, the word covers a diverse set of individual experiences, some mundane, some magical. After fifteen years of studying the subject, I feel as if I am just at the beginning of my journey, and that there can be no end to the quest "toward an understanding of healing!"

But I have come to some interim conclusions:

1) We are all part of a Universe that we do not understand. Ancient wisdom and much current thinking suggest that consciousness, information or love are its basic essence. If that is the case, then we

are all connected. We are all a part of the same thing, not isolated separate beings. And with that comes free will, and responsibility.

2) Healing, like suffering, is an integral part of our human journeys. But no one can tell you or me what to do to heal ourselves. Each of us can find our way to wholeness, integrity of body/mind/spirit and flourishing, but it is *our/your* way, and no one else's.

So, What Can You/I/We Do to Help Us All Heal?

I have been looking for a *"golden thread"* of ideas that are central to healing. The one that stands out for me at the moment is that healing is "love in action". And, if that's the case, it does point a way forwards for each and every one of us, through the new *"golden rule"*. The Christian golden rule says that you should do unto others as you would have them do to you. But, if we are all one, we can re-phrase that as

"Do unto others as if they were you, because, in a sense, they are".

So the way forward, the way to healing, is to treat ourselves and every living thing on this planet – indeed the planet itself – with love and compassion.

I started this book with a quote from Albert Einstein, and that seems a good place to end it as well:

"A human being is a spatially and temporally limited piece of the whole, what we call the Universe. He experiences himself and his feelings as separate from the rest, an optical illusion for his consciousness".

(Albert Einstein 12/2/1950).

REFERENCES

1. An excerpt of Krista Tippett's conversation with Dr. Remen, available on the internet.
2. *Explore: The Journal of Science and Healing.* July August 2017: 13(4). "A special issue on what is healing?" Pp 243–276.
3. Firth K et al. 2015 Healing, a Concept Analysis. *Glob Adv Health Med* 4(6):44–50.
4. Frank A. *Healing.* In *Encyclopedia of Bioethics*; 4th Edition, 2014; 1399–1406.
5. Zahourek RP. Intentionality forms the matrix of healing: A theory. *Altern Ther Health Med* 2004; 10(6): 40–49.

6. Hall E. *Aristotle's Way: How Ancient Wisdom Can Change Your Life*. London: Penguin Random House, 2018.

7. What is eudaimonia? Aristotle And Eudaimonic well-being https://positivepsychology.com/eudaimonia

8. Steger MF. Hedonia, eudaemonia, and meaning: Me versus Us; fleeting versus enduring. In Vitterso J (ed), *Handbook of Eudemonic Well-Being*. New York: Springer Books, 2016.

9. Carlson R, Benjamin Shield B (eds). *Healers on Healing*. New York: G P Putnam Sons, 1989.

10. Muehsam P. *Beyond Medicine*. New World Library, 2021, pp. 86–87.

11. *https://greatergood.berkeley.edu/topic/happiness/definition.

12. Dodge R, Daly A, Huyton J, Sanders LD. The challenge of defining wellbeing. *Int. J. Wellbeing* 2012; 3222-235.

13. Swayne J. *Homeopathic Methods*. Glasgow: Saltire Books, 2013.

14. Elkins DN et al. Towards a humanistic-phenomenological spirituality. *Journal of Humanistic Psychology* 1988; 28: 5–18.

15. James W. *The Varieties of Religious Experience*, 1902. Reprinted 1985, Boston: Harvard University Press, .

16. *Taylor S. Spontaneous awakening experiences: beyond religion and spiritual practice. *Int J Transpers Stud* 2019; 44: 73–91.

17. Alexander E. *Proof of Heaven*. New York: Little Brown, 2012.

18. Alexander E, Newell K. *Living in a Mindful Universe: A Neurosurgeon's Journey into the Heart of Consciousness*. New York: Potter/Ten Speed/Harmony/Rodale, 2017.

19. Radin D. *Real Magic: Ancient Wisdom, Modern Science and a Guide to the Secret Power of the Universe*. New York: Harmony, 2018.

20. Sheldrake R The science delusion: freeing the spirit of enquiry. *Coronet* 2012.

21. Storm L, Tressoldi P. Meta-analysis of free-response studies 2009–2018: Assessing the noise reduction model ten years on. *J Soc Psychiatry* 2020; 66: 193–219.

22. Schwartz SA, Woolacott M., Schwartz GE. (eds). *Is Consciousness Primary?* AAPS Press, 2020.

23. Currivan J. 'The Cosmic Hologram: The In-formation at the Centre of Creation*. Inner Traditions Bear Factory and Company, 2017.

24. Atmanspacher H and Rickles D. *Dual-aspect Monism and the Deep Structure of Meaning*. Routledge, 2021.

Epilogue

This book has been about a part of my life's journey. That journey started with my becoming an academic doctor, believing in materialistic medical sciences. It is now about working with humanities-based disciplines to promote the acceptance of the creative art of healing. But I am not certain that this is the end of the journey. I don't know where life will take me next. That's exciting.

All of us are on our individual life journeys and never quite know where they will take us. Healing is a part of those journeys, whether we like that idea or not. Everyone suffers from setbacks in their lives, such as bereavement, trauma or disease. Most of us experience all three. And we have to move on; in other words, to heal from these events. Those are continuous journeys of healing because, of course, we are all changing all the time. Healing allows us to flourish. To flourish is to fulfill our potential and become the best version of ourselves, to the benefit of those around us.

My problem with many parts of the journey detailed in this book has been that healing turned out to be about spiritual experiences and the metaphysical world, instead of the physical one. That confused me because of my upbringing as a scientist, and the culture I live in, with its total belief in materialism. The conflict has produced a lot of confusion ("How can this be, how do I explain it?"). I am still trying to come to terms with that problem, and to "process" and understand my experiences. I am rather envious of my artist and healer friends who seem to have no such problem and can accept their experiences without question or any apparent need to understand or explain them.

LIFE'S EXPERIENTIAL TURNING POINTS

We all have turning points on our life's journey. I have documented many of mine within this book. There have been quite a lot for a scientist to cope with, particularly as all of them have been "experiential" and unrelated to my knowledge and "understanding" of the world. But they have changed me. I am still struggling to comprehend what they mean, but I now know for sure that the material world that we live in is not all there is. It seems that we are a part of, or an expression of, something that is literally "infinitely more". To me, it remains inexplicable, and that is fine.

DYING HEALED

A part of my journey that I have yet to experience is dying. What will that be like, I wonder?

An aspect of healing that I have not as yet written about is the concept of dying healed. It is one that I came across early on in my exploration of healing. One of the first doctors I interviewed about healing, when asked to describe a patient whom he thought had been healed, told me the following story.

> *"He was a young man, about my age then (I was a junior doctor). He came in with dramatic weight loss and fatigue. This had initially been put down to stress at work, but he was clearly very unwell. We did a load of tests but could not find anything wrong to begin with. Then, he found this tiny lump on his body, so we biopsied that and found it was a cancer. We did not know where the primary was, possibly testicular, but it was clear that he had an aggressive tumor somewhere. He rapidly got sicker, so we had to tell him and the family that he had a cancer and that we did not know how to treat it. To begin with, he and his family reacted with shock and anger, but that soon subsided. He died a week after we had made the diagnosis, but, by then, he and his family were no longer angry or fighting it. They had been able to spend a lot of time together and say all the things they needed to say to each other; it was rather beautiful. And I had the privilege of being with him when he died, and it was very serene and felt OK. He died at peace, calmly and serenely, and his family was at peace too; I think he died healed".*

That and other stories of dying healed intrigue me. Doctors often see dying as a "failure", but it can be beautiful and an expression of the ineffable aspect of our world and of healing.

I hope I die healed.

Further Reading: The Books That Influenced Me Most

It is extremely difficult to find the literature one would most like or need on the subject of healing. There are huge numbers of books out there, most of which I have not found helpful during my research.

The POPULAR sector is full of books offering self-healing techniques, usually based on a single approach that the author uses and believes in. I would advise against this route as a way of learning about healing.

The ACADEMIC sector is incredibly diffuse and scattered, with texts written by people who are anthropologists, religious scholars, psychologists, or from many other disciplines. They often concentrate on healing within a particular culture or belief system. The problem here is that most academics live in "silos" of their own way of thinking about the world. Anthropology has probably contributed more to my understanding than any other discipline.

The MEDICAL books I have found on healing are a mixture of two main sorts. First, there are those that use the word loosely – for example, using terms like "the healing arts", when what they mean is modern medicine. Secondly, there are those that, like the popular books, are written by a health care professional who has come to believe there is one particular route to healing. Having said that, I have found several books written by health care professionals to be valuable.

There is one important journal concerned with healing within the context of medicine, *"Explore: the Journal of Science and Healing"* – published by Elsevier – which I would recommend to people interested in the topic

I thought it might be of interest to some readers to know what books and authors have most influenced my thinking about healing. So, I have listed some of them below, with a brief comment about their content. Some, I read simply because I knew, or knew of, the authors and respected them, others were chosen by chance. Here, I list some of them in alphabetical order of the main author.

Achterberg J, Dossey B and Kolkmeier L. *Using Imagery for Health and Wellness*. Bantam New Age Books. 1994. A fascinating study of a variety of mind–body approaches to healing, with the use of artistic methods of the sort I have also used.

Aldridge D. *Spirituality, Healing and Medicine – Return to Silence*. Jessica Kingsley Publishers. 2000. An excellent introduction to the concept of spiritual healing and its place in the world.

Brown C. *Afterwards, You Are a Genius: Faith, Medicine and the Metaphysics of Healing*. Riverhead Books New York. 1998. An investigative journalist enters the world of spiritual healing, witnessing and experiencing extraordinary things.

Cassel EJ. *The Nature of Healing, the Modern Practice of Medicine*. Oxford University Press. 2012. An important book by a public health physician who explores what sickness and illness are really about for people, including the spiritual element, and how to help others humanely, within a medical context.

Carlson R and Shield B (Eds). *Healers on Healing*. Putnam and Sons New York. 1989. Short essays on healing by 39 different individual healers. A superb book that is one of my favorites.

Dixon M. *Time to Heal: tales of a country doctor*. Unicorn Publishers, Lewes UK 2020. A wonderful anthology of stories from an English GP that illustrate how medicine should be practiced to facilitate healing.

Dossey L. *Reinventing Medicine, Beyond Mind-Body to a New Era of Healing*. Bravo Limited. 2000. Dr Larry Dossey has been a hugely influential figure in the field, through his books, lectures and essays. This is just one of several books that he has written about healing, but it is the one that had the biggest impact on me.

Frank A. *At the Will of the Body: Reflections on Illness*. Houghton Mifflin Company. 2002. A beautiful reflection on what it means to be ill.

Frankl VE. *The Doctor and the Soul; from Psychotherapy to Logotherapy*. Penguin Books 1952. A classic by a holocaust survivor and psychotherapist.

Greaves D. *The Healing Tradition: Reviving the Soul of Western Medicine*. Radcliffe Publishing. 2004. A passionate plea for the incorporation of healing into medicine.

Harlow T. *That something else: a reflection on medicine and humanity*. Austin Macauley Publishers, London 2021. A thoughtful exploration of those facets of medical practice, such as spirituality, that are beyond the province of materialistic science, but crucial to patients and doctors alike.

Kaptchuk T and Croucher M. *The Healing Arts: A Journey Through the Faces of Medicine*. BBC Publishers, London. 1986. A fascinating trip around many different types of healing being used in different countries.

Kaufman SR. *The Healer's Tale: Transforming Medicine and Culture*. The University of Wisconsin Press. 1993. A wonderful book based on interviews with doctors who are healers.

Kleinman A. *Patients and Healers in the Context of Culture*. University of California Press. 1980. Another classic from a renowned anthropologist.

Jain S. *Healing Ourselves: Biofield Science and the Future of Health*. Sounds True, Colorado, USA. 2021. Full of scientific references on the efficacy of healing.

Muehsam PA. *Beyond Medicine*. New World Library, California. 2021. A very valuable exploration of healing by a physician/healer.

Oschman J. *Energy Medicine: The Scientific Basis*. Churchill Livingstone (2nd ed.). 2015. An exploration of the concept of energy, from a medical/scientific, rather than a spiritual perspective.

Rankin L. *Sacred Medicine – A Doctor's Quest to Unravel the Mysteries of Healing*. Sounds True. 2022. An exploration of some healers and healing techniques, by a doctor.

Radin D. *Real Magic. Ancient Wisdom, Modern Science and a Guide to the Secret Power of the Universe*. Harmony Books. 2018. Not about healing, but a "must" for anyone in doubt about the reality of paranormal and spiritual phenomena.

Schenck D and Churchill L. *Healers: Extraordinary Clinicians at Work*. Oxford University Press. 2011. A lovely book based on interviews with some 50 doctors identified as healers by their peers.

Swayne J. *Remodelling Medicine*. Saltire Books, Glasgow. 2012. A measured argument for the need for change in medicine, and how that might be achieved.

Sweet V. *Slow Medicine: The Way to Healing*. Riverhead Books. 2017. One of my favorites; a doctor's plea for a more thoughtful approach to health care.

Index

Page numbers followed by 'f' and 't' refer to figures and tables respectively.

Printed in the United States
by Baker & Taylor Publisher Services